FALLACY

The Counterfeit of Argument

It would be a very good thing if every
trick could receive some short and obviously appropriate name, so that when a
man used this or that particular trick,
he could at once be reproved for it.

—Schopenhauer

Dedicated to

HELEN MARGARET HOLTHER
ALICE WARD FEARNSIDE

FALLACY

The Counterfeit of Argument

W. WARD FEARNSIDE

WILLIAM B. HOLTHER

A SPECTRUM  BOOK

PRENTICE-HALL, INC.

LIBRARY OF CONGRESS
CATALOG CARD NO.: 59-9517

Current printing (last digit):

17   16   15

PRINTED IN THE UNITED STATES OF AMERICA

30177-C

CONTENTS

INTRODUCTION   1

PART I MATERIAL FALLACIES

TROUBLE WITH PROPOSITIONS   10

1. Faulty Generalization, 10
   (a) Hasty Generalization, 13
   (b) Unrepresentative Generalization, 14
2. Faulty Causal Generalization, 17
3. Assuming the Cause: *"post hoc* reasoning," 21
4. Faulty Analogy, 22
5. Composition and Division, 27
6. The All-or-Nothing Mistake, 30
7. The False Dilemma, 32

TROUBLE WITH CONSTRUCTIONS   33

8. Faulty Classification, 36
   (a) Non-exhaustive Classification (Rule 1), 37
   (b) Non-exclusive Classification (Rule 2), 38
9. Misconceptions about Classification (Rule 3), 40
   (a) Reification, 41
   (b) Relativism, 49
10. Unnecessary Vagueness (Rule 4), 53
11. Over-precision, 64
12. Word Magic, 68

PART II PSYCHOLOGICAL FALLACIES

EMOTIONAL COLORATION   77

13. Emotive Language: "colored words," 77
14. Ceremony or Setting: "pomp and circumstance," 82

MISUSING AUTHORITY   84

15. Appeal to Authority: *"Ipse dixit"* or *He* says so! 84
16. Appeal to Tradition or Faith: "tried and true," 89
17. Impressing by Large Numbers: "get on the band wagon," 92

STIRRING UP PREJUDICE   94

18. Popular Passions: *"ad populum* appeals," 94
19. Damning the Origin: "consider the source," 97
20. Personal Attacks: *"ad hominem,"* 99

21. Forestalling Disagreement, 101
22. Creating Misgivings: "where there's smoke, there's fire," 102

RATIONALIZATION AND LIP SERVICE   **104**

23. Self-righteousness, 105
24. Finding the "Good" Reason, 106
25. Wishful Thinking, 107
26. Special Pleading: "having it both ways," 108
27. Lip Service, 109

BIASED MISCONSTRUCTIONS   **111**

28. Apriorism: "Invincible Ignorance," 111
29. Personification, 115
30. Cultural Bias, 117
31. The Gambler's Mistake, 119

DIVERSIONS   **121**

32. Humor and Ridicule: "lost in the laugh," 122
33. Demand for Special Consideration, 124
34. Clamorous Insistence on Irrelevancies: "red herring," 124
35. Pointing to Another Wrong, 126
36. The Wicked Alternative, 128
37. Nothing but Objections, 129
38. Impossible Conditions: "the call for perfection," 131
39. Abandonment of Discussion, 132

PART III   LOGICAL FALLACIES

LOGICAL TRUTH   **135**
VALIDITY   **138**

40. The Undistributed Middle Term, 142
41. Suppressed Quantification, 147
42. False Conversion of Propositions, 149
43. *Non Sequitur*, 152
44. Trouble with Conditionals and Alternatives, 154
45. Ambiguous Terms, 158
46. Amphibole: "double talk," 162
47. Ambiguous Accent, 163
48. Ambiguous Punctuation and Word Order, 164
49. Circular Definitions and Question Begging, 165
50. Misuse of Etymology, 168
51. Idiosyncratic Language, 170

CONCLUSION: OVERSIMPLIFICATION   **171**
EXERCISES   **173-211**
APPENDIX: SOME LOGICAL PARADOXES   **212**
INDEX   **216**

Introduction

THE FAMOUS pessimist Schopenhauer, in "The Art of Controversy," turns an experienced eye on "the art of getting the best of it in a dispute." He allows that "unquestionably the safest plan is to be in the right to begin with," but sarcastically adds that "this in itself is not enough in the existing disposition of mankind, and, on the other hand, with the weakness of the human intellect, it is not altogether necessary."

It seems doubtful that the level of public discussion has much improved in our own day. Cogency, to be sure, is admired in the scientific laboratories, just as coherence and sensitivity are encouraged amongst our mathematicians and poets. In the committee rooms of Congress, in the editorials of the chain newspapers, on radio, TV, and billboards—in all of the noise and distraction in which we live our lives, only a child or a saint could expect truth to prevail simply because it is true. Truth has a chance when Noise and Distraction are on her side; otherwise she may be overcome. And these two can and do daily prevail without her or against her.

The triumph of rhetoric is like the spread of a virus infection. When an epidemic spreads through an area, it is said to prevail there, and local measures may be taken. But to say it prevails does not mean that everyone is infected. Some persons escape infection; others are immune. It is not necessary to labor the analogy in order to show that it would be a good idea if the community could somehow develop a serum against some forms of persuasion.

Few can hope to become immune to *all* the tricks of persuasion since, like viruses, there are too many of them. People are daily exposed to appeals to blind faith, self interest, fear, prejudice, fancy. This book cannot discuss persuasion in all its variety and

1

complexity, but it can attempt to describe and illustrate some of the most dangerous strains.

Logic is the defense against trickery. The kinds of argument with which logic deals are the reasonable ones. Mistakes are possible, even frequent, in applying the forms of logical argument, and these mistakes are regarded as fallacies, many of them having been noted as early as Aristotle. We shall wish to guard against them. But the most common fallacies today are of a very different sort. It is a small comfort to know that an argument is entirely logical, that it validly derives its conclusion from its premises, and that all the rules of the syllogism, or whatever, are observed to a nicety, *if* it turns out that the premises are frauds, snares, delusions. There are brilliant tricks for getting people to accept all sorts of false premises as true (some of these tricks have been spotted since the time of ancient Greece), and these tricks of argument are so prevalent that even when people realize that something is being pulled on them, they tend to let it pass.

Arguments are a highly complicated human activity and cannot be successfully studied in a sort of vacuum, as if the language uttered and answered itself. Like Schopenhauer, we have just had some hard words for the general run of discussion. This discussion at least takes place in a world of activity and interest, is directed toward goals, and, if at all successful, takes shrewd account of human nature. It is an oversimplification to suggest a clear-cut opposition between argument on one side and persuasion on the other. The most blatant singing commercial usually contains some argument, some alleging of reasons and drawing of conclusions: buy this because it's so good. That the argument is not spelled out, that the audience has to supply the premises, generously allow a connection between them and the evidence cited, and then still accept the conclusion more on faith than reason—all this does not much matter. Even in logic books the arguments are seldom spelled out, except in the examples. After all, no one is overtaxed by the unstated premise in the argument "This man cannot vote since he is unable to read English." The argument runs:

All voters must be able to read English. (unstated)
This man is unable to read English.
Therefore, this man is not a voter.

(This form of argument is the syllogism, first described by Aristotle; he also noted the fact that in ordinary discussion one of the premises, or even the conclusion, is often assumed rather than expressly stated. Where a premise or the conclusion is unstated he called the argument an enthymeme. The unstated portion always can be supplied so that the enthymeme is expanded into a syllogism as was done here.)

One is not troubled by the ellipsis, that is, by the omission of words expressing an idea that can be taken for granted. Nor does it matter that speakers employ the embellishments, the metaphors, the richness and complexity of the living language. Ordinary speech, arising in a live situation, is not designed to satisfy the formulas of logicians. What does matter is the taking advantage of ellipsis, complexity, and verbal display to deceive and obfuscate. In this book we intend to take a look at some distinguishable varieties of fallacious argument, so that we can recognize them in the speech around us and avoid using them ourselves.

We have chosen to examine chiefly the notorious fallacies. In our descriptions we try to make it clear what the particular case before us is, and, in the examples, we try to illustrate one particular fallacy at a time, without entirely sterilizing the sample. But fallacies reinforce each other, and in a weak argument there is apt to be more than one thing wrong. In almost all cases the examples are derived from the world we live in. They are representative of actual discussion, so they are often disguised for obvious reasons, though perhaps not out of all recognition, and trimmed down to size.

The word "fallacy" is sometimes used as a synonym for any kind of position that is false or deceptive, and sometimes it is applied in a more narrow sense to a faulty process of reasoning or to tricky or specious persuasions. We will use "fallacy" in the latter sense so that one may say a fallacy occurs where a discussion claims to conform to the rules of sound argument but, in fact, fails to do so.

We classify fallacies under three heads. There is nothing compelling about the arrangement, and many individual fallacies could be placed as well under one heading as another. The divisions are: Part I. *Material Fallacies,* Part II. *Psychological Fallacies,* Part III. *Logical Fallacies.*

This arrangement can be illustrated by a figurative analogy. Suppose we compare argument to a manufacturing process which uses a machine, an operator, and raw materials. If the materials are up to standard, the operator efficient, and the machine running smoothly, the finished product will probably pass inspection. However, three kinds of things can go wrong. The materials can be below standard or poorly prepared. The operator can make a mistake—get sleepy or be distracted and turn the wrong knob. And the machine itself can break down or misfunction. In any of these three cases, the product will probably not pass inspection. If the trouble lies with the material, we call it *material;* if with the operator, we call it *psychological;* if with the machine, then *logical.* The analogy is crude, but it gives an idea of the emphasis in each section. Under material fallacies we take up faulty generalization and other contaminations of the premises. Under the psychological heading we discuss such common fallacies as emotive language. The processes of logic are rather like those of a machine, and the logical fallacies show a clear misfunctioning of forms designed to go smoothly and produce valid arguments.

We have not by any means exhausted all the things that can go wrong in an argument. What we aim to do is to produce a description of the most notorious fallacies, with some additions that today seem to deserve special notice, and to illustrate them fully.

PART I

Material Fallacies

In TERMS of the analogy of a manufacturing process (p. 4), the final section of this book will examine the misfunctioning of the formal machinery of argument, where the product is so poorly fitted together that the conclusion dangles unsupported in reason. The second source of error is the emotional tricks and appeals which distract from the process of reasonable discussion and tempt disputants to hold all sorts of untruths and half-truths to be self-evident. These, the vulgar sources of error and befuddlement, the claptrap of argument, will have their turn in the next section. There remain the errors that come from raw material of poor quality. When the material is bad, it can be small wonder if the product is also unsatisfactory, however carefully processed, however careful the manufacturer. This failure in the materials is described in the present section, where we take up some of the more common ways in which the materials of argument fall below standard.

To find good standards, the best thing to do is to examine a model product. The field of science abounds in clear examples of sound reasoning. The very model of a convincing argument built on reliable evidence is a scientific argument. Let us look at these model arguments, the demonstrations of science, and we may see more clearly how some other arguments fall short.

The various physical sciences establish their general laws by working backwards, as it were, from observational sentences, sentences known to be true in experience. The laws can be considered as premises that lead to the observations as conclusions: *if* the laws are true, the observations have to be true, too. This is the backwards effect, since, after all, it is the observations that are known to be true—the laws are inferred from them. But in the demonstrations, the arguments in scientific writing, the observations are "derived" from the laws by a vigorous process of logical or mathematical proof.

The laws are so designed as to be perfectly inclusive; that is, no known observations contradict them. Moreover, no other plausible premises are known from which the observations could follow. The laws are economically drafted: each has as wide a scope as the facts allow, and two laws never stand where one would do. Finally, all scientific laws are consistent with one another.

In all cases new observations can be predicted, not mere duplications of previous data (such as laboratory experiments in school), but actually new experiments. When Einstein published his theory, in addition to taking into account all relevant past observations in a way no other theory had succeeded in doing, he was also able to predict further observations that would be logical consequences of the laws he had discovered. The observations were made as soon as feasible, for example those connected with the bending of light rays. They "confirmed" the laws, since they could not have been predicted as a consequence of any other intelligible hypothesis.

Why, in their arguments, do the scientists treat the laws as "premises"? Why, that is, do they want to express the observations as conclusions derivable from the laws? They want to know exactly where they stand. If only one predicted observation should contradict the "law," then the latter would become a discarded hypothesis. Moreover, though the observations are derived from the law, they do not *prove* the law true in turn, no matter how numerous they are. The so-called laws remain hypotheses.

What would it mean to "prove" a law? Until the time of David Hume it had been thought that there was a "necessary connection" between the law and the observations, the sort of relation that there is in geometry between the theorem and the postulates and axioms. Hume showed that in the case of empirical laws, one can always *imagine* the sun rising in the west, gravitation working in reverse, water freezing at 100° C. But where there is a necessary connection, the contrary case is inconceivable. I cannot conceive of a prime number between 7 and 11. I cannot conceive of my being both present and absent at the same time, in the literal sense of these words. I can *say* these things, but I cannot say them without

contradiction. I can say that 8, or 9, or 10 is a prime number, but
I cannot say so and mean by "prime number" or by "8," "9," "10"
what mathematicians mean by them. On the other hand, there is no
logical contradiction at all in speaking of water running uphill.

There is no mathematical certainty, but the *probability* that the
laws of science hold is enormous. They may be regarded as generalizations with no exceptions. Moreover, these generalizations are
much stronger than the sort of naïve generalizations traditionally
discussed by philosophers of science, such as "All crows are black,"
or J. S. Mill's "All hyacinths are blue." The generalizations of science
never stand isolated. Rather, they are interwoven into more and
more complex statements, like a web drawn together at certain
points. The web endures as a whole, the strength of each strand
contributing to the strength of the others. The "induction" for a
generalization of physical science is thus not a simple leap from
positive instances, free from the occurrence of a negative instance,
to an "all" statement. It is a moving from strand to strand in a
tightly woven lattice. Everything known about the world, or nearly
everything, supports what is known about any small part of it.

Though there cannot be certainty that every occurrence will conform to the laws, throughout all time and space, there is still perfect
certainty that every known instance is derivable from them and,
moreover, that a counter instance can *not* occur if the laws are true.
The absence of a counter or negative instance is a necessary condition for the truth of a given law. The presence of such an instance
would be a sufficient condition for the falsification of the law. In
this respect, it would seem that the given law is no better off than the
generalization about hyacinths. Logically it is not, but practically it
is, even apart from the matter of cross-inference lattices just discussed. The experimental conditions are so well defined that
scientists know exactly how to test the laws. This is to say, they
characteristically know what experimental or observational procedures to set up for finding the negative instance if it has the
remotest probability of occurring. They don't have to sit around
waiting for it to show itself.

With the model of scientific law before us, what can we say
about the principles and generalizations by which we must, in our
every-day problems, attempt understanding and venture deeds?

A step-by-step comparison is hardly necessary. It is all too
evident that ordinary life wisdom is a tissue of vague categories,

where truth is relative to ignorance, which is vast, where procedures
are clumsy and blind. Far from weaving a tight lattice of systematic
investigations, individuals make isolated observations. Since man
must understand so that he may move and act, he leaps to some
hasty generalization and "induces" some broad principles from
scraps of evidence.

The common man's hypotheses sometimes fail to survive their
first test. As to the so-called laws, such as the laws of human conduct, they are often incapable of confirmation with the means at
hand ("Democracy is the most efficient form of government," "A
world state is the only check to world war"). Responsible persons
wish to act on principle, so they affirm their generalizations on faith
or pretend to believe in them while the crisis of action lasts.

This is the human predicament. It has been well expressed by
I. A. Richards. (From *Practical Criticism*, New York: Harcourt,
Brace & Company, 1929.)

> There are subjects—mathematics, physics and the descriptive
> sciences supply some of them—which can be discussed in terms
> of verifiable fact and precise hypothesis. There are other sub-
> jects—the concrete affairs of commerce, law, organization, and
> police work—which can be handled by rule of thumb and gen-
> erally accepted convention. But in between is the vast corpus of
> problems, assumptions, adumbrations, fictions, prejudices, tenets;
> the sphere of random belief and hopeful guesses; the whole world,
> in brief, of abstract opinion and disputation about matters of
> feeling. To this world belongs everything about which civilized
> man cares most.

It is not always the case, of course, that people must understand
and act at once, getting on with the evidence at hand. Sometimes
they can wait for better evidence and continue to gather it. Sometimes, when action is forced on them, they act well and meet with
signal success. What a man can always do is act in humility. He can
learn to regard his hypotheses as tentative aids to understanding,
rather than as eternal principles or absolute dogmas. When the
pressure of events forces a man to take sides, to do what he can,
he should recognize that he is engaging in a trial-and-error process,
which, though he fail, may still afford rich experience for future
guidance.

Even in the "sphere of random beliefs and hopeful guesses," there
are some reasons better than others. All of the materials out of
which the common man builds his arguments may be far from

scientific standards, but some are considerably further than others. There are many occasions of error in the gathering and arranging of the evidence from which to build arguments.

In an argument this evidence must be marshalled in a way to lead somewhere. Where it leads is called a "conclusion." Evidence cannot lead to a conclusion unless it is carefully organized in a cogent way, that is, unless it can be cast into the form called "premises." The premises not only must lead to a conclusion, but they must be true to the evidence also. Making sure that the premises are true to the evidence is a problem of meaning; premises must *mean* no more than the evidence supporting them. Moreover, they must be intelligible and clear, for the conclusion will be vague or haphazard if the premises are—you cannot get out more at the end of an argument than goes in at the beginning. Casting the evidence into the form of cogent premises, with the language clear and intelligible, is also a problem of meaning. The whole process, then, of setting up true premises for an argument is a matter of *meaning*, of what is called "semantics." There are two fairly distinct problems:

    a. is the evidence truly and fairly represented in the premises?

    b. are the premises which represent the evidence clear and intelligible?

A simple example may make these necessary distinctions clear. If one wished to make an argument to show that certain forms of advertising are good for the consumer as well as for the business man, he would want to be sure that the general propositions he was advancing as premises represented the facts as they are, and that the classification of the kinds of advertising treated was clear and consistent. Could he assert (a) that *all* advertising must, say, appeal to some real need of the consumer? Is the distinction (b) between, say, prestige sponsorship of a symphony orchestra and direct product pushing clearly drawn and easily applicable?

We shall first treat the problems of stating the facts right, of correctly representing the known situation in the premises. Here occur the familiar fallacies of hasty generalization, *post hoc* arguments, faulty analogies. After treating of these and related fallacies, we shall turn to the problems of vague classifications, word magic, and the rest of the nightmare horde that haunt the semanticist.

TROUBLE WITH PROPOSITIONS

The premises of argument are embodied in propositions—sentences that set forth the claims made about the materials. Sometimes these propositions assert that certain conditions obtain. The conditions are well enough understood, but the claims made are exaggerated or unwarranted in some other way. Perhaps they are too broad—all fire engines I have ever seen are red, but I leave out the qualification ("I have ever seen") and simply state "All fire engines are red." Sometimes the relationships among the facts are misinterpreted—I eat lobster and have nightmares, so I announce as though it were a universal law: "Lobsters cause nightmares." If a speaker takes certain well understood precautions, he can avoid unwarranted claims in his premises.

In this section we assume that the materials are as well in hand as they are likely to be, or at least as is necessary for making responsible assertions about them. The troubles treated in this section, then, come from going beyond or counter in some way to the evidence. In the next section "Trouble with Constructions," the troubles are more subtle, since they are interferences encountered in the actual formation of the notions about the evidence, related together or otherwise modified in the propositions. For the present we assume that the constructions are suitably precise and that the problems come from their use in propositions, rather than from their formation in experience.

1 · *Faulty Generalizations*

Unlike the scientist, the layman lacks techniques for testing generalizations. Laboratory instruments, trained technicians, controlled conditions—these are all missing. There is no system for testing a generalization through all the multiplicity and complexity of the probable cases. Consider a very ordinary instance: "No human act is truly disinterested. Every man's generosity has somewhere a core of selfishness in it. Every man wants to get something when he gives something, if only self-approval." The "truly" takes care perhaps of the anonymous benefactor and similar alleged cases of disinterested generosity, by defining them away. But in all the deviousness of human relations, what means are available for searching out this core of selfishness? The constructions seem serviceably clear, but where can the evidence be found? Could all agree on what the evidence for confirming or falsifying the generalization might be? For instance, can any one suggest a test case that would be crucial for exposing self-interest, if present, in an act of pronounced generosity—something like the crucial experiments of science?

These considerations have led skeptics to claim that in the business of daily life a principle of indifference operates. Many decisions are a gamble in which the dice can *not* be loaded, that is, in which there is not even a crooked way to anticipate the cast of fortune. And wagers, so to speak, are dictated by compulsive magical practices, mere habit, or wish-thinking. This is Richards' domain of random beliefs and hopeful guesses.

The facts fail to confirm the skeptical view of everyday thinking. Almost everybody who acts on principles and guides his present choices by his past experience meets in a thousand details of life with more successes than misfortunes. On the whole, intelligent people invest their money well, they order their human relationships pleasantly enough when they order them at all, they raise their children in mental and physical health. This cannot be all blind chance, balanced out by the bankrupts, the multiple-divorcees, and the heart-broken parents of delinquent juveniles. Disasters happen to very intelligent people, and sometimes "through their own fault." But by any common-sense standard of intelligence, they fall on them less often than on the uninformed and the unprincipled.

Information and principles, when expressed in language, take the form of generalizations. The language has a very limited number of ways to express generalizations. We usually have to say "all *x* is *y*," or "no *x* is *y*," or "most *x* is *y*," or "*x* somewhat resembles *y*," or some paraphrase of these. With increasing statistical and actuarial information, we are sometimes able to speak of the percentage of cases or the incidence of a trait. Sampling techniques guarantee to some extent an even distribution, so that the relatively small number of cases examined will provide reliable information about all the cases. "Children from homes with an income *i* will become juvenile delinquents with a probability of *p*." "*X* percentage of married couples owning their own homes will divorce as compared with *y* percentage of those who pay rent."

Though the body of statistical information is growing daily, most generalizations on which laymen must base their understanding of the world they live in cannot claim any such precision of meaning. "Only psychopaths have no loyalties." "Brain washing and psychological torture prove what the Inquisition failed to demonstrate, that every man has his breaking point." "Child psychology will probably never develop an adequate safeguard against sibling jealousy."

These and thousands of similar statements seem entirely meaningful—that is, they are true or false. They are sweeping; they are unprotected by sampling procedures or careful statistical sifting. Yet they or principles like them are indispensable in thinking about important problems.

The model of the statistical generalizations, nevertheless, throws light upon the nature of other generalizations. It is scarcely two generations since William James sent out the first known questionnaire (he wanted to find out if persons who had lost their legs felt that they had sensations in the missing members). In that brief period everybody has had many surprises as beliefs deriving from untested experience and "general knowledge" have tumbled over one after the other. The reflective man has learned a measure of caution.

He has also learned that when he says "all," "none," etc., he often means "almost all," "hardly any." In the realm of human behavior no (that is, hardly any) generalizations hold one hundred per cent. Even in medicine, a matter of chemistry and physiological structure, people occasionally recover from "incurable" diseases, walk around on fractures, and shoot themselves through the head without doing noticeable brain damage. As to common-sense beliefs in the psychological and cultural spheres, they remain tenuous to the point of being diaphanous.

Statistical findings suggest caution before placing confidence in universal statements. Sampling methods suggest extreme care in order to be representative. The refinement of questionnaire techniques suggests ways in which to ask questions so as not to influence the answers. The traditional "inductive" fallacies (see p. 13 ff) can be interpreted as infringements of rules justified by these procedures.

The positive criterion for testing a generalization is the literal truth of the proposition as stated. If the generalization claims "all," or "none," then one counter instance makes it false. "Finding the counter instance" is the great task of refutation in law courts, scientific journals, the learned controversies in philosophy, criticism, social science. It is also the most likely tool in the debates and discussions of every-day intelligent living.

Yet one must not pedantically carp at enthusiastic and sweeping statements which can be simply and plausibly recast without damage to a position. If a speaker says, "All power corrupts," he need not be rebuked. One can mentally add "by and large."

The two most common forms of faulty generalization are jumping to conclusions and selecting the cases. Let us take these up briefly and exemplify them.

(a) *Hasty Generalization:* "jumping to conclusions"

The fallacy of generalization from too few cases consists in drawing a general conclusion on the basis of an experience with particulars, which statistical science shows to be insufficient in view of the size of the unit examined, or, as pollsters say, the "population." Even where there is a lack of time or money to prepare a proper actuarial survey, there is no excuse for ignorance about the minimum size of the sample—the man who talks to a few people in his office and to his neighbors and then makes a bet on a presidential election deserves to lose the bet.

EXAMPLE. Peter is eating Jane's Frozen Peas when he breaks a tooth on a pebble hidden among them. He tells all who will listen never to buy another Jane's product.

COMMENT. Tired of hearing this complaint, Peter's wife points out that one bad experience with a box of peas does not constitute wide acquaintance with Jane's packaged products. It is not even a fair sample of Jane's Peas.

EXAMPLE. "Professor Ballast is insufferable, and I will have nothing to do with him. He struck his wife when she reminded him of his promise not to borrow more money."

COMMENT. It is easier than in the previous example to feel sympathy with this general conclusion, which likewise stems from a single instance. Sometimes behavior is revealing because it is so far from the norm that a single instance indicates a bent of character.

Although it is true that more instances would provide a better foundation for judgment, in a life situation one would hardly await numerous examples of unpardonable conduct before one felt secure in the conclusion "This man is insufferable."

EXAMPLE. Consider the following proposition: "The proverbs of the language preserve generalizations that have stood the test of time. They embody the experience and wisdom of the race."

COMMENT. Several things are wrong here, but the present concern is primarily with insufficient cases. The speaker presumably refers to such expressions as "A stitch in time saves nine," and "A bad penny always returns." But proverbs often contradict each other: "Look before you leap," "He who hesitates is lost." Or, "Two's company, three's a crowd," "The more the merrier." Or, "Absence makes the heart grow fonder," "Out of sight, out of mind." Counter instances have shown that the generalization about "generalizations that have stood the test of time" is false.

EXAMPLE. A student of contemporary literature writes, "So-called science fiction is a waste of time. I have waded through nine novels and many short stories by the better known writers in science fiction, and I find that their plots are feeble, their characterizations implausible and the science in the fiction is fantastic and largely irrelevant to the action." In answer, the editor of a science fiction magazine points to two examples of well constructed novels in the field, which have had a deserved success.

COMMENT. The editor's argument, citing counter instances, is legitimate in testing the critic's unfavorable generalization. The generalization "All science fiction is bad writing" is exploded by pointing to one good story or novel. In the everyday use of language, people are not so strict. The critic here need not be interpreted as saying that *all* science fiction writing is bad. He is establishing a critical judgment and describing the *genre* as a whole. It is clearly a "waste of time," as he says, to read for hundreds of hours in order to find one or two good stories.

(b) *Unrepresentative Generalization*

Though people in the ordinary case will not be able to sample a widespread population, in the manner of a Gallup poll, knowledge of sampling techniques ought to make them shy of regional, occupational, and other differences. Polling experience abundantly demonstrates that even a very extensive acquaintance with particulars does not warrant a universal conclusion unless the particulars enjoy a representative dispersion. If a minister should poll every member in a large metropolitan congregation of a certain church on, say, capital punishment, this will not enable him to predict with any assurance the division of opinion country-wide, even in the same religious denomination.

The extreme instance of unrepresentative dispersion of cases is the misrepresented selection. Many people have an impulse to suppress the counter instances: consciously or unconsciously they vitiate the evidence by selecting only a part of it. They look exclusively for evidence that will support an idea, with the result that they overlook the opposed evidence. The selection may take a more subtle form: no actual case is suppressed, but the sample is chosen to avoid damaging cases. Side-walk interviews held on prominent shopping streets are often of this sort. An investigation of the effectiveness of TV advertising could be made to yield decidedly different results, depending on whether the survey was made near a college campus or in an underprivileged part of town. Much cited in this connection is the *Literary Digest* poll which predicted the election of Landon over Roosevelt in 1936. An egregious error resulted from an inadequate sampling technique: in 1936, apparently, millions of Democrats could not afford a telephone, or had no time for questionnaires, or had not formed the middle-class "clerical habit" of answering them.

EXAMPLE. A famous historian writes: "Military coalitions usually fall apart before their objective is attained. So it was with the coalitions which opposed Louis XIV, Frederick the Great, and Napoleon I."

COMMENT. The writer is suppressing, one hopes unconsciously, evidence against his generalization. The academese "usually" does not let the good scholar escape the charge of giving a false generalization, unless he is prepared to show that an adequate number of instances justify the assertion "usually." To hedge against contradiction by employing *without evidence* "usually" or any like words is to make unjustified assertions. In this case, the exceptions to the statement are many—for instance, both Louis XIV and Napoleon I were ultimately defeated by coalitions that remained intact against them. Incidentally, on August 31, 1944, Hitler stated in a conference of his generals, "All the coalitions in history have disintegrated sooner or later. The only thing is to wait for the right moment, no matter how hard it is." Thus, in the hope that the allies would fall out among themselves before his defeat, Hitler justified prolonging World War II until battle raged in the streets of Berlin. One may conjecture that Hitler's generals would hardly have dared to subject his generalization to an impartial discussion, and that all present had reason to indulge in rationalization (see #25).

EXAMPLE. Professor Peter is talking to a colleague. "Engineering students generally study hard. I have three engineers taking my sophomore course, and they're all hard workers."

COMMENT. The professor should be allowed some leeway in expressing ideas in a casual conversation. At least, he is trying to cite confirmatory evidence for his opinions. The danger is that, having advanced an idea, he will look for cases from now on that confirm it, rather than examining a representative group of instances. Moreover, the number here is so far too small to permit any but the most hasty generalization.

EXAMPLE. Overheard on a bus, "That Maud is illiterate. She says, 'I ain't got none' for 'I haven't got none.'"

COMMENT. That the correction is also "illiterate" is not the point of this example. The word "ain't" is a sort of shibboleth for the semi-educated; those who use it brand themselves as linguistically hopeless. For the better educated there are many other crucial cases, such as the use of "none" for "any." The interesting thing is the actual presence of such definite criteria. Consider the example of the professor who struck his wife (see pp. 13-14). On the basis of this one act, people are ready to condemn Professor Ballast as being socially hopeless. No one asks if the act is representative. The question "Out of a thousand hours with his wife, how many does Professor Ballast spend striking her?" seems ridiculous. Similarly, people don't require to know how often a speaker says "ain't got" for "haven't got." One occurrence of certain traits is felt to be "representative" enough for the purpose of judgment. But care must be exercised in the extent of the judgment. A speaker who says "ain't" may expose himself as belonging to a certain linguistic group or as employing a certain dialect, but it does not follow that what he says in his idiom may not make excellent sense, or that his speech may not evidence candor and sense. As to men who strike their wives, whatever the provocation, they reveal a serious character fault, and they will be judged accordingly by their associates. Again, it does not follow that their character is all fault. Many men with dangerous tempers have been known to be generally kind, considerate, gentle. The problem, then, in these cases is not that the generalization is hasty or unrepresentative, but that the judgments based upon it may go beyond it. From "bad grammar" to "stupid speaker" is an easy but snobbish step. The leap from "bad temper" to "bad man" is unwarranted and uncharitable.

2 · *Faulty Causal Generalization*

People ordinarily speak of one event causing another when the two events belong to two classes related according to the following rule: every event of the first class is closely followed in time by an event of the second class. Imagine two classes of events, say (1) the class of lightning flashes, and (2) the class of thunder claps. The rule implies that if lightning causes thunder, then every flash of lightning will be followed by a peal of thunder. It will be seen that the classes of events are constructed so that there is a paired relationship between members of the first class and members of the second. We know how to construct the first class, relative to the second, since we know how to put each member in a one-to-one correspondence with members of the second class. Do we know how to construct the second class relative to the first? Well, we know that there will be a member of the second class for every member of the first, but we don't know from the rule of construction whether or not there will be some members of the second class left over. In terms of lightning-followed-by-thunder, we know that every instance of lightning will cause thunder, but the rule doesn't tell us whether or not every instance of thunder has been caused by lightning; perhaps some other way of violently disturbing air masses can also cause thunder. Still, accepting the generalization "lightning causes thunder," we should not regard any atmospheric electrical display (say northern lights) as lightning unless it is followed by thunder.

Causal generalizations are not theoretically different from other sorts. Thus they are subject to the ordinary ills of generalization;

they can be hasty and selective. Yet, the complexity of the causal relationship is such that errors here are more common and harder to detect.

Some of the complexity arises from the fact that very often there is a class of events when there is no evident class of causes. People develop high fevers, and fever seems a definite phenomenon. Automobile tires go flat, and flat tires are remarkably different in a recognizable way from serviceable, inflated tires. Since we start with a noticeable class of effects, it is a class of causes we wish to discover. In such cases a class of causes is constructed according to the pairing-off rule. It is well constructed if and only if every instance in it is followed in time by an instance of the class of effects. If every instance of a puncture is followed by an instance of flat tire, we can say that punctures cause flat tires. But the class of flat tires, though pretty evident to motorists, is still not so well constructed, considered as effects (of course, in its turn it is a cause of other effects). We don't know that every instance of a flat tire is paired off with a puncture. Maybe this present instance is paired off with a leaky valve.

Since most drivers have wide experience with flat tires, and tires are relatively simple man-made things, few are apt to make a false causal generalization about them. In more complex cases, the causal relationship may be obscured; though the class of effects is unmistakable, it is not well constructed relative to a class of causes. Fever, for instance, is caused by a wide range of infectious diseases; each instance of infection is neatly paired with an instance of fever. Thus the presence of fever is small help to a physician in diagnosis. As "diagnosis" means "ascertaining the cause of an illness," the physician needs a wider range of effects before he can distinguish between, say, a common cold and the onslaught of polio.

From these considerations it can be seen how the most important false generalizations about causes occur by taking the class of effects to be well constructed relative to causes. If by far the most frequent pairing-off of flat tires is with punctures, but still not all, generalizing from this factual base to the statement "Every flat tire is caused by a puncture," is obviously a false generalization. In this form, it would be recognized as one, inviting as it does reference to counter instances: "What about leaky valves?" The mistake is more likely to occur in a concealed form: "That tire must have a puncture." In such a case the false generalization is in a suppressed premise:

"Every flat tire is caused by a puncture. That tire is a flat tire. Therefore, that tire must have a puncture." We have just seen that the class of effects is not necessarily well constructed, just because a class of causes is—in this instance punctures relative to flat tires.

It *may* be well constructed. The advance of physical science is marked by a progressive narrowing of the classes of effects so that after the pairing-off with the classes of causes, there will be no instances left over. If something comparable were feasible in medicine, doctors would not talk about fever, but about *x*-fever, *y*-fever, etc., so that the wide class could be replaced by smaller classes determined in such a way that each had its own unique class of causes, where each instance of one is paired with an instance of the other, with no remainder.

In the ordinary case, speakers are able to say that one thing is *the* cause of another only as a sort of convenience. They mean it is the cause with a high degree of probability. If someone should say that public ownership of electrical power in Southern California is the cause of the rapid growth of industry there, he presumably would accept the emendation "everything else being equal, such as available transportation, good labor market, etc., between Southern California and some other area." "The cause" here means "a cause selected because it is the important difference." Persons lacking scientific training quite naturally tend to understand "the cause" to mean what it says. When they do not know any other cause, they suppose that what usually happens always happens and argue with irrefutable logic from false premises to what may be a false conclusion.

EXAMPLE. Peter develops hay fever whenever exposed to goldenrod. He takes his family for a drive in the country but soon begins to sneeze and cough. "The goldenrod must have bloomed early this year," he exclaims, and turns the car towards home.

COMMENT. Peter's statement is an enthymeme. Expanded, his reason for cutting short the drive becomes "The cause of my hay fever is the presence of goldenrod. I now have hay fever. Therefore I am in the presence of goldenrod. Therefore, goldenrod must have bloomed early this year." Peter may be right. But other things may cause the symptoms of hay fever besides goldenrod, as people allergic to one thing are commonly allergic to several. It is wise to turn the car around; the only thing his family might question, if they feel like splitting hairs, is Peter's reasoning, not his action. The example, nevertheless, has its interest, as it shows the common belief that the class of effects is well constructed, simply because the class of causes is, so that one is entitled to make a strict conversion (see #42) from "Every instance of x is a cause of y" to "Every instance of y is an effect of x." This could be so only on the interpretation of "the cause of y is x" as "The only cause of y is x." In the case of hay fever and similar phenomena, this interpretation is almost certainly false.

EXAMPLE. It is sometimes argued that the ultimate cause of war is human aggressiveness, and thus, as long as human beings are aggressive, there will be wars. Hence world peace organizations and disarmament programs are doomed to failure.

COMMENT. The word "ultimate" presumably means a cause behind the proximate causes. The cause of a murder victim's death may be injuries in the organs in the head, in turn caused by contact with the blade of an axe. But "the cause" here refers to the intent to kill on the part of the murderer. Similarly, World War I was touched off by the assassination of an archduke, but historians speak of economic, social, political factors as being causes, and the incident at Sarajevo as being the "occasion" of the ultimatums and mobilizations. Those who propose the above argument are saying that behind these economic and other causes there lies still another cause, which is *the* cause, namely, the aggressiveness of man. Western man is culturally aggressive, but there is no evidence for asserting this aggressiveness to be incurable. At least theoretically, world peace organizations, like national and civil institutions, could make it possible for communities to live in world harmony as they now so often do in neighborhood harmony. This is incidental. The real trouble with the argument is that it goes too far back in the causal chain. It is as if one should say "The cause of the axe murder is the frustration of the middle class." Many things are interrelated in a spreading causal nexus, but in law and common sense speakers limit their causal generalizations to as few classes as seem sufficient to explain the phenomena and thus to guide their conduct. One says, not that the cause of wars is human aggressiveness, but that *a* cause of economic and political conflict, which may or may not lead to war, is human aggressiveness. And sometimes, over-aggressiveness will lead to war even where there is no real opposition of interests. This pushing back of causes can go on indefinitely: the cause of war is the nursing habits of mothers—there is evidence that some aggressiveness may be explained as a result of putting small babies on a rigid feeding schedule!

3 · Assuming the Cause: *"post hoc* reasoning"

The trouble with *the* cause arises from complexity in this construction of the classes. But there is a vulgar error in talking about causal relations which comes from a false generalization about causation itself. This error takes the form of supposing that because something follows something else it is caused by it. One feature that all paired constructions of causes and effects have in common is that the effects follow the causes. This is a necessary feature, but it is by no means a sufficient one for constructing the classes of causes. If it were sufficient, everything that preceded anything else could be regarded as a cause of it. Astrology would be science instead of superstition, since there are configurations of the heavenly bodies antecedent to every event in the world. My plucking a red rose yesterday would also be a cause of my nosebleed today. When the classes of events belong to the same realm of phenomena and are closely related in time, their connection seems more plausible. If the first event is political and so is the second, the propinquity may be very convincing. Many persons who put no stock in astrology would still nod amiably if someone should say, "The death of President Roosevelt caused the cold war."

The sufficient conditions for a well-constructed class of causes are similar to those for any well-constructed generalization—lots of representative cases and no counter instances. Putting the necessary and sufficient conditions together, we may say that one thing is a cause of another if and only if, in numerous and representative cases, every case of the one is followed by a case of the other.

Post hoc means "after this." The words refer to assuming without proof that a prior event explains a subsequent occurrence. The *post hoc* error is called "vulgar" since it is not only common but also ignorant. Magic, superstitions, old-wives tales, and political debate abound in instances of *post hoc*. The first example involves a special feature that deserves notice.

EXAMPLE. A student for his term paper makes a study of European wars and notices that in the years preceding the outbreak of recent wars there occurred an increase of armaments among the

belligerents. He states as the thesis of his paper, "Increased armaments appear as one of the major causes of European wars."

COMMENT. The increase of armaments and the outbreak of war
may both be the effects of the same cause or causes. Friction and
tension between nations can result in (a) armaments and (b) war.
The armament race precedes closely in time and belongs to the
same realm of phenomena as the outbreak of war, but this is not a
sufficient condition for saying that war is an effect of it. The possibility of a cause having several effects makes it difficult in involved
situations to see, where one effect precedes another in time, that the
former is not a cause of the latter. Laboratory workers attempt to
isolate factors in the complex and to alter them one by one, in the
hope of producing some of the effects alone. Where they succeed,
experimenters know that they are dealing with linked effects. Where
the events resist isolation, the experimenters accept a causal connection, the earlier standing as perhaps an intermediate cause. If it
were possible to experiment with whole nations and epochs,
sociologists might discover, by isolating economic, political, psychological factors, whether armament races are linked effects of
antecedent causes or in fact are an intermediate cause of war.

EXAMPLE. A testimonial reads, *"Relax* tablets relieved my headache. You can end your headache troubles, too!"

COMMENT. This is the crassest sort of *post hoc* reasoning, even
assuming the sequence of events true and the opinion offered in
good faith. The fact that the body rids itself of many ailments is
overlooked when attention is centered on the little pink pill. No
doubt the fact that our present age expects wonders from medicine
explains the persistent popularity of worthless patent medicines
whose patrons discover themselves "cured" after they have taken an
alleged remedy. Of course, *Relax* pills may be effective against some
headaches: we shall never establish this by such testimonials.

4 · *Faulty Analogy*

An analogy is the assertion that things which resemble each other
in some respects will resemble each other in some further respect. It
is thus a generalization predicting the occurrence of class characteristics. We are constantly applying our knowledge of one thing to

another. If a friend asks us to help him repair his Chevrolet, we get to work on the basis of what we know about our Ford. If we are wondering whether group medicine will work in the United States, we will look up the record in Sweden or England.

Let us suppose that x and y are members of class F, that is, they have the property f in common. Members of a class, of course, often share more than one property—the members of some classes share innumerable properties, for instance the class of human beings. To argue by analogy is to suppose that since x and y, members of class F, have properties f_1, f_2, f_3 . . . in common, they will also share some further specified property f_m. Thus

$$
\begin{array}{cc}
x_{f_1} & y_{f_1} \\
x_{f_2} & y_{f_2} \\
x_{f_3} & y_{f_3}
\end{array}
$$
therefore, as x_{f_m} then y_{f_m}

Now it is always possible that y will not show the property f_m, that the analogy will break down. Indeed, every analogy must break down at some point since the class members are similar but not identical. Though generalizing by analogy is dangerous when only one or two similarities are known, it is good reasoning if the number of essential qualities known to be shared is very large. But we must always be prepared for the point of "break down." There is no sure rule for predicting this point, though there are rough guides. The more characteristics shared by objects, the narrower the class is in its extension. In other words, as we add characteristics, we keep potentially limiting the number of individuals that qualify. For instance if we start with the class of human beings, and then add the requirement "male," we cut out about half the members of the original class. Then if we add "over eight feet tall," we have brought our class down to a roomful, if that.

The fewer the essential characteristics shared, the wider the class. Plants, from the simplest lichens to the giant redwoods, share only the most general biological characteristics. A very wide class like this, of course, has sub-classes, but if certain common traits in some sub-class are discovered, there is a low initial probability that other members of the parent class will also share these characteristics. I find that carrots and turnips have certain things in common. Can I risk a prediction about squash and onions? About orchids and seaweed?

Faulty analogy consists either in assuming that shared properties will continue indefinitely to be found in new members, or in assuming that it is highly probable there will be *some* other shared property in a class so wide that there is only a low initial probability of finding any other shared properties relevant to the purpose at hand.

EXAMPLE. Legal arguments often take the form of showing that a given case falls under a precedent, which is to say that it is analogous to some previously decided case. And the courts commonly decide the meaning of a statute by examining whether or not a particular situation is analogous to the situation with which the statute was designed to deal. The case of *Omaha and Council Bluffs Street Railway Company vs. Interstate Commerce Commission* (230 U. S. 324) will illustrate legal arguments founded on analogy. The Supreme Court had to decide whether the statute granting the Commission jurisdiction to regulate "railroads" applied to a streetcar line which crossed a state border. Some state courts had previously held streetcar lines were railroads in the sense of the statute; others had held they were not. Mr. Justice Lamar gave the Supreme Court's decision as follows:

> This conflict of state court decisions is not so great as at first blush would appear. For all recognize that while there is similarity between railroads and street railroads, there is also a difference. Some courts, emphasizing the similarity, hold that in statutes the word "Railroad" includes Street Railroad, unless the contrary is required by context. Others, emphasizing the dissimilarity, hold that "Railroad" does not include Street Railroad unless required by the context . . .

Mr. Justice Lamar then proceeded to examine whether the similarities of streetcar lines and railroads made the two analogous *for the purpose of* regulation by the Interstate Commerce Commission. He pointed out that railroads were not characteristically local in their business, they connected with other lines to move freight across the country, they were prone to engage in rebating, pooling, and discrimination (which the statute was designed to regulate), they operated elaborate stations and terminal facilities. Streetcar lines, on the contrary, were primarily local, rarely connected with other lines covering widespread areas, did a passenger business unsuited to rebating, pooling, or discrimination, and generally picked up and deposited passengers on the street. Noting these differences, the

Court decided that a streetcar line could not be included by analogy as a "railroad" subject to Interstate Commerce Commission regulation.

COMMENT. This instance is typical of the careful application of analogy to settle a legal problem. The comparison is limited to similarities and differences which are relevant to the question at hand. It is quite possible that on the next day the Court might have considered a streetcar line included by analogy as a railroad for the purpose of taxation or for some other purpose in which the similarities might be more relevant than the differences.

EXAMPLE. King James I of England was wont to argue that as the monarch is the head of the state, republicanism is demonstrably false. If you cut off the head of a body, the other organs cannot function, and the body dies. Similarly, if you cut off the head of the state, the state may flop around awhile, but it is due to perish in time or become easy prey to its neighbors.

COMMENT. This kind of argument is sometimes called "figurative analogy." It is only in a figurative sense that a state can be compared to a living body. From such comparisons no generalizations about further relevant shared characteristics are at all probable.

Figurative analogy may be safely employed only by way of illustrating one's meaning. In order to explain the changes one may expect to experience in passing from youth to age, I may, in a purple passage, write: "Life is like a river. It begins as a joyous brook, matures into a powerful stream, and finally creeps on sluggishly until it is lost in the sea." No one would be apt to draw from this and from his knowledge of rivers principles about the conduct of business or human relations.

EXAMPLE. Nature Lover Peter has observed that the Humpback salmon dies after spawning in the rivers of the Pacific Northwest. He observes a "run" of King salmon in the same region. "All these salmon," says Peter ruefully, "can never return again to the sea after spawning."

COMMENT. The class of salmon is a very narrowly constructed class, but it is still only highly probable, not certain, that what is true of one sub-class (species) will be true of all. Were Peter a better naturalist, he would discover that King salmon, unlike the Humpback, survive spawning and swim merrily back to the sea.

One highly effective device for refuting an opponent is to exaggerate his contention by asserting "Then you must also believe that . . ." or "This is the same as saying . . ." Such phrases commonly introduce an extension so that the discussion turns to considering the problem in the light of some allegedly analogous situation.

EXAMPLE. Paul, ignorant of the niceties of disputation, says, "I believe the city ought to collect the rubbish as a municipal service. The present system of private contracts has produced poor service and led some people to duck the rate by throwing rubbish away on streets and vacant lots." Peter, in pretended astonishment, cries, "The next thing you will ask us to do is to go into the transportation business with municipal buses and into the power business with a municipal power plant. Step after step you will take us down the road through municipal ownership to full socialism."

COMMENTS. Paul proposes one particular change to be made independently of municipal participation in other programs—which may or may not have merits irrespective of the "road to socialism." Peter's strategy in argument is: first, to extend the discussion to matters he considers more clear or favorable to his contention; second, to refute these other matters by demonstrating or assuming such action unwise; third, to conclude that the refutation disposes of the original—and allegedly analogous—proposition. Paul's only recourses are to decline the extension, declare it not analogous, or point out he is advancing one particular question and will examine *its* merits.

One further device of faulty analogy is common enough to deserve separate mention. It is so common, in fact, that it has been given a name: stereotyping. If an individual belongs to a class, then the individual possesses the characteristics common to the class. But that is all that the individual necessarily has in common with the other members. Stereotyping consists in lumping all sorts of individuals together and treating them as a unit for propaganda purposes, simply because they share one or a few common properties recognized by some familiar term in the language. It is this last matter of the familiar class name that seems to distinguish stereotyping from other varieties of faulty analogy. Political novices are often astonished to find Republicans voting with Democrats on some bills. Even parents are sometimes agreeably surprised when their own teenage children show no interest in hot-rod racing, unpleasant hair styles or the current popular music idols. The stereotype of the Republican seems to include the notion of "always fighting the Democrats"; that of the teen-ager seems to involve enthusiasm for the singer Simper Smirk and the tomato slice haircut.

EXAMPLE. A real-estate broker tells a colleague, "I don't have to worry about this deal. The buyer is a musician, and everybody knows musicians are babes-in-escrow." A few weeks later the broker ruefully confessed to the same colleague, "The deal fell through. I thought a musician would be a pushover, but it turned out that he knew as much about property values as I did."

COMMENT. All musicians know something of music. After that they are not a "harmonious" group.

EXAMPLE. Yankees will be Yankees and Southerners will be Southerners, that's for sure.

COMMENT. If this is a tautology, then it will be perfectly safe to base an argument on it. But the chances are that this is the so-called pregnant use of the terms—compare "Out West, where men are *men.*" Translated, then, the example means something like "Yankees will be sharp-traders, narrow in their regional interests, taciturn like Coolidge, etc., etc., as well as being residents of New England or deriving from there. Southerners will drawl, believe in keeping "Nigras" in their "place," prefer to live in ruinous buildings whose white Grecian columns are entwined with honeysuckle, etc., etc., as well as being residents of certain states below the Mason-Dixon line or deriving from there." It is evident that, like other faulty analogies, regional stereotypes constitute an unwarranted generalization of the grossest sort: these people live in certain regions; therefore, they are bound to be marked with all the traits of certain neighbors. The use of a stereotype, then, as a premise in argument is always otiose. "Southerners are Southerners. So-and-so is a Southerner. Therefore . . ." What? Only that he lives in, or derives from, the South.

5 · *Composition and Division*

Related to faulty analogy is the *fallacy of composition;* this is to assume that what holds true for each member of a class standing alone will hold true for all members of the class taken together. Since a whole sometimes does and sometimes does not exhibit the characteristics of its parts, it is not possible to *assume* that parts and whole will share the same characteristics in any given case. Illustrations are easy to produce. Someone might argue that since each member of the Supreme Court possesses his own personal prejudices, the decisions of the Court as a whole are bound to be the product of these personal elements. In fact, the very reason for group decisions is that a pooling of knowledge makes for sounder judgment than any individual member of the group is apt to produce.

Incidentally, the fallacy of composition sometimes turns on the ambiguity of "all." Often "all" means "each instance." Thus the sentence, "All residents of these pueblos are Pueblo Indians," translates into "Each person, if he's a resident of these pueblos, is a Pueblo Indian." But sometimes "all" provides a way of talking about a totality (or *Gestalt*) that cannot be taken as simply a sum of its parts. No one would suppose that when Caesar wrote, "All Gaul is divided into three parts," he meant "Every instance of Gaul is an instance of tripartite divisibility." Whether or not the word "all" actually occurs in reference to a totality, there is danger in assuming that what is true of the whole is true *in the same way* of each of the parts, and, conversely, that what is true of the parts is true of the whole.

EXAMPLE. A lobbyist points out, "A tariff on meat will benefit the stockgrowers, a tariff on coal will benefit the coal miners, a tariff on toys will benefit the toy manufacturers, a tariff on any commodity will benefit the producers of that commodity. Therefore, a tariff on all commodities will benefit everybody who produces any commodity—and that is the whole country in one way or another."

COMMENT. Since producers are also consumers, tariffs on everything may well bring more total costs than total benefits. Also, multiplication of tariffs inspires retaliation and creates other complications which cut down international trade and threaten domestic production.

EXAMPLE. An economist writes, "Each individual will further his own economic interest to the best of his ability. The result is that all individuals together—society as a whole—thereby achieve the maximum possible economic advancement."

COMMENT. This cardinal assumption of Adam Smith's *laissez*

faire economics is nowhere maintained in pure form today. Experience has shown that while the efforts of individuals seeking their own welfare contribute to the economic advancement of society in some types of production, they lead to duplication and waste in other areas. Consider the result of unregulated, competitive exploitation of an oil field.

The *fallacy of division* lies in assuming that what holds true for all members of a class taken together is necessarily true for each alone. This assumption is the converse of composition. Of course, what is true of all is often true of each, but not *necessarily* so. For instance, a general may strive to preserve the fighting efficiency of his army as a whole by giving orders which will result in the fighting efficiency of some units being destroyed. Less melancholy examples can easily be adduced.

EXAMPLE. A city alderman proposes, "The City revenues have fallen off. I propose a 20 per cent across-the-board cut for all City Departments. We'll just have to get along with four-fifths of the service we've been used to."

COMMENT. It is incorrect to assume that a 20 per cent budget cut will result in services differing only proportionally from the previous standard. Possibly reduced financial support will result in proportionate reduction of service in some departments, other activities may become unfeasible, and still others may not be noticeably affected. Further, the effects may be qualitative as well as quantitative. Street sweeping may be quantitatively reduced, while the City Engineer may quit and a competent replacement be unobtainable.

EXAMPLE. A famous lecturer says, "The credence given to Marx's economic interpretation of history is extraordinary. Why, Marx's own life denies his theory. Born the son of a lawyer with a comfortable place assured to him for the asking, still he chose the hard and penniless life of a political exile. If economic motivation had so little appeal for Marx himself, how could he believe all history to be determined by the economic motivations of mankind?"

COMMENT. The lecturer's observation is thought provoking. Marx's own life does indeed provide a striking instance of a man whose primary motivations were non-economic. Even if Marx's point is right that all society organizes itself along the class lines of economic interest, it would be an instance of the fallacy of division to suppose that what is true of all taken together, need be true of each individual. Economic motivations might be a least common denominator sufficient to determine class interests even though no one person was primarily motivated by them.

6 · *The All-or-Nothing Mistake*

Though truth is sometimes a matter of black or white, much more often it ranges through a whole spectrum of colors. One catches a train or fails to catch it. An electric light is on, or it is off. On the other hand, a government will never be simply "good" or "bad," for here the range of possible variations is infinite. Where a situation requires a relative judgment, it is a fallacy to wrap up a judgment on it into one hasty bundle labeled All or Nothing, Good or Bad, Blameworthy or Blameless. This kind of thinking peoples the mind with simple heroes and villains instead of characters that are true to life.

The all-or-nothing mistake assumes a naked dichotomy where no such simplification is warranted. Mr. Justice Frankfurter has called this "the great either–or." For example, an office holder may declare that others must either favor his policies or oppose them. This position overlooks the possibility of indifference as well as favoring some policies and opposing others. The assumption that there is no middle ground is a favorite weapon of persons desiring to force others to take sides in black-white terms even though the problem is not simple and though its fair solution requires an evaluation of several possibilities. Hitler takes shrewd account of this in discussing propaganda:

> The task of propaganda is, for example, not a weighing of the various rights, but the exclusive emphasis of the one advocated by it. It has not to inquire objectively into the truth, so far as it favors the other sides, in order to represent it to the masses in doctrinary honesty, but it has to serve its own side continuously. . . .
> This feeling [i.e. the thinking of the masses] is not complicated, but very simple and conclusive. There are not many differentiations, but a positive or a negative, love or hate, right or wrong, truth or lie, but never half so and half so, or partially, etc.
> Hitler, *Mein Kampf*

No one can wholly avoid this fallacy of treating complex things as if they could be divided into simple extremes. Sometimes action has to be taken according to an unambiguous decision even though a two-fold classification is unrealistic. Doctors squirm when the lawyer demands whether or not a certain individual shall be pronounced sane or insane. Medicine is more complicated than the gates of an insane asylum, yet someone has to know when to swing the gates open or shut. Again, the shortness of time and the demand for effective action forever press toward decisions which a man would blush to defend in the abstract. In the polling booth the claims and counterclaims, charges and analyses, promises and issues—all the vast complication of the campaign—must be reduced to simple votes for or against candidates, yes or no on propositions. The citizen most aware of the complexity of issues and personalities has no more choice of alternatives than the most irresponsible elector.

Where there is not the demand for an immediate decision, impatient individuals commit a fallacy when they cut through complexity as if everything has to be decided by simple affirmation or rejection. "Spare me the details—is it good or bad?" This is the "sentiment" of the masses which Hitler says is the function of propaganda to exploit. To consider the all-or-nothing fallacy important chiefly as a tool of the demagogue is to miss its universal range. It is a constant attendant in discussion, as the following examples will attest.

EXAMPLE. The chairman of a prize committee: "In the case of all these prizes, you should notice that honor is often a more important motivation than money."

Mr. Peter: "You mean that money doesn't matter?"

COMMENT. A crude example though not unknown in live discussion. To suggest qualifying an idea is often interpreted as full rejection by one who makes an intellectual habit of all-or-none.

EXAMPLE. "The only way to convince this union crowd is to hold out until they're too damned broke to strike any more. You treat 'em kind, and they take a mile. Get tough, and they'll knuckle under."

COMMENT. Better call in a mediator! The speaker *may* be right in his assessment of the particular union. But where there are many possibilities in a situation, the chances are that any only-way solution is an unwarranted attempt to cut through a complex problem.

EXAMPLE. Paul: "Is Henry intelligent?"
                  Peter: "Sure he is."

COMMENT. In casual conversation people don't insist on precision. But what can asking for or conceding Henry's intelligence mean? Men are not sharply divided into the intelligent and the unintelligent. Paul and Peter probably know this and in context understand each other well enough.

EXAMPLE. The Communist Manifesto: "The proletarians have nothing to lose but their chains. They have a world to win."

"Workers of the world, unite!"

COMMENT. Proletarians! Lives, property, freedom may be lost. The world may be less than "won." But let no one underestimate the power of a slogan.

7 · The False Dilemma

Everybody, unfortunately, has experience with true dilemmas; that is, when one is forced to choose between undesirable alternatives. To have this operation is dangerous; to delay is to risk illness or even death. To study tonight is to give up the party; not to study is to risk flunking the test. To go to the party *and* study is to give up all sleep. In a false dilemma, the speaker represents the situation as offering only undesirable alternatives when the facts do not warrant it. One of the given alternatives may actually be neutral or even desirable, or, more frequently, an unstated alternative exists which is at least neutral. In other words, the false dilemma turns out to be no dilemma at all. The all-or-nothing fallacy and the false dilemma are related since each involves ignoring alternative positions. The relation of dilemmas to the rules of classification is explained on page 39.

EXAMPLE. There is a famous Greek dilemma. One of the sophists advertised that any pupil of his would win his first case at law or not have to pay for the course of instruction. A pupil completed the course, announced that he did not expect to practice law, and refused to pay the sophist for the course. The sophist sued, and the pupil entered the following plea: "If I lose this case, according to the agreement I do not have to pay, as it is my first case. If I win it, I do not have to pay by the judgment of the court." The sophist replied: "On the contrary, if you win this case, you have to pay, according to the agreement. If you lose it, you must also pay, according to the judgment of the court."

COMMENT. It is not known how the case was decided.

EXAMPLE. A farmer can never expect to make much money. Either the farmer raises a bumper crop and finds that the price is low, or the price is all right, but he finds he has only a meager crop to dispose of.

COMMENT. This dilemma is false since it overlooks the possibility of government subsidies and price supports as well as other factors. Refuting a false dilemma by pointing out an additional possibility which is not undesirable is called going around or between the horns of the dilemma.

EXAMPLE. Abbé Sieyès, a figure in the French Revolution, posed this famous dilemma concerning a bicameral legislature, "If the second chamber agrees with the first, it is superfluous; if it disagrees it is pernicious."

COMMENT. This is a false dilemma since disagreement of the second chamber is not necessarily "pernicious." One may question either of the assumptions of a dilemma, namely, that the alternatives are exhausted or that all the alternatives are alike undesirable. Refuting a false dilemma by pointing out that one of the alternatives is not undesirable is called taking the dilemma by the horns.

TROUBLE WITH CONSTRUCTIONS

The previous section, starting with the supposition that the evidence was fairly well in hand, was concerned with the problem of knowing what could reasonably be asserted about it. There was no question as to what the situation involved, and it was assumed that the classifications and general notions were serviceable. All cows are brown—the problem was the handling of *all*, rather than

cows or *brown*. Does the evidence warrant saying *all* or only *some?*
The notions *cows* and *brown* were assumed to be clear and intelligible. In this section the interest centers on the formation of
the notions themselves, rather than how they are related together
in propositions. The most difficult problems in managing the materials of argument arise in the forming of notions and classifications and the like. We shall use the term *constructions* to cover all
notions and abstractions. All abstract thinking proceeds by selecting aspects of the situation and making constructions out of them.

Some constructions are relatively easy to understand—*cows,* for
instance—a three-year old can form the notion of a cow. The
names such simple constructions bear are well known terms in the
common speech. Every user of the language can learn the proper
construction and hence the correct use of the name. The class
name "child" represents a construction made up from certain things
in the world, children, markedly distinguished from other things:
babies, adults, and, for that matter, elephants. The construction
reflects the *situation* in the world in a rather obvious way. A
speaker, if pressed, can give at least rough conditions for a proper
use of the term.

$$\longrightarrow \qquad\qquad \longrightarrow$$

class name *means* construction *stands for* situation

As the class name is often a familiar term in the common language
and the situation is the state of affairs in whatever aspect of the
world is under discussion, the only subjective part is the construction, though, perhaps, since the speakers communicate the construction, this part should be called "inter-subjective."

All constructions involve at least implicit classification—babies
are grouped under the heading "babies" and children under "children." Now speakers are constantly making new classifications. For
this reason some constructions do not have a traditional name in
the language, and a name must be made up for them. It may be
a new word or a whole new phrase made up of old words, but
whatever it is, it often names a construction that stands for characteristics of the situation not previously remarked. Since all writing and speaking of point proceeds by drawing attention to fresh
groupings of things, it is evident that anybody who wants to make
a contribution in discussion must understand the elements of classifying if his constructions are to be intelligible.

Suppose a boy gets from his uncle a bag containing a hundred marbles. And suppose this boy has a little sister who wants to play with the marbles. The little girl begins to sort them. First she arranges them by color, green with green, red with red. Then she sorts them within the colors, clear glass with clear, cloudy with cloudy. There are some hard to classify: opaque agates, little dull clay balls, marbles of mixed colors. She has disappointments. Though she is very fond of purple, there are no purple marbles. And some of the prettiest blues have little chips and flaws.

The boy says his sister is silly. *This* is the way marbles should be sorted. He first pretends to shoot with each one, then sets aside one of the "aggies" and two of the chipped "migs" as "shooters." The rest he arranges in several orders, regardless of color or marbling. The least mig, he tells his sister, is worth ten of the "dough babies," but the best migs are worth ten of the worst, and the aggies are worth at least ten of the best migs. A good shooter is worth the lot; in fact, it is beyond price, but he won't know if there are any good shooters until he has tried some out in competition. His sister doesn't understand anything he is talking about and decides it is really boys who are silly.

Here are only a hundred marbles. Yet it is at once evident that there are a great number of ways to classify them. If they are sorted as to color, there will be empty classes, purple for instance. If "cloudiness" (marbling) is the criterion, then the clay marbles present difficulty: they are not marbled, but they are not transparent, either. If cost is to be the consideration, then there are two obvious ways to put them in order: monetary value, for agates are relatively expensive, or trade value, which seems to depend on the fashion or taste of certain boys in the neighborhood—one marble "costs" ten others. And so on, indefinitely.

The *situation* is present. It would be a truly "silly" error to assume, because the marbles are classifiable as to color, that there must be somewhere a purple marble. And maybe there will not turn out to be a first-class shooter in the bag. So the situation puts a limit to the number and kinds of constructions. And the names ("shooter," "pretty ones") or the descriptions ("worth ten of") must *mean* the constructions. This is all we intend by these terms, and there is no metaphysical commitment in the notion of the "situation."

Even in the simple cases of classification, there can be trouble.

It will be seen that difficulty can arise over where to put marginal cases. When this happens, the classification may carelessly omit them altogether—they get left out. Sometimes the classification seems to require putting the same object under two coordinate headings. In this event, the classification does not function in respect to that object, for the general function of a classification is to *separate*.

From these considerations, since the time of the early Greeks certain criteria of classification have been enforced. They can be expressed simply, and we shall try to state them in a set of rules. The fallacy of violating any of the rules falls under the general head of "faulty classification."

Rule 1. The classification must be exhaustive. (The dough babies must not be left out, simply because they don't fit the division of *clear* or *cloudy*.)

Rule 2. The classification must be exclusive. (Cross-classifications are permissible—cloudy-red marbles—but there must be what is sometimes called a *fundamentum divisionis*, which prevents putting something under two coordinate headings.)

Rule 3. The classification must be adequate to the purpose for which it is designed. (The little girl's classification of the marbles into colors, etc., though perhaps suitable to the purpose of the little girl, is not adequate to the game of migs.)

Rule 4. The divisions of the classification must be precise enough to avoid serious marginal cases. (If boys don't usually agree on, say, which marbles are shooters, then this construction is vague.)

8 · *Faulty Classification*

The violation of each of the four rules gives a different fallacy. Some of the rules, however, are more complicated than others and will be treated here at greater length. There are many ways in which a construction can be vague (Rule 4), and it will be useful to distinguish several of them in the discussion. Similarly, the third rule is related to some misconceptions about the nature of classification, and we shall also wish to discuss these at length. The fallacies of non-exhaustive or non-exclusive classifications should be relatively easy to understand, and one or two examples will

probably suffice. So under the present heading, though all viola-
tions of the rules are properly regarded as "faulty classifications,"
we shall take up only the failures to be exhaustive and exclusive.

(a) *Non-exhaustive Classification* (Rule 1)

To criticize a classification for being non-exhaustive is to assert
that it does not take account of the whole situation. It is always
possible to divide, that is to classify, the situation so that everything is regarded as one thing or another without remainder:
beautiful or non-beautiful, true or non-true. Such divisions are
model classifications as to being exhaustive, but they may be far
from adequate to a given purpose (see #6). The difficulty arises
when the classification is supposed to distinguish important characteristics in the situation.

In argument, where the classifications are often more complicated than cases like the marbles, one way to test a position depending on them is to search for elements in the situation which
have got left out. If one finds such elements, it by no means follows that the classification is deliberately selective (see #1) or
deceptive. It may just be careless. It is often possible to correct
classifications that leave something out by a more careful attention to the basis of division.

EXAMPLE. Traveling Salesman Peter has submitted his expense
account. A few days pass, and the boss calls him in: "I understand
the $421 for plane fare, the $128 for hotel bills, the $84 for dining
out, and the $37 for entertaining. But what is this $202 for miscellaneous?" Peter shrugs, "Oh, that's for things I couldn't fit in."

COMMENT. Possibly Peter will satisfy his boss, but if he uses
the same principles of accounting in his income tax returns, he
can expect a visit from the treasury agents. This example is not
an argument. It merely illustrates the frequent use of the feeble
"miscellaneous" heading to take care of classifications which are
not exhaustive.

EXAMPLE. Overheard on a bus: "She never says a kind word,
and when she does, she doesn't mean it."

COMMENT. The speaker here has made what is called an Irish
bull, that is, a statement that on the face of it is contradictory
nonsense: "I'll never forgive you until the day you die, if you should

live so long." The Irish may use the bull for humorous effect, but the speaker in the example presumably recognized that the distinction "kind or unkind" didn't cover all the evidence, and that a third division "only apparently kind" was needed.

EXAMPLE. A critic writes, "Ivy Compton Bennet and Paul Goodman, to name two, are lively writers pointing to new directions. Yet important modern novels fall into three classes, all unfortunate for contemporary letters. There is the historical novel, more or less carefully reconstructing a period or a situation of the past and exploiting it to give us an understanding of our heritage. This is the proper function of the historian or biographer, not of the novelist. There is, secondly, the psychological study, which purports to convey by literary means insights into personal relations. This seemed a promising field initially, but all the novels of this school are failures, and now it is evident that failure is inherent in the method. Finally, there is the novel of manners, in the tradition of Jane Austen and Henry James. But this tradition is exhausted, and what we get today are problem pieces and regional studies, like those of the southern school."

COMMENT. Even if it can be assumed that the critic's eliptical arguments convey sound judgments—that, in fact, each of the three classifications mentioned has failed and is now creatively useless, the unspoken conclusion that the modern novel is in a bad way as a literary form follows only if it is true that there are no other varieties of novels than those mentioned. There seem to be many interesting novels that do not fit the categories of the critic, some of them also very different from each other, for example the novels of Ivy Compton Burnett and Paul Goodman, whom the critic himself mentions.

(b) Non-exclusive Classification (Rule 2)

A classification is non-exclusive when elements in the situation get put under more than one co-ordinate head. The trouble here can sometimes be corrected by choosing a different basis of division. A simple artificial example would be for someone to attempt to divide animals as "cold-blooded" or "vertebrates." Since reptiles, fish, etc., are both, this classification does not operate for these important sections of the animal world. The classification is easily corrected by distinguishing first among the vertebrates and invertebrates, then perhaps among the cold and warm-blooded animals. The shark then is properly classified as species vertebrate, sub-species cold-blooded; elephants as vertebrates, warm-blooded; crabs as invertebrates, cold-blooded. This is not very profound, but it is at least applicable to the animal world.

One way to examine an argument dependent on a classification is to test whether or not the classification is exclusive. If it is not for any one case at all, then there is a possibility that the classification is not applicable to the case or cases at issue in the argument. If the classification is faulty in general, then it may be faulty in important particulars. Again it should be observed that the fault may not be deliberate. It is very hard to make adequate classifications, and the classifier may simply not have noticed that his divisions are not applicable to certain elements of the situation. The thing to do is to examine the *fundamentum divisionis*, the basis of the division, and see if the classification can be repaired.

EXAMPLE. Peter argues, "You either save your money or you invest it. If you save it, you get caught in the inflation, since money in the stocking will buy less tomorrow than it will if you spend it today. If you invest it, you run the risk of losing it. They've got you going and coming."

COMMENT. Many forms of savings are relatively free of risk—deposits in banks, government bonds, and some types of investment trusts. The accumulated interest is normally larger than the rate of inflation. In the case of sound stocks and some real estate, the value inflates with the rest of the economy. Peter's argument is a false dilemma.

All arguments pose a dilemma insofar as they rest on classification. The dilemma becomes a false dilemma when the classification is faulty. False dilemmas turn on a non-exclusive classification whenever one of the alternatives is not as represented, just as it will be non-exhaustive whenever there is a third alternative. In this connection it will be instructive to review #7 and see if you can decide which of the dilemmas cited there get their plausibility from non-exhaustive classifications, which from non-exclusive, that is, which violate Rule 1 and which Rule 2.

9 · *Misconceptions about Classification* (Rule 3)

The problem of the relation of classifications to the situation is a difficult one, and thinkers have often gone wrong on it. In fact, the theory of "sets" or classes is still a very busy field in mathe- matics and logic. What we say here about classification and con- structions in general must perforce be elementary and partial. We are interested in fallacy: in this connection two main misconcep- tions of the function of classification have led to broad errors in argument. These errors are related to the philosophical systems of Platonism and relativism, but we shall try to characterize them without a long digression into the history of philosophy.

Classifications are expounded in general terms, the so-called uni- versals. This means only that when speakers use general terms in the language, such as "man," "woman," "child," they are classifying objects in the world according to certain traits or referring to the class of such objects itself.

1. Peter is a child.
2. The child is the father of the man.

In (1) the speaker says that Peter belongs to the class of the child (children). In (2) the speaker says something in general (hence "general terms") about children, as well as about fathers and men. General terms like "child" mean certain constructions, and the constructions in turn obviously stand in some way for the situation. All children have a great number of traits in common. The situation in the world of human beings seems to impose a construction for "child," so that a language which lacked a term for the child-construction (that is, one can imagine, had only a word for *person,* which provided no guide to age or maturity) would certainly seem to lack a much needed term. Perhaps it would be correct to assume that the construction *child* is so much needed that every language has one or more names to mean it. In this common-sense way of talking about general terms, it will be seen that there are two notions at least that will stand examination. What can it mean to say that the situation in the world "imposes" a construction? What can it mean to say that a term is "needed" for a construction? Reification and relativism give very different answers to these questions, and each can lead to serious error.

In connection with Rule 3 (that classifications must be adequate for the purpose for which they are designed), we will argue that these errors arise from a misunderstanding of the role of purpose. Reification holds that the structures are imposed by a suprasensible world, and that the only purpose that the classifier should have is to learn to know them as they are. Relativism holds that there are no structures in the world or anywhere else; there are just totally discrete particulars. Hence in relativism no limits are set to the activity of the classifier, which is anyhow a mere exercise in fiction. We shall take up these misconceptions in turn in the form in which they result, for argument, as fallacies.

(a) *Reification*

In the *Phaedrus* Plato says that classifications should not proceed, as a bad carver might, by cutting up the situation just anyhow, but should break it "at the joints." The assumption is that there are natural structures in the situation which it is one's duty to discover. These structures are closer to reality than other characteristics, which are mere accidents due to the recalcitrance of the material in taking shape in imitation of the idea. The idea is in a heaven, and it is "ideal," that is, perfect, changeless, timeless. The things of this palpable world try to imitate the ideas, with indifferent success. The ideas, the eternal structures, are after all free from the gross embodiment of sense experience, in their pristine perfection. What you have got to do, unless you want to hack away as a bad carver, is to discover the natural structures, those closest to the ideas. Then your classification will produce neat joints and chops.

This view has the common-sense merit of recognizing that constructions stand for characteristics of the situation. It has the disadvantage of a great unprovable assumption, namely, that the characteristics referred to by the "natural" constructions are somehow more real than the other characteristics present. The preferred status of some structures over others is that the Platonists prefer certain *purposes* over others in classifying. These purposes turn out, on analysis, to be precisely those purposes imbedded in a culture and so traditional in their view of the world that they are felt to be natural and get built into the language. They have names in the common speech, such obvious names as "man," "redness," "goodness." Language seems to render this Platonism a natural thing to believe, and it is not surprising that it makes a strong appeal. This is not only a view that the division between, say, child and man is a natural division; it goes deeper. The term "redness," for instance, since it exists in the language, would seem to be a term for something, to name something, just as "the New York Central Railway" names a very complicated and ramified system. It does not seem farfetched to assume that, since redness has a name, it must exist. "Red is a primary color," is a perfectly legitimate expression in the language but one implicitly making an astonishing claim. Does this not seem to say that there exists a class of colors, rather like the class of children, and that red is a member of this class? Not this book or this country schoolhouse, of course, but redness itself, the redness that makes red the surfaces of this cheek or this rose. The inventor of language was a Platonist. Modern Platonists adhere to what they call the "perennial philosophy," and they acknowledge this philosophy has a "natural piety toward language."

There is more to Platonism than advice to eschew new-fangled terminology and modernistic or otherwise reprehensible ways of looking at things, that is, of making constructions. The senses can never give knowledge of redness, only of this red object or of that —and even the best example is not perfect. The senses, likewise, cannot give knowledge of *child*, only of Peter or Paul or Hazel. But these particulars can grow old and die, and knowledge must be an ideal ageless perfection. There is no point in a feeble copy. However clear the photograph, one would prefer to see the person. However typical the person, one should prefer to know the Idea. Peter or Paul or Hazel are imperfect copies of the ideal "child." Thus, in Platonism the ideal child and redness are conceived of as existing purely, of floating about, as it were, ready to enter into particular bodies or surfaces.

This *reification*, thing-ization, of preferred constructions is a fallacy when it leads to mistakes in argument. Philosophers may do as they choose in deciding what things are "real" and what are not. But when they carry over their reifications into other fields, then they are asking for unnecessary trouble. The history of science, of affairs, even of mathematics has been troubled for generations uncounted by demands for "real definitions," assertions that something *is* because it *must* be, denegations of whole areas of inquiry as unreal and wicked.

Reification, then, is the "hypostatizing" of entities, that is, the making of abstractions into substances. It is the assumption that *child* exists (in a Platonic heaven) over and above Peter, Hazel, Ethel. It is not necessary to make this assumption even if language suggests it. Universals, such as "redness" and "child," can be interpreted in a way that makes no philosophical claims as to whether or not the constructions they name refer to entities in the real world. This way of handling them is called *Reduction.*

Reduction is a rule asserting that any sentence containing a general term, if the general term designates an intelligible construction, can be reduced to a sum of sentences containing mention only of particulars. Abstractions ("redness," "justice") are included under general terms. Thus, A reduces to a_1 or a_2 or a_3 . . . or a_n, where A is in a sentence containing the general term, and a_1, a_2, a_3, etc., are sentences referring only to particular instances. Thus the sentence, "A child needs security," as far as the child-construction goes, reduces to "Peter needs security, or Hazel needs security, or Ethel needs security," and so for all children. "Red is a color," similarly reduces to a mention of red books, red balloons, and other objects. The word "color" in "Red is a color" points out that whenever an object is red it is colored, that is, belongs to the larger class of all red, green, blue books and all other colored objects. This may seem a strange kind of "reduction," involving, as it does, expansion to unlimited numbers of sentences—in the case of "child" one, in fact, for every individual young human being that now is, ever was, or ever will be. The "reduction" consists in the boiling down of general terms to particulars. The difficulty presented by the great number of sentences is only practical. Theoretically, it is soon clear how the process works out for the sentences in question, and since the series are fairly orderly, a sort of induction can be applied to show the reduced content of the general terms. (In point of fact, it seems that children actually learn the use of general terms in much this way.)

Consider "Peter is a child." This begins immediately to give the extension of the class by naming one member. Reduction of "child" in this case begins by simply designating a class member by its proper name. When the extension of the class is evident, the general term can be eliminated another way: it is now possible to single out essential characteristics which Peter shares with Hazel and Ethel and other children and then to say that Peter has these

characteristics, thus giving the necessary and sufficient conditions
for verifying the sentence "Peter is a child": Peter is human and
aged y years, where $y = $ a number under 12.

What reifiers do is resist the rule of Reduction. For them the
question "What is a child?" is not a question of how "child" is used
in the language, or rather, it is a question that asks for *more* information, namely, what a child really is. In addition to Hazel,
Ethel, Peter, and all the children, for the reifier there is another
entity in the world, *child*, which Peter, *et al.*, in their different and
imperfect ways partake of, share in, embody. Similarly, with colors,
there is this red object, and that, and moreover redness, the idea
which enters into teacher's pencil, Mary's blush, the Russian flag.
Redness and child exist together in heaven, along with Justice and
bed (Plato's most famous examples).

In these simple cases reification is not apt to lead to confusions
of the sort "Is redness red?" or "Is childness childish?" At least in
the arguments about ordinary affairs, it more often leads to pseudo-
philosophical meanderings about whether justice is an absolute or
relative good, whether art can be for art's sake, whether a savage
dog which is not man's pal is really a dog after all.

Suppose someone to argue, "The true friend has never yet been
found. Damon was not a real friend of Pythias, David of Jonathan,
Johnson of Boswell. Real friendship implies absolute equality, an
equal sharing—a having of 'all things in common.' Otherwise, one
will have the advantage of the other. And since there can be no
absolute equality in all things, even among identical twins, there
can be no real friendship in the world. Perhaps there can be
friends among the angels, but certainly not among men."

How can such an argument be met? It is set up in such a fashion
that no evidence can possibly refute it. The speaker hypostatizes
an entity, apparently in heaven among the angels, of true friendship, which involves (a saying of the ancient Greeks) "having all
things in common." Then he demonstrates that this kind of sharing
is impossible in the sense of an *equal* sharing, which is certainly
one sense of sharing. By what is apparently a heavenly intuition,
the speaker knows that true friendship implies equal sharing. Since
such equality is impossible in the nature of things, therefore, true
friendship is illusory.

The only possible answer is to point out to the speaker that the
way one learns how to use the term "friendship" is precisely by

observing how it is applied in the cases of Damon and Pythias, and other friends. This is obviously a high-level abstraction, involving references to many kinds of behavior—speaking well of each other, being helpful, liking to be together, having mutual trust and confidence. But it can in principle be reduced to particular events under each kind. What would the speaker say if one pointed this out to him? Presumably that he knew all this sort of thing, that his point was precisely that all this was *not* enough to constitute friendship. There is no way to answer such an argument. As long as the speaker persists in the habit of making a thing out of an abstraction and of saying that some other thing is clearly not that thing, he is at once so right and so wrong that argument is impossible. Obviously nothing on earth is identical with anything else on earth, to say nothing of something in heaven which is at once immutable, atemporal, aspacial, perfect.

The firm way to deal with suspicious abstractions in argument is to demand their reduction to particulars. If the opponent cannot or will not show that such a reduction is possible in principle, then further discussion is pointless, since no evidence or counter-argument is relevant. One finds oneself involved in an unruly discussion. But if reduction is admitted, at least in theory, then it is possible in principle to test the argument. It may be possible to find a counter instance, to make experimental application, to verify or falsify.

The examples are designed to show some chief varieties of reification.

EXAMPLE. Case history of patient J.S. Young man, 28, complained to his pastor that his wife, in-laws, and associates at work were all "persecuting" him. Pastor sought the help of clinic, reported to clinic that there seemed to be the following grounds for the young man's complaint: Investigation showed J.S. aggressive, accusing those around him of plotting against him. These persons retaliated by avoiding his company, talking about him behind his back, and generally behaving badly towards him. His wife, especially, resented his jealousy and finally left him. What caused the pastor to seek the help of the clinic was the fact that J.S. refused to see how he was responsible for the way others behaved towards him. He maintained that everybody he knew had been "got to by a secret power." His wife and his friends were in fact, he claimed, the agents of that power. At his last interview with his pastor, J.S. threatened the pastor with a knife, claiming that the pastor was also an agent, trying to win his confidence in order to betray him. *Diagnosis.* Paranoia. Patient's social relationships are disturbed by his self-destructive tendencies. These he projects into an outside independent agency. *Recommendation.* Confinement and extended therapy.

COMMENT. J.S. actually was being persecuted in a way. His own aggressive behavior and distrust had alienated his wife, his relatives, and his associates. They avoided him and "talked about him." But notice that J.S. does not mean by "persecution" a construction that reduces to the sum of any particular occurrences in the behavior of others towards him. Instead, he sees all this as being inspired by a "secret power." He feels persecuted by a power, a kind of Platonic entity which is the *cause* of all the particular occurrences of persecution. The point is that there is a class of events having the common property of acts of persecution; the reification consists in making this property into an independent entity in the world, lying behind the acts and mysteriously causing them. It can be easily seen in this case that such reification is insane. It may be harder to detect the insanity in more ordinary cases.

EXAMPLE. Commissar Petrov writes in *Pravda,* "Loans to smaller nations, subsidies, bilateral trade agreements, mutual defense pacts with the inevitable concomitant of air bases and arms supplies—all of these have an obvious policy behind them of forming aggressive alliances against the Peoples' Democracies. This is not even in effect denied, for the United States admits that its basic policy in the Cold War is 'defense' against communism. But what is denied is that all these activities reveal another policy, a deeper and more underlying strategy. This is the indispensable policy, in fact, of all monopolistic capitalistic nations: colonialism. All these activities of the United States carry out the capitalist necessity of imperialistic colonizing of so-called backward areas. The frank colonialism of the last century is no longer possible: the empires of Great Britain, France, the United States can not stand anywhere against the political aspirations of downtrodden peoples. So, as the powers are forced to yield political empire, with the other hand they impose an economic-military empire on the same peoples. Thus the activities of the United States serve two purposes: they attempt an aggressive encirclement of the Peoples' Democracies, and at the same time they enslave the backward areas in a new-style colonialism."

COMMENT. This argument, like most of the arguments of dogmatic Marx-Leninism, bases its proof on a reified entity. Starting with the common characteristic underlying the diverse activities of U.S. foreign policy, defense against communism (which it interprets as aggressive alliances against the "Peoples' Democracies"), the proof then alleges another common characteristic, colonialism. It is certainly possible that the United States could be doing two things at once. But what is the evidence for this second purpose? *Pravda* cites only contradictory evidence, the break-down of empire (apparently referring to the new-found independence of India, the Philippines, etc.), and alleges that this has led to a "new-style colonialism." There is a curious sentence about the "indispensable policy" of "all monopolistic capitalistic nations" being colonialism. And this is then referred to as a "necessity." The reader of this article is now in the presence of an Entity. Like the secret power of the previous example, this construction of an indispensable policy cannot be reduced to any supporting evidence, nor refuted by any contradictory evidence. The writer, as a Marx-Leninist, is speaking of a "truth" more basic than any mere accidents embodied in historical events. If pressed to explain, he would presumably cite other and still more fundamental entities—the "logic" or determinism of historical process, the dialectic of the class struggle. A rule attributed to the nominalist William of Occam warns that "entities are not to be multiplied beyond necessity." This means that you do not keep on appealing to entities, such as colonialism or the secret power, to explain what is already sufficiently understood. As such entities go beyond all possible evidence, they are unarguable. What, if not evidence, can possibly support or refute them?

EXAMPLE. King Aroo overhears one character reproving another for throwing away his future. Now King Aroo had just learned that his own future was nothing but a smear of tea leaves, so he begins looking through ash cans for the future that got thrown away. (This is from Jack Kent's famous comic strip for March 6, 1957.)

COMMENT. King Aroo's search is funny because the reification is so concrete that it might be something found in the ash can.

Superstitious people seem to use the term "Future" as if it named a sort of country where events are already taking place which in time will be reproduced on this earth. These events can be dimly seen in crystal balls, tea leaves, cards, palms of hands. All you have to do is wait for them to arrive, like a letter already in the mail.

EXAMPLE. "The State is the divine idea as it exists today . . . It is the absolute power on earth; it is its own end and object. It is the ultimate end which has the highest right against the individual." Hegel.

COMMENT. King Aroo deserves a smile. Not so Hegel. His is a reification which, unfortunately, has millions of followers. The "State" its own end? What mystic thing is a state that *can be* an end apart from the welfare of individual people?

"No, one thousand times, No! The supreme end is the individual, and collective institutions should have no more hold over him than is needed for his own individual development." Salvador de Madariaga. (Quotations from Hegel and de Madariaga are taken from Sontag and Beddie, *Nazi-Soviet Relations.* New York: Didier, 1948, p. VIII.)

Personification (see #29) is a mark of reifying. Amateur psychologists often speak of the Ego or the Id as alternative souls presiding by turns inside the head (like the "ghost in the machine" derided by the philosopher Gilbert Ryle). Amateur strategists say things such as, "Strategy dictated the policy of island hopping." If this means only that strategical considerations led to the plan of island hopping, there can be no objection—economy "dictates" the use of personification in numerous more or less literary sentences (including some in this book). But if the speaker resists such a reduction of *strategy,* then a new thing has been born into the world. If one wants to waive aside such military considerations as subordinating operational tactics to over-all designs—there are these considerations, of course, but also something else much bigger, namely, Strategy, or even Grand Strategy, which not only controls the plans but also, somehow, the planners, who are its instruments —then shake hands with Strategy and introduce him to Id and Ego.

Poets can get very different effects from that of King Aroo by the use of similar devices. Jean Cocteau depicts a character in a diligent search, not for his own future, but for his own death, as if there were a special (not just a different) death for everybody. In his *Orpheus* the same poet personifies Death as a woman surgeon. Other writers speak of a character's life as a mystical *Gestalt*—a sort of space in which the drama of his fate is worked out: the world is a stage and human beings are puppets moved by destiny. The Greeks personified the fates as the Eumenides, and T. S. Eliot depicts the Eumenides howling outside the window in *Family Reunion*. Such devices are of the utmost importance in literature, where they effect a dramatic economy. It is philistinism to complain of reification in poetry—there is no harm in the device, provided it is understood as a play of imagination.

(b) *Relativism*

Relativism stands at the opposite extreme from reification. If you want to render an account of a situation, the Platonists say that you must select for your classifications only the essential characteristics, the essential being those that make the situation what it is because they reflect the eternal reality. For the relativists, no characteristics are essential or even intrinsic. None are more "real" than any others. The relativists are impressed with the obvious fact that situations can be classified in any number of ways—thus the criticism of classifications must center on the purpose of the classifier. Since his freedom in making constructions is without limit, but since he does in fact choose one set of constructions over the others, why does he choose as he does? Well, he chooses to suit his purpose. The relativists add that since there is nothing in the situation to fix his purpose, it must be given by something extrinsic. This extrinsic purpose will be found in the preoccupations of the classifier, his preconceptions, the peculiar concerns of his times, the unique interests of his class.

Relativists are thus poles apart from Platonists: there are no *real* characteristics in the situation, as the reifiers think, to determine the constructions. The model of the nominalist or relativist explanation is the famous case of the ass that was placed exactly equidistant between two bundles of hay. Only the relativist ass does not starve to death in indecision, but makes a choice. This choice is not determined by anything in one bundle of hay to make him prefer it to another—that would be an intrinsic consideration. No, his choice is some extrinsic matter, such as the habit of always turning left to his dinner. Of course, there are more than two bundles of hay, for there is an indefinite number of possible choices in classifying situations.

Relativism bids us consider the case of the historian who sits down to write an account of, say, a battle. Thousands of objects are involved—men, guns, weapons. Thousands of events transpire —melees, charges, cries and deaths. The historian cannot know all of these. Moreover, he already knows more than he can use, in most cases. What does he do? He talks generally about the movement of wings and centers, about the breaking and holdings of fronts, about advances and retreats. He selects and arranges the materials and in so doing imposes a structure on what is essentially structureless. In short, as he cannot know all the facts and cannot use even all the facts he knows, the historian's structure is an invention of his own. It will be determined, not by the data, but by his own values, prejudices, needs, social or political commitments. If this is true of the account of a contained story, such as of a single battle, how much more so must it be of large "wholes," such as the history of the Punic Wars or, for that matter, of the Roman Empire.

The historian does not tell the truth about the past; he does not even tell a lie. (This assumes he doesn't fabricate evidence or conceal facts.) For relativism there is no truth beyond the particulars, that is, the actual documents and other data. There is only fiction. One account will be as "true" as another, for all accounts are relative (hence "relativism") to the narrow intellectual and moral concerns of the writer. As these differ characteristically from age to age, it will be necessary for each generation to rewrite history for itself. Charles Beard speaks of the views of the historian as being "arbitrarily established." F. J. Teggert says that an historian may seem to be presenting a picture of some distant time but that he is perforce speaking with the "voice of his own generation," and giving tongue "to the ideas and aspirations of his own community."

Relativistic theories have serious implications beyond the technical problems of writing and evaluating history. The Roman Empire is obviously a very large, multiform "situation," but other persons besides historians often must try to understand situations that are quite manifold and complex enough. It may well be that no constructural machinery can be devised that will adequately classify the events of the Roman Empire. But it does not follow from this that all situations are impervious to understanding. Even historical situations are not always vast and unwieldy, and relativists could hardly maintain that there is a difference in essential *kind* between historical and other events.

It is not so much the size and complexity of a situation that makes relativists despondent. It is the predicament of theorizing in general. They believe, *in principle*, that since the account of any situation involves classifying, that is, selection and arrangement, the account is not of the situation but of the bias of the classifier. What you get from an account of the battle is not an understanding of the battle, but an insight into the historian. So expressed, relativism seems a form of the fallacy of origin (see #19); that is, it invites you to pay no attention to the truth of what is said but only to the source of the remarks. But more is involved. It is a theory that, since the selection and arrangement are never in the situation but only in the mind, and since an account is simply the presentation of the selection and arrangement, there *can* be no understanding of the situation. All that there is to understand is a construction of the mind.

Of all the possible selections and arrangements, the man making the account chooses that particular way which best implements his purpose. In this sense the account is strictly relative to the purpose, and it is good to call attention to this relativism, for an understanding of the account must involve the concerns of the man making it. Our way of saying this is given by Rule 3. The classification is, we say, in fact *determined* by the purposes of the classifier. But does it follow that his account is not of the situation? The account is in fact *limited* by the situation. There is no reason to believe that the account of large situations (the Punic Wars) is different in anything except complexity from the small situation (say, the hundred marbles). Perhaps despondency over very ambitious history-writing is justified. But even Gibbon and Toynbee are bound by limits, and these limits are clear in the data. Aside from the obvious negative limits (Hannibal lacked H-bombs in his attacks on Rome), there are recalcitrant facts that also must be taken into *all* accounts (Hannibal failed to break Roman resistance). Historical and other vast situations present the characteristics they have and no others, just as do all situations. These characteristics are in principle classifiable, and the account can then be evaluated according to the well understood rules of classification. Evaluation of the purpose behind the account is an important matter, but it is a different matter.

EXAMPLE. Peter says to his wife, "Why are you reading those book reviews? Criticism is a farce. One critic likes what another critic cannot stand. Jones in the *Tribune* says that a book illustrates courage under adversity and that the characters are finely drawn and true to life. Smith in the *Gazette* says that the theme of the same book is that virtue is its own punishment and that the characters are puppets manipulated by a clumsy writer. Which is right? Neither! Each critic finds in the novel what he is looking for, and everything in the book proves anything you care to say about it. Why? Because there is no *novel* except in the reader's head, and what the reader likes and doesn't like depends entirely on his taste. This is why the old saying 'There is no disputing about taste' is so wise. What would two critics be disputing about? Two separate novels, one in the head of each. If it is silly to dispute about 'fictions,' it is silly to write or read criticism."

COMMENT. In a sense, there is a novel in each reader's mind, but it hardly follows that these cannot be very similar in salient respects. The events in a novel can certainly be classified in various ways, and the choice of ways will be determined by the purpose of the critic. This purpose, in turn, may be causally related to his taste. Similarly, the characters in fiction do and say things that are subject to various interpretations, just as people behave in life. But we do in fact understand each other. This is to say, our account of each other's character makes it possible to predict behavior, to get along together, to cooperate. In a similar sense, good critics give insight into the characters in a novel and elucidate the action. There is nothing mysterious about this. If the purpose is to find hidden motives, then psycho-analytical constructions throw light on the characters of a novel as of life. If the purpose is to show how the behavior is socially or economically directed, then the speech and actions will be ordered in a different way. A good novel is a rich and complex texture, and it will support many interpretations.

EXAMPLE. Student report: "I know a lot of historians think that President Jackson's quarrel with the Bank was a misfortune for the country. This merely shows how they feel about banks and about Jackson. As for me, I happen to feel different about things. I happen to admire Jackson. The historians have a right to their opinion, and I have a right to mine. After all, no one can say which of us is objectively right, since there's no way to run the nineteenth century over again without Jackson."

COMMENT. "Objectively" here suggests the model of a laboratory where experiments can be "run over again." There are clearly other senses of "objectively," such as "in conformity with the evidence." Jurors cannot run a murder over again to see if the accused did in fact kill the victim, but they can nevertheless bring in an objective verdict. In this model, unlike that of the laboratory, objectivity in a verdict ("opinion") implies a verdict in line with the evidence and free from the "subjective" elements of personal passion or bias.

This is all rather obvious. What is important to note about the example is the widespread supposition that "everybody is entitled to his opinion." This is simply absurd in the *kind* of case under consideration. The student is not entitled to an opinion counter to informed historical judgment, just as a juror is not entitled to an opinion counter to the evidence. If the present book can be said to have a general thesis, it is that nobody is entitled to an irresponsible opinion on anything.

10 · *Unnecessary Vagueness* (Rule 4)

The fourth rule of adequate classification (see p. 36) requires that the divisions must be precise enough to avoid serious marginal cases. Let us briefly resume the account of the model of a scientific law (see pp. 5 ff.) to see how classifications are set up in science. What needs to be added to the previous discussion is that science characteristically defines the divisions between the categories in terms of measurable properties.

One of the first things that impresses the young student of science is the difference between scientific and ordinary vocabularies. When he now uses such terms as "mass," "force," "energy," "velocity," he must use them exactly. The student finds that they are precisely defined; in fact, they are specified in mathematical equations. All the categories to which the student is introduced turn out to be almost perfectly determined. The laws and observations are expressed in terms as free from vagueness as it is possible to make them, the language of measurement and precise definition. Compared to the language of ordinary affairs, that vapor of vagueness, scientists use a language that seems a relatively perfect instrument of communication.

The precise determination of the categories becomes possible in science because the phenomena dealt with are concrete: they can be measured. This means that the laws are so formulated as to be open to test by procedures of the laboratory and of the trained observer. It means, moreover, that the definitions can in all typical cases be stated so clearly (since they are given in measurable units) that these definitions make explicit the necessary and sufficient conditions for the application of the terms: a given thing or event is an instance of a particular category if and only if such and such. The characteristics, as they are measurable, provide criteria for classifications that are unmistakable and final. The lines between the categories are cleanly drawn, so that a marginal case is a great rarity, calling for a redefinition of the terms involved.

To anyone acquainted with the clarity of scientific classifications, further description will be unnecessary; to anyone without scientific experience, unintelligible. What can be said about the clarity of nonscientific classification? Surprisingly, the case is not always desperate. Mr. Richards in lamenting the imprecision of "the sphere of random belief and hopeful guesses" (see p. 8) allows that there are "rules of thumb" in "the concrete affairs of commerce, law, organization and police work," and speaks of "generally accepted convention" being helpful there. He is not interested in these fields, but let us see what these conventions and rules of thumb are like.

If your bank sends you a statement reading, "Your account is overdrawn," you know exactly what evidence will render this sentence true or false. You know the conditions of the category of overdraft: subtract your withdrawals, plus charges, from your deposits; if the figure you get is minus, the sentence is true; if plus, false—supposing neither you nor the bank keep inaccurate records. Thus the category "overdraft," like scientific categories, is defined in terms of necessary and sufficient conditions: you are overdrawn if and only if the figure determined as above is minus. Many commercial expressions are far from vague.

Mr. Richards also exempts the law. It is true that the legislatures and the courts make a great effort to define legal categories so that the characteristics of all the basic classes can be accurately determined. "The people of the State of N. charge that on or about 7:00 P.M. EST, October 5, 1957, at 100 First Street, City of X, County of Y, the accused committed an act of burglary, to wit . . ." The dates and times, the names of the people and places, are of course almost always unmistakable. What of the category of burglary? This is determined exactly enough for all but rare cases. A court applying common law will instruct the jury to find the accused guilty if and only if the prosecution has proved that at the times and places specified the accused did in fact

a. break and enter
b. the dwelling of another
c. in the nighttime
d. with intent to commit a felony (not necessarily theft).

All these four elements are, in turn, defined to make each concept as precise as possible. To "break and enter" refers to any entrance without authority even though no door or window is moved and even though the accused only reaches in with an arm or hook; "dwelling" refers to any place of abode and its immediate outbuildings; "nighttime" receives a statutory definition as so many minutes after sunset; while felony is generally defined by statute as applying to any act punishable by a certain penalty, commonly over one year imprisonment. The trial will involve attempting to prove that the accused committed certain acts (as specified in the dots following "to wit" above) which fall within the legal category of burglary.

But legal categories, since crime and other social relations can be exceedingly various, are sometimes unfortunately vague. Many problems do not lend themselves to crisp definitions even though jurists might be willing, as with the case of separating *day* from *night*, to adopt an arbitrary definition for the sake of clarity. Sometimes it is not helpful to press for arbitrary definitions, since they would not be useful in solving the problems. For instance, "negligence" or the establishment of guilt "beyond a reasonable doubt" cannot profitably be defined in an arbitrary way. In law as in less rigorous fields there are categories that resist either reduction to particular cases (precedents) or precise definition.

Let us turn from the fields of law and commerce to Mr. Richards' area of "random belief and hopeful guesses." It must be admitted at once that many important constructions are relatively very vague. Particular instances may be instructive.

1. Peter is bald.

The construction *bald* is vague. Let us see just in what the vagueness consists. It is possible to construct a scale from one extreme condition of a man's head to the other:

bald		?		hairy-on-top	
x^1 x^2 x^3		x_4		x^5 x^6 x^7	

In the every-day situation represented here, people use the term "bald" without knowing at precisely what point they would be unwilling to call a man "bald." For x_1 there is no doubt, and his dome shines afar. For x_2 and x_3 only very charitable persons would hesitate to employ the description, though there may be a fringe and a combed-across wisp. As to x_5, there is a good thatching over, albeit a little thinning in front. But x_7! His hair springs up, it seems, from every possible minute spot: you feel there is not room for another hair, and nobody would call him bald. What about the wide range where x_4 is? Well, people may say that x_4 is balding, getting bald, losing his hair. Some actually say that he *is* bald.

If "Peter is bald" is a case of x_4, then there is a broad range of possibilities concerning the condition of Peter's scalp. Moreover, the borders, so sharply drawn on the scale, are in doubt. Some users of the term might not distinguish between x_3 and x_4. Other users might not distinguish between x_4 and x_5, as we have.

Is this vagueness an insurmountable disadvantage? If it were to become important to know for every man whether or not he is bald, scientists could certainly set up one arbitrary line in the middle of the scale somewhere. They could say: "bald if fewer than 5000 hairs on the head." But note, if it *were* important, the importance would surely lie in a tie-in with something else, artistic ability, say, or mathematical genius. In such a case, the arbitrary number of 5000 hairs might be no help at all. The definition of baldness would depend in part on the proved relationships to the tie-in, and scientists would draw the line only where evidence of connection with genius or the like warranted doing so. Again, that evidence might not prevent a rather vague border.

The possibility of precisely setting limits is not the important thing about the usage represented by (1). Though at the present time nothing much would be gained by setting such strict limits, it is still possible to use the term "bald" in a very definite way. In the case of x_1, as contrasted with x_7, the difference is striking. Avoiding, then, the vague range and staying well to the extremes, a careful speaker can say "Peter is bald" and communicate very effectively to those who know Peter. At the same time, the speaker does not exclude the possibility that Paul, who may have quite a number of hairs compared to Peter, perhaps is also bald. The speaker leaves Paul's case open. Obviously, it would be a very narrow view of the function of the categories of description to deny the right to say that Peter is bald just because one cannot say whether or not Paul is bald (but see #11).

This consideration enables us to give a sufficient condition for deciding when a term is too vague for reasonable communication. We shall say that *when there is no clear case, no x_1 on a scale, then the term should be rejected for vagueness.* It will be evident that many constructions of the language pass this test. In spite of areas of vagueness, there are cases where nearly perfect communication is possible. "Child" and "redness" are quite precise enough for the needs of ordinary communication. Other constructions are becoming more clearly defined day by day. With the application of statistical analysis, the refinement of observational techniques, the discovery of linguistic and semantical principles, informed speakers today are in a position to make many judgments with a degree of intelligibility that would have been impossible only a few years ago. Despite its conceded limitations, I.Q. measurement provides a more exact description of mental ability than vague terms such as "capable" or "bright." Let us take another instance for the purpose of exploring the application of the rule for excluding vague terms.

2. Chivalry implies the ideal of womanhood.

There are here two constructions, *chivalry* and *ideal of womanhood.* Certainly these constructions are vague to the point of being diaphanous. The borders of the concept are almost hopelessly fuzzy. Can such constructions be excluded by the rule? One feels that (2) is saying something; it is not mere nonsensical mouthings. In fact, sentence (2) itself provides some help: any likely elements the speaker includes in the construction of *chivalry* apparently will be related in some sense ("implies" is a very vague term in common usage) to elements in *ideal of womanhood*. But the latter is no less vague than *chivalry*. Still something is gained.

What of the technique of reduction? Clearly this technique will not work unless there are some clear-cut particular instances. What particulars would all users agree upon? In the case of *bald* there would be no reasonable doubt about x_1, though the term does not reduce as readily as other abstractions, such as "redness"—it passes the test. Would informed users of "chivalry" unanimously regard this deed of Sir Lancelot as germane? What of this decree by King Arthur? Or, more generally, this practice of wearing a lady's colors in tournament? This body of amorous song? This search for the Grail?

Probably not unanimously. Nevertheless, a conscientious historian could specify certain feelings, beliefs, attitudes, as they reflect themselves in various language samples and cultural practices and weave themselves in and out of medieval institutions, such as courtly love, and thus roughly specify the development of chivalry in the history of the Middle Ages. The historian's difficulties are legion in such an enterprise, but they are in degree surmountable.

As the term exists in the common language, it is to be ruled out by the condition for excluding vague usages. But this is not to say that it is entirely meaningless. What happens when the speaker of (2) intends an observation about behavior of today? When this is the case, how is (2) to be interpreted? Presumably the speaker can refer to feelings, beliefs, attitudes, and the like, which resemble the historian's construction called "chivalry." In the common usage, as opposed to the careful historical usage, it would seem that such terms as "chivalry" merely point in a direction. It is as if one gestured casually to the north when asked where Nome is. Even a general direction is something, and there is no occasion to condemn the common usage of terms represented by "chivalry." But in responsible discussion, one can expect something more. In the case of the speaker of (2) referring to today, he can be reasonably held responsible for a knowledge of some historical specifications and, moreover, for a list of contemporary developments which he has in mind when speaking of chivalry.

One thing remains to be noted about sentences of the type represented by (2). This is the danger of reification (see pp. 41 ff.). Language encourages its users to suppose that there exists a structure corresponding to the constructions named, that there is a kind of Platonic entity in the nature of things. A term like "chivalry" names, of course, the construction of the users, but people feel that their construction more or less corresponds to strands of reality. Instead of saying that speakers and writers construct a class by relating one cultural or social phenomenon to another and calling it, for convenience, "chivalry," some speakers tend to suppose that strands or structures of in-themselves-related phenomena, however poorly realized in any actual place at any actual time, have a basic reality which men perforce notice and name. It is natural to assume that the way to achieve a sensible notion of such a term is to study, yes, the actualizations of the ideal in its poor embodiments in France and England, say, but at the same time to hold in view the pure concept itself.

Yet *chivalry* can be used by conscientious writers and speakers. They do not have to suggest a reified perfection crudely embodied in some Medieval institutions. They can realize that they are exploring a construction-for-convenience of cultural attitudes or practices, and the like. As to the vagueness of such terms, what is required is that one designates the particular instances intended. Presumably these will lie in the "direction" of the common use. If this is done carefully, the speaker can be as clear as he needs be for communication. Finally, there remains to be discussed a class of usages which have been called vague from the earliest times.

3. Man pursues the good.

Value terms are an instance of terms that resist reduction, in spite of heroic efforts on the part of recent writers. (They may have been the instance that led Plato to his theory of ideas.) "Man pursues the good" illustrates a use of "good" so far impossible to analyze. There are indeed many uses of "good" that can be reliably reduced or that can be translated, without loss, into a group of sentences not employing "good" or its synonyms. "That is a good design" translates into a sum of sentences about the adequacy of the design, its economy, qualities it has that many people find pleasing. If the condition is added that "good," as well as describing such things, also expresses the approval of the speaker and invites an appropriate attitude on the part of the listener, then the result is a sort of translation for "good" in "That is a good design," that few will object to. Like many other abstractions, it turns out to be a shorthand expression for something complicated, but not impossible, to spell out. Similarly, if one says, "Money is a good," it is possible to reduce this meaning of "good" (as in "goods") to things desired by people. If one should say, with Aristotle, "It is a good to have a good," restatement would yield, without much loss of content, something like "People feel a satisfaction in the having of something they desire as well as in the thing itself." A great many usages of value terms can be analyzed in this way, but almost certainly not all of them. Dewey and his school 'seem in error when they suggest that all usages can be so analyzed because most can. There still remain uses of (3) in ethics and religion that do not yield to reduction.

Can we say of these cases that they are so vague as to be useless? Well, we shall not say so, in spite of the condition of exclusion. Let extreme positivists legislate as they choose, few will obey them. For our part, we prefer to hope that analysis in years to come will teach us the secrets of these terms.

In conclusion, we can draw together the tentative findings of this section. People are always making new classifications, tinkering with old ones. The best we are able to suggest is a few rough and ready rules to follow in making or testing classifications, rules which a careful arguer employs. As we saw (pp. 36 ff.), a classification must be able to separate elements of the situation. The rules of classification can be observed only if the characteristics are given, at least implicitly, in a way clear enough for others to apply them and come up with the same results. This will not be possible unless there are at least some indisputable applications of the construction, as with the case of baldness, or unless the user of the term gives it such applications himself by pointing to unmistakable examples of what he has in mind. Let us summarize these observations.

1. *Peter is bald.* The unmistakably bald person is called "bald" by all users of the conventional term. Despite some borderline cases, the construction is useful. If Peter's case is marginal, it can be dealt with by further description: "getting bald," "thinning at the temples."

2. *Chivalry implies the ideal of womanhood.* The sentence points in the general direction of certain (or uncertain) feelings, beliefs, and attitudes. The terms can be employed where a mere indication of such general meaning is sufficient, that is, where the notions are not crucial for the discussion, as when the speaker is merely blocking

in a background. Otherwise the speaker must show by citing instances some clear applications.

3. *Man pursues the good.* The meaning of such statements is beyond our analysis. However, note that other uses are serviceably clear: the speaker of "That is a good design" considers that the instance before him carries out effectively the principles of design. (These principles and their application to the given case can be explained on demand.) This use of "good" is not hopelessly vague, though there may be an ambiguity with ethical and other uses of "good."

Apparently the vague usages in question are approved for argument? Not exactly. The qualifications are important. Let us gather them together:

a. a merely directional use of such terms as "chivalry" is permissible only when nothing central to the argument hangs on it.

b. vague terms in argument may be employed in a crucial place only when there are clear applications and these are the cases under discussion. If a marginal case becomes important, then a satisfactory decision must be made for this case.

When arguers make up new constructions and give them new names, they often specify the application with care and clarity. If they neglect to do so, someone will sooner or later find a counter instance and explode their balloon. But when arguers use the old abstractions, like "chivalry," which designate constructions very vague indeed, being merely general directions of use, then they are in danger of getting into such trouble that even finding a clear counter instance would be a real help. They do not know the borders of the construction, but fail to observe that they do not know them—after all, "chivalry" occurs in the language and is defined in the dictionary. They cannot disentangle the various characteristics; they have notions of two or more unrelated strands of phenomena floating in their constructions, like letters in alphabet soup. These vague abstractions can be illustrated from almost every conversation, every popular non-fiction book, every student paper or speech, many a lecture on literature, history, social science.

EXAMPLE. Dialogue overheard in the Forum:

First Citizen: I don't want war, but I do want our lost territory back.

Second Citizen: Well, friend, do you want the lost territory back even if it's going to take a war to get it?

First Citizen: I don't want war, as I say. But if it's going to take a war to regain the lost province, then we will have to beat our plowshares into swords.

Second Citizen: I see what you mean. You don't regard war as a good thing, but you want to regain the lost province even more than you want to avoid war."

First Citizen: I guess that's right.

COMMENT. Second Citizen has pressed this dialogue to clear up the vagueness of First Citizen's assertion; the reply reveals the relative intensity of his "wants." Vagueness in the common language is nowhere more pronounced than in the case of words designating choices: "want," "desire," "hope for," "like." These can range from the slightest predilection to the most intense. Consider the range of meaning possible in the simple assertion "I like ice cream." I might be affirming my preference for ice cream over any other food, or I might mean that only cream pie and tapioca pudding stand lower in my order of desserts. Vagueness arises from failure to limit the range of choice-words: "I like ice cream best of all."

EXAMPLE. A grocery company was indicted under a statute making it unlawful to charge "unjust or unreasonable" prices. The attorneys for the defendant argued that the statute violated the constitutional provision, "In all criminal prosecutions, the accused shall . . . be informed of the nature and cause of the accusation." The court upheld the defendent's contention since the term "unjust and unreasonable" did not reduce to clearcut acts so that an individual would know in every case whether or not his contemplated act would be a violation of the law. (Example founded on *United States vs. L. Cohen Grocery Co.*, 1921.)

COMMENT. Barring vague descriptions of crime is one of the protections for individual liberty enjoyed where a rule of law prevails. Fairness to individuals requires that the terms of the criminal law be so phrased that there can be no doubt as to whether or not an act is illegal.

EXAMPLE. A literary quarterly publishes an article arguing that "responsiveness to the Zeitgeist" is the chief mark "of genius of the true poet." This is in the first paragraph. On the second page we read "Artistic sensibility always reveals itself in a fresh wonder at language."

COMMENT. None of these constructions is intelligible, and the sentences are nonsense. Terms like "Zeitgeist" and the dogmatically positive use of "reveal themselves" suggest, moreover, a strong leaning toward Word Magic (#12).

EXAMPLE. Professor Peter lectures his class in sociology: "The matrix of cultural usage provides for the necessary safety valve of a few non-conformists. The deviates, however, must conform at least to an accepted-rejected pattern of non-conformity. They may be non-conformists only in a prescribed way: not all patterns of non-conformity are open to them."

COMMENT. Professor Peter is probably trying to say something, maybe something interesting. But there is a difference between paradox and open contradiction, and the difference often reveals almost at sight the difference between intelligible constructions and the kind of vague thinking that leads to the verbiage of the pseudo-scientists. One would like to bang Professor Peter's heads together and make him talk sense.

EXAMPLE.
"Give to the Midgets' Rest Home. You can take it off your income tax."
"Relax your tired blood. Take Elixir of Ambrosia."
"Panty Waists are tighter."

COMMENT. Without such vagueness modern advertising would be impossible; it's of the essence. "Take it off your income tax" can, in law, mean only "take it off your income before computing the tax, *if* you use the long form and not the standard deduction for charity, local taxes, etc.," but you are not supposed to think of that. "Tired" is so vague in everyday usage that it seems hardly a metaphor to apply the adjective to blood, but what can it mean? "Tighter," "better," "smoother," "longer lasting," "less fattening"— than what? "Better," perhaps, than the worst in the field?

EXAMPLE.
"-ism"
"-ist," "-ite"
"-er"

COMMENT. It is superfluous to illustrate the tiresome exploitation of these vague formations. In political controversy, a "communist" can be anybody from a card holding Communist Party member to a patriotic clergyman who twenty years ago foolishly allowed his name to appear on the letterhead of the American League for Peace and Freedom. "Peter is a Morrisite," "Peter is a deceiver." Do these mean that Peter once deceived or habitually deceives? that he agrees with Morris on some particular, or that he follows him around day and night like a disciple? The use of these formations in argument brands the speaker as naive or vicious. Look back to the previous sections. Do such terms as "relativism" or "reifier" offend against this principle?

11 · *Over-precision:* "logic chopping"

Some persons, apparently impressed with the rule of reduction and other modern techniques, would reject the extreme-case criterion for permissible vagueness as far too generous an application of Rule 4 (p. 53). It is not enough for them that all would agree on x_1: there must be agreement on all cases in the range. That nobody is likely to deny Peter's baldness does not qualify "bald" for precise usage unless unanimity is also possible on Paul and Henry, whatever the state of their scalps. Some writers blame the vagueness of terms in common usage for an alleged lack of progress in social science and for much of the confusion in politics and other activities of everyday life. They demand of every general term that it carry with its use the method of its reduction. As to marginal cases, they are to be eliminated by formal definition or by exact distinction.

Vagueness, they say, encourages reification and Word Magic (see #12). The existence of a certain usage in the language does not guarantee anything about any entities in the world. The name "Zeus" is a proper name, but there is no god. The difficulty with "the good" or "chivalry" is that the use of these terms often commits the speaker to a belief in Platonic entities, since the tendency in language to give *some* content to words leads speakers to reify when no content from reduction is possible. Moreover, a belief in a Platonic superchild does not matter for communication: the term can always on demand be reduced to this young person or that. But abstractions such as "chivalry" cannot be reduced since the concept is not well enough constructed to permit its users to state the conditions for applying it. They can, of course, provide an *ad hoc* definition, but then they might better have avoided the term altogether and with it the confusion with common usage and its likely reification.

For these reasons the extreme-case criterion is held to be too broad. It is not enough to eliminate the merely directional usages of terms such as "chivalry," but such terms as "bald" must also go. The fact that there are clear-cut cases misses the objection to vagueness in language: this is that there are any cases *not* clear-cut. Let speakers adopt the practice of defining each term as it occurs: this will eliminate marginal cases as they arise. There is no reason to put up with indecision about them and to tolerate vague uses. So goes the positivist argument.

Most of these strictures are directed against the vagueness in certain social sciences, psychology, sociology, history. Many of the key concepts in these sciences seem to the critics merely evaluative and literary. Can psychologists precisely state the characteristics of projection, of repression, of sanity itself? On the contrary, they are unable even to specify the level of abstraction for these constructions, much less show how to reduce them to particulars. Can any anthropologist state with clarity the conditions that will indicate for every human trait whether or not that trait is "culturally determined?" These criticisms imply that it is always desirable to give precise rules for the usage of terms, and that it is always possible to do so.

Sigmund Freud and Margaret Mead could, indeed, define their terms and be done with it. The definitions would perhaps be arbitrary, but they could be clear. But what is the problem such writers face? Is it merely to define, say, "repressions," that is, to provide an exact list of characteristics by which psychologists can judge whether or not any given human activity can be arbitrarily designated "repressive"? Or is it to explore a situation believed to involve a basic psychological mechanism? Reflection will show that the task of the scientist here is not to set up artificial systems, but to found tentative constructions on the description of some clear (extreme) cases. In the bewildering complications of fact, these early constructions may be found ultimately to be as basic as was originally thought—in which case they will by degrees become entirely explicit and uniquely determined in scope—or they will be found unproductive—in which case they will be discarded or replaced. In the meanwhile, the investigator is usually aware of the vague and tentative character of his key concepts.

It is a form of perfectionism (see #38) to reject the best available on the grounds that it is not the best conceivable. What is happening seems to be a rejection of serviceable usages for the sole reason that there are cases that are marginal or doubtful. We have stated that the function of classification is to separate, and the criticism of the marginal case seems well taken. How can the rules of exhaustion and exclusion operate if the construction is littered with doubtful cases? But we have also stated that where these are crucial they must be decided. We now add that this decision can be recognized as tentative where a formal division would not further the understanding of the situation, but on the contrary would be arbitrary and artificial. In a discussion where the marginal cases are not at issue, it is captious to reject a construction simply because such cases exist. This amounts to refusing to allow the term "bald" when Old Marbletop is being pointed to, simply because there is a gent, Old Brushacross, who is nowhere around.

In such instances we say that the criticism is fallacious. There is nothing wrong with the extreme-case uses of construction, when the alternative ("'bald' means 'fewer than 5000 hairs on the head'") is purely arbitrary. If there are *some* clear cases, as with "baldness," "repression," "culturally determined traits," the historian's "chivalry," then the uses are permissible unless greater precision is possible without artificiality. This is admittedly itself a vague criterion of permissible vagueness, but it must serve the present purpose—which is only to characterize the fallacy of requiring an unnecessary precision. The fallacy is easily recognized in *its* extreme forms: wholesale rejection of vast areas of human inquiry as "nonsense," pedantic hair-splitting and logic-chopping over constructions that are the best available and good enough for the purpose, the ironical bark in discussion, "I can't understand that!" "What does that mean!"

EXAMPLE. Professor Peter writes in the *Historian's Quarterly,* "It is bad enough to see this term *romantic* in undiminished circulation amongst music critics and literary historians. What does it mean to characterize Beethoven's Opus 28 as romantic? Or Byron's *Don Juan*? The sonata contains the notes, chords, movements it contains. How can these add up to some non-musical entity to be designated as *'romantic'* and thus automatically grouped with *Don Juan,* as well as with Gothic revival, the agony of a perverse love, trap doors and ghosts? But when an historian, who should know better, seriously sets out to specify clear-cut, extreme cases of the romantic impulse in diplomacy and political agitation, then we have seen everything. I can only say that Professor Paul's latest tome may be program notes or literary *obiter dicta,* but it is hardly history."

COMMENT. It is true that terms such as "romantic," "classical," even Professor Peter's "history," are frequently used in literary and popular contexts in a merely directional way. No precise content can be given to them, and it is not even clear if there is an extreme case. Yet Professor Peter's attack itself refers to fairly definite areas of content (trap doors, ghosts)—almost all literary critics agree in regarding the appearance of Gothic props in novels and poems as marks of what they call the romantic movement. Moreover, Professor Paul apparently is at pains to find "clear-cut, extreme" cases of practices in diplomacy and politics which he is proposing to call romantic, since they lie in the general direction of what is ordinarily called "the romantic movement." At any rate, he must use some term to cover the phenomena he is describing, and all that can reasonably be required is that he provide some clear cases, even if he must leave it open whether or not other cases are to be so characterized.

EXAMPLE. Overheard in a bull session: "You say that whatever morality involves, it's bound to include people helping each other in time of need. You cite rescues at sea and loans to friends, even considerate advice to troubled spirits. This is the way all you moralists talk. You list noble deeds that, of course, everybody approves of, then treat them as if they were a class of similar things, give them a name, like "helpful," and think you have proved something, I don't know what. All you have done is cite cases, which may or may not have something in common, and wrapped them up in a vague meaningless name. I still don't know what it means to be helpful, and I don't think you do. Look! What if the man at sea were dying of cancer and didn't want to be saved, or if your alcoholic or whatever didn't want your advice—maybe he needs his vice, not advice! How would it be helpful to interfere then? Answer me that!"

COMMENT. The providing of particular cases was apparently

designed to free the term "helpful" of some of its every-day ambiguity. The critical attack does attempt to test the extreme-case instances by imagining counter-examples, but even though such may occur, surely there are many rescues that are desired just as eagerly as the rare one is not. The intention obviously refers to such cases. Is the designation of such cases as "helpful" un- justified? It will be noted that the critic seems himself to have de- rived from them a clear enough notion of "helpful" to pose counter- cases; he asks, "How would it be helpful to interfere?" If he would accept the term as now specified in the light of rescues, ad- vice, loans, the critic might then find out what his interlocutor thinks he has proved—presumably that being helpful is a moral good.

12 · *Word Magic*

In the discussion of classes we saw that the existence of a name does not guarantee the existence of any corresponding entity in the situation. Suppose you start with a construction, say a fairly clear one like *child*. The name "child" means the construction *child*, right enough, but the point of the analysis was that there is no need to suppose that the construction *child* stands for a Platonic entity in the world. This is to say that, by the process of reduction (see pp. 43 ff.), you can interpret the construction *child* in ordinary usage by reference to Junior, Sis, *et al.*, and do so without committing yourself to a belief in a child in Plato's heaven, who never grows up, whose hands are never in need of washing, who is parentless and sexless. Reduction is possible in principle for even the highest level of abstration; even the use of vague terms, like "chivalry," in careful contexts, need involve no reification.

There are other terms, however, the use of which usually implies the existence of entities in the situation unverifiable in principle. The usual occasion of the use of such terms as "destiny" and "fate" provides no clue for reduction and strongly suggests hypostatization of entities. Such use is commonly called Word Magic. The name, like a spell, conjures an Entity into being. In recent years much attention has been paid to Word Magic, and this phenomenon of language has become an important part of the much discussed "tyranny of words." There has, however, been a certain vagueness in the notion of Word Magic itself. Most writers seem to include every sort of reification and make no distinction between reified uses of, say, "child," and of "destiny." At other times writers seem to include all constructions not firmly anchored in the situation, such as an infant's notion of Santa Claus, and thus indifferently regard simple mistakes due to ignorance of "the furniture of the world," as instances of this fallacy.

We shall want to use "Word Magic" in a less vague way. We shall exclude cases of ordinary hypostatization, where the constructions, such as *child* or *red,* can be given a straightforward analysis free of metaphysical commitment. We shall also want to exclude mistakes due to ignorance. Sentences about centaurs, elfs, ghosts, cannot be reduced, it is true, but they do not essentially involve reification of entities—for they might be uttered in good faith apparently on good authority and constitute simple mistakes. Perhaps we have already sufficiently discussed reification. We want, however, to take a look at the centaurs and ghosts. But let us first consider the following case.

a. The Average American smokes 7.472 cigarettes a day.

Only a very naive person would suppose that "Average American" designates any class of people, especially people so carefully measuring their consumption of cigarettes. Those who are not so naive know that there may in fact be no one person who smokes exactly 7.472 cigarettes every day, or any day. They will know how to interpret such idioms and the sort of evidence that will confirm or falsify the generalizations. A mistake here is due to ignorance, but the ignorance differs from the example (c) below about the centaurs. The ignorance here is of a rather ordinary convention of language to give a shorthand summary of complicated factual material, rather than ignorance of the kinds of things there are in the world.

b. The centaur is a mythical beast.

The logical analysis of this sentence, which needn't detain us here, shows that, though it probably seldom misleads, it is still a misleading way to speak. The use of "is" where there is no reference to existing things *can* get confused with the use of the term to imply existence, and hence is misleading. The sentence, "The President is an elective executive," states that for every case where somebody is President he is an elective executive and, moreover, *there is such a case.* Sentence (b) is of the same form, but can one say, "For every

case of centaur, this is a mythical beast, and there is such a case"?
Well, it is only the form that is misleading, not the sense, since the
form is contradicted by the sense (of "mythical").

c. "The centaur is half man, half horse."

Unless the context contradicts the form of this sentence, there is
nothing to show that the construction *centaur* is unanchored, that
no referent can be found in the widest situation known. Now suppose this sentence were to be found in a medieval travel book and
that you are a student in a little cathedral school. If you believed this
sentence to be true, that is, that "there is such a case," would you be
guilty of Word Magic? One does not quibble over the use of this
term if he points out that the *chief* mistake you have made, at the
worst, is a reliance on insufficient authority (see #15). You have
not traveled yourself over the world—how do you know what
animals are in it? Unless you have deduced *a priori* (see #28) that
centaurs are impossible, the most that one can expect of you in
your ignorance is a certain skepticism. In the Middle Ages—and in
many other times and in many places—people have made mistakes
of this sort. They have eaten the horn of the unicorn ground up.
They have fed ricecakes to ghosts. They have kept the werewolf
from the door with wolfbane or garlic. They have burnt witches.
They have trapped demons in trees and rocks. These practices involve magic, but, as we shall use the term, not Word Magic. The
spells and other linguistic incantations seem a consequence of a
mistaken belief in something, rather than the other way about. The
belief is theoretically verifiable. We may never encounter a centaur
or a werewolf, but we should certainly recognize one if we did.
Let us take another case.

d. Phlogiston makes the fire burn.

Chemists have found no "principle of combustion," in the sense
that Newton found a principle of attraction. The problem is not
the name "phlogiston." If there were such a principle—every case of
combustion involved its operation just as every case of the attraction of bodies involves gravity—the name "phlogiston" of course
would serve as well as any other. Yet the existence of this name
has apparently led astrologers and mystics to state that the chemists
must be wrong, that fire must be a uniform element in nature, that
there must, therefore, be a uniform principle involved in all com-

bustion. To this day arguments to this effect can be found here and
there. With this use of "phlogiston" one enters the presence of
Word Magic. No longer can simple ignorance excuse. The fallacy
here occurs only in comparatively rare cases where the existence of
the word magically guarantees the existence of the entity: we have
the name, let's find the thing. This is like the celebrated case of the
genius who argued that opium must put people to sleep by virtue
of a "dormitive agent" and set out to find that agent in all cases of
soporifics.

The situation being what it is, no unique principle of combustion,
no unique dormitive agent can be found. Looking for one in advance of knowledge of the nature of things is not a fallacy. Persisting
in the search after the situation is understood, simply because of the
existence of the name (or, of course, of a useless construction,
whatever its name) we call Word Magic.

We come now to usages that *automatically* involve Word Magic.

e. It was Peter's destiny to build houses.

How can this sentence be confirmed or disproved? If Peter dies
without building a single house, we might inscribe on his tombstone:
"Here lies Peter. His housebuilding destiny was unfulfilled." Or if
Peter dies after building fifty houses, we might then write: "Here
lies Peter. His destiny was to build houses, and he built fifty of
them."

The very sense of such terms as "destiny" is that no verification of
sentences of the sort of (e) is possible. The clause "he built fifty
of them," does suggest a sort of evidence, but it is easy to see that
it is not a condition of having a destiny to build houses to have
actually built a number of them. This is made clear by the usage
about a destiny being unfulfilled.

Take the case of "Sylvester has luck at the races." If this means
that Sylvester encounters a higher instance of successful bets than
normal expectancy promises, then the sentence amounts to a shorthand way of saying a rather complicated thing. But the practice of
touching wood, wearing special colors, compulsively avoiding certain locutions—all these suggest that, in our culture, *more* is meant
here than a mere shorthand expression. If the speaker uses "luck"
to mean a force in the world which is, at least temporarily, on
Sylvester's side, does this usage not deceive him into entertaining a

thesis which, the world being what it is, is in principle unverifiable? For (e) you might try, "Peter had an interest in building construction and in residence contracting." This is a less picturesque sentence, but at least the conditions are known under which one is willing to say that a person has an interest in doing something, even when he is prevented somehow from doing it. But if your interlocutor is unwilling to accept this or another verifiable paraphrase, if he says something like, "Yes, of course he had an interest in it, but he also had a destiny to do it, I tell you!"—if this is the best you can get out of him, then you can only tap on wood and cast a counterspell.

All such cases differ from ignorant mistakes about what the situation is, in that they cannot be falsified. No amount of evidence can reach them. Thus they can be separated from sentences about centaurs and ghosts. They have it in common with reification that they imply metaphysical presuppositions, but differ from these in that no alternative interpretation is possible in the ordinary occasions of use. *Child* can be analyzed by the rule of reduction to escape any metaphysical entity, though the Platonist will not accept the reduction. But with "destiny" the construction the term names cannot be reduced. Word Magic, then, is that instance of reification where there is no alternative non-metaphysical interpretation and where the construction cannot be verified or falsified in principle.

This is the last fallacy we treat under the general heading of material fallacies. When mystics go so far along the line of Platonism as to persist in using terms that can be given no reference at all to any known situation, it is obvious that psychological factors are involved. We might more wisely have placed this fallacy in the next section, where everything is tinged with magic or, alternatively, where most of the language is incantation. We would have done so, except for the obvious connection with reification. Even in discussing that fallacy, the prime example that suggested itself was the case history of an insane man. But at least the poor fellow had some evidence to support his belief that a secret power was after him: he produced detailed accounts of how this power was operating (see pp. 45 ff.). In the case of Word Magic and in many of the cases in the next section of this book, the psychology seems entirely unhinged. This is the witches' coven, the necromancer's magic square. It is the arena of babbling and madness. It is, in short, the everyday world of leading articles, politicians' platforms, TV commericals, and common gossip.

EXAMPLE. On February 24, 1920, when National Socialism was an obscure movement, a meeting was held during which the Party Program was announced. The size of the audience and the enthusiasm for the Program exceeded Hitler's most sanguine expectations. Hitler uses the following language to describe the thoughts that he says ran through his head as the audience filed out of the hall:

> A fire had been lighted out of whose flames in time to come a sword was bound to arise that should win again the freedom of the Germanic Siegfried and the life of the German Nation.
> And beside the coming upheaval I felt strode the goddess of inexorable revenge for the act of perjury of November 9, 1918.
> Hitler, *Mein Kampf*

COMMENT. Notice some general things about this passage. It is highly metaphorical, it is impassioned, it is even inspired. There is nothing particularly reprehensible about being impassioned or inspired, if a writer can sincerely achieve these states as Hitler probably did on this occasion. As to metaphors, figurative language does not of itself involve special difficulty. The metaphors can often translate to prosaic statements; these may be flat and involve a loss of emotion and color but perhaps no loss of substance, if there is any substance. Let us take a closer look at a few of the particular expressions here.

1. "A fire had been lighted out of whose flames in time to come a sword was bound to arise . . ." This translates to something like: "A movement had been started, and out of this beginning there was bound to come some day an armed political power." Here it is not the metaphor but the notion of "bound to" that causes difficulty. "Bound to" suggests inevitability. The laws of gravity obtaining, if you drop an apple it is "bound to" fall. The expression suggests the operation of a law of nature. But there is nothing in the knowledge of political or social nature that could constitute evidence that the acquisition of power is ever inevitable. If Hitler had been killed by a bus on his way home from this meeting, or if any of a thousand other quite possible contingencies had arisen, would the National

Socialist Party nevertheless have been bound to acquire power in Germany?

2. The words ". . . to win again the freedom of the Germanic Siegfried and the life of the German nation" are also metaphorical. They presumably mean something like "German freedom and prosperous unity." These are the things that are going to be "regained" by the power that is bound to come from the beginnings of the movement. It is readily conceivable that a strong political movement could restore freedom of action to a nation and help it to unity and prosperity.

3. What is the "goddess of inexorable revenge" who is now walking about? Revenge is an intelligible concept; it means something like a consistent motivation to pay back evil with evil. Perhaps the goddess is the embodiment of that motive in Hitler, or even, so to speak, in his movement. But what can be inexorable about a motivation? The word "inexorable" applied to human motivations shows that magical abstractions can be adjectives, as well as nouns like "destiny," just as "bound to," used in similar situations shows that verbs are also available for concocting spells of Word Magic.

4. The date November 9, 1918, makes it evident that by "act of perjury" Hitler is referring to the proclaiming of the German Republic. At least, that is when the Republic was proclaimed. Whether one approves or disapproves of this action, there is no chance that it can be taken literally as "perjury." "Perjury" is lying under oath. It is hard to understand what metaphor occurs here. The likely thing is that the term is simply extended, for its emotive connotations, to mean the public act which the speaker detests and wants his audience to reject.

EXAMPLE. Peter, a docile follower of the party line, declares, "The dialectic of the class struggle requires the inevitable overthrow of capitalism."

COMMENT. This example is similar to the first—compare the use of "inevitable" with Hitler's "inexorable" and "bound to." If by "dialectic" is meant "clash of opposing political and economic classes," then the outcome will be decided by the course of events and the strength of the interests involved. If by "dialectic" is meant "the resolution of apparently opposed propositions," this will be a logical exercise, irrelevant to the world of political and economic struggle. Finally, if by "dialectic" is meant some underlying principle of historical development, like Spengler's law of decline or Toynbee's law of response—and this is the way the Marxists and Hegelians talk —then it is another magical abstraction, and there is no point in adducing evidence from history, since none is relevant. This use of "dialectic" and other Marxian terms is not simple reification, since, aside from how Marxians feel about them, there is no way at all to make the constructions available (as the historians can *chivalry* —see #10) to the ordinary users of the language.

PART **II**

Psychological Fallacies

 BEFORE AN audience of children, a debate about diet between a physician and a confectioner would be won by the confectioner, hands down. Before an adult audience, a politician armed with the tricks of persuasion and versed in rhetoric may overturn an engineer or soldier even though the subject is a specialty of the latter, say the building of defenses or harbors. Persuasion flatters the appetites of the audience and has a great advantage over a cold appeal to reason. This has been recognized at least since the time of Plato, and the above examples are from his famous attack on rhetoric, the *Gorgias.*

It is more interesting for all of us when speakers become excited, when they gush or rant, make us laugh, conjure our sympathy, cozen and beguile us in a hundred ways. "Instead of working on your opponent's intellect by argument, work on his will by motive; and he, and also the audience if they have similar interests, will at once be won over to your opinion, even though you got it out of a lunatic asylum," says Schopenhauer, lampooning the level of public discussion in his day. Sarcasm aside, it is easy to agree with Schopenhauer that a man entering on a controversy "must know what the dishonest tricks are," since he will certainly have to meet them.

It is evident that even a sound argument can still be urged on listeners with all sorts of emotional embellishments and with the help of various psychological appeals. If we are going to mean by "fallacy" faulty reasoning in argument, then these appeals and devices are not real fallacies. Yet, whether or not there is an actual error present in the machinery of the argument, some of these psychological tricks have been listed among the fallacies from the earliest times—such devices as name calling, flagrant appeals to prejudice, flattery, ridicule.

All these tricks are practiced for distraction, disturbance, diversion. They confound the issue, they play up special interest, they rely on appeal and dazzlement. In short, they put people off guard, or by shifting the focus of discussion from a close preoccupation with the facts and their cogency, they seduce to the colorful or dramatic or disturbing. Sometimes the speaker will intend, by letting his audience look up, as it were, from a lengthy examination of the issue, only a momentary relaxation. Such a respite is often welcome. At other times the audience may find themselves led away altogether into watching or participating in vigorous displays or noisome forensics. Without becoming hypercritical of every embellishment and sparkle, we can still learn to recognize these for what they are, an added grace by the way.

EMOTIONAL COLORATION

Playing upon emotion to color the case and distract from a close scrutiny of the issue is the most common of all fallacies. It is present in degree in almost all instances where there is any other disturbance. Indeed, the possibilities of name calling, prejudicial epithets, flag-waving, and the whole sorry display of public emotion are so commonly exploited by all classes of men under all sorts of conditions as to seem a part of our natural equipment, like the ability to laugh and cry. No one needs to learn them. As soon as we begin to converse and to enter upon public discussion, we find ourselves endowed with the knack of generating, as people say, more heat than light.

13 · *Emotive Language:* "colored words"

Language has great emotive power. There are several hundred names for the most subtle distinctions in moods and emotions, some ranging from the warmest acceptance to the most resolute rejection, others lying in a rainbow from the complicated attitudes of languor, ennui, and indifference at one end, to wonder and dread at the other. Certain names of emotions have even the power

to evoke in degree the states they refer to. "Astonishment" raises
the eyebrows a little, while "terror" can raise the neck hairs.
"Nostalgia" brings a wistful smile, and "regret" a gentle pained
expression.

The descriptions of some emotions or moods also convey attitudes toward them. Consider Bertrand Russell's conjugation. "I
am firm." "You are obstinate." "He is pig-headed." "Firm" here is
an instance of what the linguists regard as ameliorative connotation, "obstinate" and "pig-headed" as pejorative in increasing degree. Yet these three sentences could refer to the identical situation. Such words as "charming," "kindly," "reasonable," at once
designate and praise certain qualities, while "liar," "coward," "fool,"
designate individuals of certain characteristics and in the same
breath condemn them. Some expressions when applied to persons
are so offensive that it becomes a matter of honor to resist them.
This leads speakers to hunt paraphrases for them, so that "bastard"
becomes "illegitimate offspring" and "lie" becomes "misstatement."

It may be instructive to analyze the pejorative term "lie," as it
occurs, say, in the sentence "S is a lie." This is a simple sentence,
yet it is deceptively simple, since it is true only if it meets each
of four conditions:

    a. S is false.
    b. The speaker of S knows that S is false.
    c. The speaker intends to say S.
    d. The speaker intends a hearer to believe S true.

Each of these conditions is necessary. We do not say that a man
lies if what he says is true, no matter if his intention has been to
deceive—we say he tries to deceive us. Nor do we say he lies,
though what he says is false, unless he knows that it is false and
does not say it by mistake. And we will not regard him as a liar,
though he knowingly and intentionally utters a false sentence, unless he intends to deceive by doing so—he might be merely employing irony or sarcasm: "Now *that* was a smart thing to do!"
Although each is necessary, these four conditions are not sufficient.
They merely take care of the sense of "lie," or the *denotation* of it.
There still remains the *connotation*. One does not seriously say
to a man, "That is a lie" unless one also intends to insult that man
or disparage him. For the term connotes contempt, anger, revul-
sion.

The complexity of the analysis for a familiar term like "lie" illustrates the difficulty of rendering an adequate account of the various functions of language. The expressive and evocative functions are so far from fully explained that the linguists and psychologists have not yet developed any but the crudest tools for investigating them. We hear a little about pejoration or euphemism. We read about "effect modeling" and get the notion that smiling language, as it were, induces us to smile back. Poets talk about a communication of feeling, and propaganda analysts tell of the universal tendency to believe a Big Lie if it is big enough, or the effectiveness of endlessly exasperating a captive audience.

We have little reliable knowledge about the emotive function of language, but we have, all of us, a considerable acquaintance with the possibilities. We employ emotive effects with nearly every sentence we utter. "Pass me the bread, Honey." "My, you look swell today." "That old viper!" We choose words in harmony with the emotive meanings we wish to convey. And we observe our own susceptibility to nuance and rhythm and color when we encounter them in the utterances of others. Hans Reichenbach observes, "Language is the most effective tool for interfering in the inner life of others." We use this tool adroitly or clumsily, according to our abilities. Yet we do not understand it. We are like the small boy with the electric train, who knows how to work it but doesn't know how it works.

For our generation, ever since writers such as C. K. Ogden and I. A. Richards drew attention to the importance of the emotive function of language, there has been a tendency to deplore the inevitable accompaniment of imagery and rich connotation as a source of error and unreason. The advance of science has provided many models of precise communication, free of disturbing feelings and tone. Writers have felt that political discussion and other whole areas of human intercourse could profitably follow these models. As early as Plato, in fact, objections have been vigorously urged against the tendency to substitute persuasion for rational conviction. Plato and many since his time have seen the systematic exploitation of emotive function of language as an attempt to obscure sound judgment and pervert truth. Yet Plato himself wrote a noble style.

Today the attack on "colored terms" and the "tyranny of words" is often pressed with great persuasiveness and force. Few would

wish to maintain the extreme position that every serious attempt
to communicate need resemble a logical argument or a bank ledger.
Everyone with an ear for language protests measureless and un-
rhythmic periods and undramatic arrangement of parts. To say
nothing of these subverbal elements, who would wish to deny a
speaker the right to choose his language consciously for its emotive connotation? Speeches can be made dull by an unimaginative
vocabulary; poetry would be impossible. Fancy transposing:

> The Curfew tolls the knell of parting day,
> The lowing herd wind slowly o'er the lea,

into

> The Curfew sounds indicating the end of the day,
> The herd of mooing cows walks slowly over the pasture.

Sensitivity to the associations of words is a mark of skill in expressing and comprehending ideas. There are times, quite apart
from euphony and embellishment, when the truth can be served
only by frankly emotive language. This world has its fools and
cowards and liars. Shall speakers always find euphemisms? What
polite word should Hobbes have substituted for "fools" in his fine
sentence, "Words are wise men's counters,—they do but reckon
by them; but they are the money of fools"? Label fools as such
and don't suffer them gladly. Don't speak of torturers and assassins
as "custodians" and "liquidators," or, as Orwell has it, of hate as
love, of starvation as discipline, of war as peace.

If a bad ear for connotation leads to absurdity, linguistic cyni-
cism makes a lying use of the emotive resources of language.

Where, then, is the fallacy of emotive language? Fallacy lies in
the *abuse* of the power of words to evoke response. The abuse
may occur when a speaker begs the question under discussion by
formulas of praise or blame. Or it may gradually arise over a period of time so that no one can say precisely that the fallacy occurs
here or here—as when a speaker excretes an atmosphere of passion in which sober talk becomes impossible. Where there is *passion* there can scarcely be *dispassionate* examination of an issue.
The angry man cannot easily think—nor can the flattered man,
either.

Lacking a comprehensive theory of language, we can only observe and experiment. We certainly ought to do so. We can begin
with one thing we do know: no study of language can get off the

ground if it fails to distinguish between the referential function of words and the power they have to convey mood and feeling. Perhaps one who has learned to make this discrimination will begin to acquire some mastery over language; one who has not learned is captive to a powerful trifle.

EXAMPLE. A commentator harangues the radio audience: "This deliberate plot against the American people . . ."

COMMENT. Several of these words have powerful emotive connections. "Deliberate" and "plot" are prejudicial: they do two things at once, describe and denounce, like the word "lie." Incidentally, our own reference to the speech as a "harangue" is also prejudicial. "Harangue" is a word chosen to assure an unfavorable judgment, for nobody respects a harangue.

EXAMPLE. Overheard in a commuters' train: "Suckers and malcontents are always with us, always ready to support visionary schemes to get something for nothing out of the state. That's the way I look at the Desmond Bill."

COMMENT. This is merely name calling.

EXAMPLE. Comrade Peter, in 1940, wrote of the fall of France as "a prearranged sell-out in this imperialistic war between contradictory forces of the right vs. the right." In 1942, after Hitler had violated his entente with Stalin, Comrade Peter wrote in the same journal: "Martyred France is rising in Resistance to fight on the side of the people's armies of east and west in the war to destroy fascism forever."

COMMENT. There are here actual contradictions in the logical material, though they are more implicit than spelled out. But the striking things about Peter's changed "line" is that *each* position he takes is reinforced with a cynical and practiced choice of terms to produce the emotion desired.

EXAMPLE. "Governor Jones stands for freedom, integrity and efficiency in government."

COMMENT. Emotive responses are pleasurably aroused by these words. Propagandists identify this technique as the "glittering generality."

EXAMPLE. Real estate ad: "You'll enjoy the hearthside charm of this two bedroom cottage. Lovely neighbors, attractive landscaping. All the built-in comforts essential to cultured living. Priced to sell."

COMMENT. Better look for termites yourself.

14 · *Ceremony or Setting:* "pomp and circumstance"

Everyone has found himself roused by military music or by cadence in marching, by bunting and colorful displays. Ceremony is a powerful stimulant, sometimes a Pied Piper leading a people into disaster. Or it may elevate the feelings of the audience, as in a religious service. There is no call to condemn ceremony as such. The color of public occasions is part of the joy of life; it is capable of reinforcing attachment to institutions and ideals. But these should be such as to win loyalty on their own merits—people should give consent, like a bride, for reasons of worth and promise, not for the sake of a public ceremony.

Very different from the inspiration derived from public display is the influence exerted by the setting. The physical circumstances forming the background of an argument often affect the notice the argument gains. The same words uttered by the President before a joint session of Congress and by an acquaintance on the next stool of the Trolley Diner have, because of the difference in setting, entirely different penetrating power. The same salesman will sell more with the same sales-line when he has his hair trimmed and his trousers pressed than when he has neglected his appearance. A change in the appointments of office or a store will likewise affect sales. Yet the President's argument is no better than that of the fellow sitting on the next stool—by hypothesis it is identical—and the same sales pitch varies in effectiveness with setting. Setting covers the physical environment of an argument. It is at worst an embarrassment, at best an adornment; truth stands resolute in both rostrum and soap box. Yet arguments that might be listened to with respect coming from the one may be laughed at when coming from the other.

EXAMPLE. The Nazis fully understood the appeal of pageantry. They made masterly use of the contagious excitement stimulated by masses of men, colorful banners, trumpet blares, parades of troops marching with flawless precision, honor guards standing in motionless files, spirited songs, and cries of *Sieg Heil*—all this was deliberately organized to stir the emotions of the people, to emphasize the omnipotence of the leaders, and to provide a setting which would make even commonplace utterances seem of deep significance.

COMMENT.

> On the other hand, the National Socialist meetings were indeed not "peaceful" meetings. There the waves of two views of life clashed against one another, and they ended not with the humdrum singing of one or another patriotic song, but with a fanatical outbreak of popular and national passion.
>
> Hitler, *Mein Kampf*

A display of confidence is, in effect, a type of setting. Personal bearing—tone of voice, dignified posture, a candid eye on the person addressed—can make a vital difference to the practical effectiveness of argument. Salesmen, advocates, leaders—all cultivate these attributes in order to gain by the "confident manner." Indeed, not to display at least a moderately impressive personal demeanor is to invite the audience to discount the value of what is said. If they do so, however, they are committing the fallacy of origin (#19).

EXAMPLE. An Army captain gives a training lecture to his military police unit. "You must outdress every other outfit on the post. People obey orders from those they respect. If you have to reprimand a soldier when you are on police duty, the chances are that you and the soldier will have been total strangers up until that moment. The soldier will size you up by the tone of your voice, by your posture and dress—if these are superior, you aren't going to have much trouble. But if you're sloppily dressed and not snappy in your bearing, then watch out."

COMMENT. The captain is making shrewd use of the fact that men are influenced by setting as well as reason.

EXAMPLE. Mr. and Mrs. Peter stop with a crowd listening to a street orator. "Let's go," says Peter to Mrs. Peter, "He'd make more impression on me if he had a shave."

COMMENT. Mr. Peter may be expressing merely a reluctance to consider argument from such a source (see #19). As expressed, his reluctance is an instance of reliance on setting—if we can regard a stubbled chin as a setting for a speech.

MISUSING AUTHORITY

Genuine appeals to reason found in speeches or discussions are the bones of formal argument and the flesh of evidence. But discourse is usually more than naked reason; it is adorned with many embellishments designed to persuade or to please. Strictly considered, these embellishments are irrelevant. Practically considered, some of this irrelevant material may be advisable. The speaker will often want to adapt the tone of his speech to the occasion or to the mood of his audience. He will want to show the importance of the issue, to bring home a realization of human problems that may lie outside the experience of the average person. For instance, if a speaker is bent on proving that more money must be allocated for the rehabilitation of juvenile delinquents, he may find it helpful to describe some case histories. Here a good speaker resembles a novelist: he gives his listeners a sort of "knowledge-of-acquaintance" concerning human situations where before they may have had only a detached "knowledge-about" the problems involved.

If this sort of appeal, though logically irrelevant, is practically justified, there still remain many sorts that are not. The appeals described in the following fallacies often serve to take advantage of the ignorance of the audience rather than to overcome it. They play on prejudices and misconceptions instead of meeting them squarely. And one must very often suspect that, unlike some fallacies which are the result of ignorance or carelessness, these appeals are dishonest in intent.

15 · *Appeal to Authority: "Ipse dixit" or "He says so!"*

In this day of specialization, all men must rely on authority in the fields of technical information. Since no one can be a specialist in everything, even specialists must defer to each other. The mechanic consults the doctor about his health, the doctor consults the mechanic on the maintenance of his car, both consult an accountant when they make out their income tax. In argument, as in everyday matters, it is entirely proper, indeed inevitable, that authorities be called on for information. It is not, alas, inevitable that source material derived from authorities is always used fairly. Source material should be given the weight due to an authority if and only if the source is (a) personally reliable, and (b) qualified as an expert.

An authority is *personally reliable* in the same way that anybody else is. The chief conditions to watch for in questions of personal reliability are these:

1. There is reason to believe that the witness is telling the truth as he sees it, or at least no reason to suppose he is lying. The witness, for example, is not an habitual liar. If he were, it would be foolish to trust his words even though he might know a great deal about the matters he is reporting on.

2. There is reason to believe that the witness is disinterested, or at least no reason to suppose him swayed by bias. A highly biased or partisan report would convince no one who recognized it as such. Such reports, even from acknowledged experts, usually result in learned confusion at the best.

3. There is reason to believe that the witness is conscientious, or at least no reason to suppose that he has not been attentive to the problem and diligent in gathering data. Casual statements from a witness, however competent, who has been too busy or too lazy to investigate properly, ought not to be regarded as authoritative.

An authority must be *qualified as an expert* in the field in which he is cited. Expert qualifications show the following marks:

1. The authority is clearly identified. The assertion "A leading expert says . . ." is a device of slovenly journalism. How can it be a proper appeal to authority? Since the expert is not named, his qualifications cannot be examined.

2. The authority has professional standing. The qualifications of experts are properly judged, not by laymen, but by fellow experts. The standing of a surgeon should be established by his colleagues, not by the size of his practice or by his popularity among his patients.

3. The authority is current. Darwin is a great name in biology, but before relying on Darwin as an authority, one would want to check present opinion in the science. In some fields today the growth of knowledge is so rapid that a few years or even months may suffice to render an opinion obsolete.

4. The authority is expressing an opinion within the field of his special competence. Einstein may have held very worthy opinions on world peace, but he was not to be regarded as an expert on international relations just because of his reputation in physics. It is of course possible—and this may have been the case with Einstein—for a man to be expert in several fields, even as far apart as physics and politics.

5. The authority in the opinion cited must hold representative views in his field. Where there is controversy, it is not proper to cite one side without acknowledgment of the other.

It is easier to see merits of these criteria of personal reliability and expert qualification than it is to apply them in some practical cases. Just how is the bias of a source to be determined? Just how can it be learned whether an article or a book is representative of settled opinion in a field?—or even is really current? There will be no neat answers to these questions. Yet it often happens that they must be faced. Until there are experts on choosing experts, a man who wants reliable information will have to do the best he can.

Again, even where opinion comes from an impeccable source, human experience suggests care in applying it. Even the greatest expert is human. Revision in science is almost synonymous with progress, and where there is revision, there usually is correction. Life problems of great importance are wisely referred to more than one authority in order to fend against human error. It is good sense to pay for consultation of several surgeons before putting one's life under the knife of any one of them.

Sometimes the surgeons disagree. This is always a perplexity to the layman. Should he accept the opinion of the majority, or of those best qualified as far as he can judge, or of those who are clearest in their explanations? One certain thing emerges from substantial disagreement among authorities, and this is that human knowledge has not reached a satisfactory degree of certainty in dealing with the matter in question. A conflict among experts spotlights the risk of error.

This is a small satisfaction. It is a false generalization, however, to conclude that one man's opinion is always as good as another's. Although it is obvious that, where all knowledge is subject to revision there will always be uncertainty in the world, this does not amount to conceding that an ignorant guess is as good as a responsible opinion There are whole bodies of problems best submitted to experts—from TV repair to astro-physics. It is perhaps the most difficult question of all to determine, in the practical situation, which problems fall into the group to be sent to the experts, and which do not. No expert can tell a man how to vote or judge for him basic political issues. At the other extreme lies technical information: here the layman is entirely at the mercy of the expert. The problem, as often, is one of the marginal cases.

The value of expertise varies with the state of human knowledge. Where the field is exact, knowledge is the property of the expert. Where the problem is a matter of taste, of moral judgment, of the application of life experience, there may be wisdom, but knowledge in the technical sense is lacking. Knowledge, then, is the field of expertise, and it is for knowledge that the layman appeals to authority.

In summary, an appeal to authority is proper where the problem is technical and the expert cited is qualified and personally reliable. Otherwise, the appeal is suspect: at best the speaker may not realize what is required for a proper appeal to authority; at worst he may be trying to give some opinion of his own a weight it would not have without the aid of great names or unidentified "expert opinion."

EXAMPLE. A senator argues, "George Washington warned against entangling foreign alliances. Invited on all sides to internationalist adventures, we should remember the wisdom of the Father of our Country."

COMMENT. Granted that political scientists consider George Washington to have been astute, the admonitions of his Farewell Address are clearly obsolete. If the first President could be brought back to life today, it would take him years to acquire an understanding of the present world situation. His reputation for being astute might be tarnished if it turned out that he would change none of the many opinions he held in 1798, including, quite possibly, the opinion quoted.

EXAMPLE. Sign on a billboard, "Thousands of physicians smoke Whank Cigarettes."

COMMENT. The testimonial is a stock in trade of advertising ballyhoo. Thousands of physicians also go without sufficient sleep. This is not even a forthright appeal to authority, since it is not the opinion of the physicians that it cited but their practice. Perhaps we are supposed to get the idea that if the physicians smoke Whanks, we may safely smoke them also, that the practice of smoking Whanks comes from the established opinion that they are not bad for us. There is no evidence offered for such an "opinion."

EXAMPLE. Peter and Paul are talking about the control of atomic energy. "I am impressed by Oppenheimer's views on this problem," says Paul. "Oh," rejoins Peter, "I don't care what Oppenheimer thinks or says about controlling atomic energy. He's a theoretical physicist."

COMMENT. Peter is right in insisting that any man, even one as outstanding as Oppenheimer, must be qualified in the field in which he expresses an opinion before his view is entitled to any special weight. The remark, "He's a theoretical physicist" seems to indicate that Peter regards high qualification in one field as somehow operating as a disqualification in other fields. This does not follow.

EXAMPLE. Overheard in a library, "Look! This Webster's Dictionary says that 'primp' means 'dress up' or 'preen.' So that's what the word means and not something else."

COMMENT. The "authority" of a dictionary is a special case. Dictionary definitions have no finality, for the editors of a dictionary do not lay down what words *should* mean. Rather, they base their definitions upon research into how the words are *in fact* used by educated speakers of the language. Some words are reported as having a colloquial or slang use. Thus a reputable dictionary is authoritative in the sense that it is a scholarly report of how words are used in practice. Though a dictionary "binds" no one, he who wishes to use a word in an unusual sense will do well to point out the special meaning that he intends or he will run the risk of being misunderstood.

There is a special misuse of authority which is notorious under the name of *quoting out of context.* This may be done in either of two ways that seem especially attractive to the unscrupulous. The first is for one to make out through a suitable manipulation of the text that an authority is on his side. This is done by omitting distinctions, exceptions or qualifying remarks, or by otherwise distorting the text. The second is to treat the opponent as a sort of authority of his own position and to pounce upon something he has said that can be used against him—if the rest is ignored. A brief example of each of these tricks will suffice.

EXAMPLE. A man tells his wife that they should not eat eggs or other forms of animal fat, because, according to an article in a medical journal, fat causes heart attacks. His wife dutifully eliminates the undesirable foods from the family diet, at great trouble in preparing the menus.

COMMENT. If the husband had quoted the article correctly, he would presumably have mentioned all sorts of qualifications and restrictions on the statistical correlation between excessive accumulation in the body of animal fat and the incidence of heart attacks. He would, moreover, have mentioned to his wife that a certain amount of animal fat is necessary in the diet for health. The layman is particularly liable to quoting scientific authority out of context through innocent oversimplification (see p. 171).

EXAMPLE. One of the most flagrant uses of an opponent's own words against him occurred during the campaign of Upton Sinclair for the governorship of California. Billboards made it out that Sinclair was a hater of America, the Flag, God, and Motherhood. The quotations in all cases were out of context.

COMMENT. Sinclair was no politician. As a writer he had frequently used vigorous expression and epigrammatic style. Many politicians do not permit themselves sharply worded statements, for these can look damaging in or out of context.

16 · *Appeal to Tradition or Faith:* "tried and true"

Some of our traditions, our religious or political tenets, represent policies or basic decisions in the light of which we will wish to examine certain proposed courses of action that involve a group to which we owe allegiance. A nation may be committed to going to war when its allies are attacked, a political party to instituting a particular economic reform, or a church to propagating the gospel according to its interpretation. Where an appeal to these basic policies is relevant for deciding on a course of action, it is always in order. Where the appeal is not relevant, it cannot be proper, as, for instance, where the proposed course of action on its face is no more a consequence of the basic tenets than the alternative courses of action. Where this is the case, the question is what means will best carry out the policy. At other times the basic policy itself is under question; in this case an appeal to it merely states the very issue which is being decided. Such an appeal cannot be in order. Thus, there are two main kinds of improper appeal to tradition or faith.

The first occurs where the discussion concerns ways and means for implementing a group's basic decision. Here an appeal to principle obfuscates the issue by hinting that one party is forsaking or at least conveniently forgetting it. The discussion should properly turn on a consideration of what is called expediency: does the proposed course of action meet the situation? Is it feasible? Let us look at an instance of this first kind of improper appeal to tradition before turning to the second.

EXAMPLE. Peter belongs to the Tin-Workers International Union, Local N, a union, like most unions, committed to the fundamental policy of striving for higher wages for its members. The membership in a certain factory is called upon to decide whether to arbitrate or resort to a strike. Peter addresses the members: "Friends and Brothers, we are pledged to do all in our power to obtain higher wages for our members. It is in our power to strike. Therefore, I move that we go on strike."

COMMENT. The manner of Peter's appeal to the policy of his union obscures the issue by suggesting that the alternative proposal is counter to this policy. The question before the members is *which* course of action will more effectively further the purpose of raising wages. Incidentally, there is also another fallacy in Peter's argument (see #45).

The second kind of improper appeal to the basic decisions of a group occurs when the group is called upon to question the basic decision itself. As circumstances change, groups sometimes find themselves having to re-examine the commitments which originally brought their members together. National examples are the changed attitude toward monopoly since the early days of trust busting, and the diminishing reluctance of some leaders to surrender part of national sovereignty to a world organization. When a proposal to change a policy—to modify a traditional practice or recast a fundamental objective—is under discussion by the membership of a group, it is clearly circular to attack the proposal as undermining the established order. It is irrelevant to argue that the basic decision is fundamental or hallowed by usage and loyal observance—though, of course, these factors will make some proposed changes seem revolutionary and of the gravest concern. Yet whenever the soundness of the established order is being challenged by responsible persons, then the justification for the commitment should be re-examined. The re-examination may result in modifying or renouncing the commitment. It may result in reaffirming it. To reaffirm is also to make a new decision. When reason prevails the group will make such a decision (since it concerns by definition matters of fundamental importance to the group) only after conscientious re-examination. The thing to notice here is that for the very reason that people do not lightly propose the overturning of fundamental commitments, it is all the more disorderly in discussion either to be continually making emotional appeals to them when they are not in question, or to beg the question by mere reiteration of the basic commitment which the group is being asked to re-examine.

EXAMPLE. Paul is reading the Congressional Record for 1919. He discovers the debates concerning the entrance of the United States into the League of Nations and reads the following statement by Senator Peter: "I am an isolationist and intend to remain one. The Wilsonites are subversive of the American tradition, a tradition hallowed by our great founder and by thirteen decades of American history."

COMMENT. The tradition of isolationism amounted to a basic decision of American policy thoroughly entrenched in the structure of our international relations prior to 1919. Those men (the "Wilsonites") who favored joining the League of Nations in 1919 were in effect challenging the soundness of the tradition itself in the light of World War I. Such a challenge is always in a sense subversive: it is a proposal to "subvert" a tradition. To call the followers of Wilson subversive was, thus, merely to state that they were challenging the tradition, a fact obvious to everybody—with an emotional suggestion that it was wicked to do so. Now if Senator Peter had carefully examined the proposal, he earned the right to reaffirm his adherence to the principle of isolationism, supposing his continued acceptance of the tradition to remain unshaken. But he could justify his continued adherence to the tradition only by showing that it was sound, not by an irrelevant reference to its venerated source or long standing establishment.

17 · *Impressing by Large Numbers:* "get on the band wagon"

Mere numbers constitute a sort of pseudo-authority. Sometimes a speaker will bolster his position by pointing out that there are many who hold his belief, buy the brand he is selling, or support the candidate he favors. Though it is pleasant to be in step, to conform, to go along, to ride a band wagon, truth is not always democratic. Even unanimity is not infallible.

The authority of mere numbers commonly amounts to no more than mass suggestion or unquestioning acceptance of tradition. Obviously, what "everybody knows" is not necessarily true, for once "everybody" knew that the earth was flat, that monarchs ruled by divine right, that disease was caused by evil spirits, that slavery was necessary. Informed support of democracy today does not involve the conviction that the majority is always right. Perhaps, while no system as such will guarantee wise government, democracy at least has the advantage of allowing citizens to "kick the rascals out."

Of course, everything else being equal, large numbers do often have a wisdom and authority. We saw that an expert is qualified by being recognized by those familiar with the field, and the more of these the more qualified the expert appears to be. Here it is sensible to be impressed by the numbers of other experts who hold an opinion. Even in matters not commonly thought a field for expertise, people are justified in admitting numbers to help form their opinion wherever those numbers can evaluate the facts and arrive at a reasoned judgment.

EXAMPLE. An editorial presents this argument: "All the world knows that whenever people are free to choose between the life they have experienced under Communist rule and the life offered by free institutions, then great numbers leave Communism, even at high personal cost. Over a million refugees have fled Eastern Germany to become displaced persons in Western Germany, while the movement from Western to Eastern Germany remains negligible. When 75,000 Chinese and North Korean prisoners of war were given the choice of returning to their homes or facing the uncer-

tainties of a life in exile in South Korea or Formosa, 22,000 chose
separation from their families and native land. Regardless of
whether one looks at Indochina or Hungary or the other Communist satellites, the story remains always the same: streams of
exiles and the merest trickle of those seeking repatriation. And let
us note that those leaving Communism have lived under it."

COMMENT. Telling argument here. Individuals who have *lived*
under Communism are rather like experts at such a life. Moreover,
in matters of experience which intimately concerns them, ordinary
people are in a position to judge. Granting this, the numbers are
impressive.

EXAMPLE. Salesman Peter, representing a perfume manufacturer, urges a prospective customer, "Fifty thousand women can't
be wrong."

COMMENT. The world presents, unfortunately, a daily spectacle of tens of millions of individuals holding wrong beliefs and
consequently following courses disastrous to their social and individual welfare.

EXAMPLE. A noted philosopher explains in an interview, "Eminent minds have come to the conclusion that in our civilized world
the evil in man prevails over the good. As Hobbes put it, 'The life
of man is solitary, poor, nasty, brutish, and short.' If I am accused
of pessimism, all I can say is that I have lots of company and
famous company, too."

COMMENT. That many philosophers have become disillusioned,
including eminent men among them, is no guarantee that such an
interpretation of life is adequate or even meaningful. Hobbes, incidentally, was talking about the conditions of life in a putative
"state of nature" before the benefits of government. Hence the
reference to Hobbes involves quoting out of context (see p. 88).

EXAMPLE. A housewife to her husband: "Yes, I have heard
about the fund raising campaign for the new recreation center.
Why, half the social lights of town have endorsed the idea. A look
at those endorsements convinced me that we should support it too."

COMMENT. There is both a rational and an irrational possibility in this common situation. The good housewife may be reasoning, "These people would endorse only sound ideas. They endorse this idea. Therefore, this idea is sound." In this case, she is
adopting the idea she regards as supported by the favorable judg-

ment of reputable people who, she presumes, have enquired into its merits. On the other hand, she may be swayed by the prestige of prominent names; she may be adopting the idea because it comes from sources that she considers beyond question. If so, she is a casualty of the bandwagon technique.

STIRRING UP PREJUDICE

Prejudice is an opinion held without reasonable grounds: it takes the form of a decided preference for something or aversion to it. One man may favor foreign aid, luxury taxes, or nonrepresentational art; another may firmly oppose the very same things. An appeal to prejudice shrewdly represents a position as coinciding with whichever bias the speaker supposes to prevail in his audience. Such an appeal is evidently different from an examination of the merits of a given proposal—or even of general tendencies and policies relating to the proposal.

It is often presumed that the strongest bias an audience has is toward its own interests, especially its economic and social interests. Correspondingly, whatever threatens the audiences self-interest is a likely area of negative prejudice. Clever speakers take advantage of this—and of their audience—to exploit greed or snobbery or fear. But clever audiences learn to discount *ad populum* and *ad hominem* appeals and to pay attention to the arguments *ad rem,* if any. *Ad populum* means "to the people," and refers to stirring up group prejudices; *ad hominem* means "to the man," and refers to appeals to these same prejudices usually by the round-about method of personal attack on the character or motives of an opponent. These Latin terms show how long these fallacies have been recognized; a naive person might be surprised we still have them with us. The remaining expression *ad rem* means argument "to the issue," and refers to those unadorned arguments that stick to it.

18 · *Popular Passions: "ad populum appeals"*

The appeal *ad populum* or "to the people" is characteristic of addresses to the uninformed. (Bacon named them "idols of the market-place.") The man who conjures with racial or religious hatred, the agitator who stirs passions by pointing to the evils of colonial government without acknowledging any of its accomplishments, the demagogue who resorts to name calling and in this country brands proposals which he does not like as "communist" or "fascist" or in the USSR similarly applies the word "capitalist"— all these are either relying on popular passion or invoking the self-interest of the crowd. Mark Antony's funeral oration is an often cited instance of this maneuver. The issues that the Roman public was called upon to face were, (1) Had Caesar been guilty of conspiring to overthrow the Republic? and (2) Should any action be taken against the assassins? Mark Antony's speech says nothing of the issues. Instead, he reminds the audience that they once loved Caesar,

> You all did love him once, not without cause.
> What cause withholds you then to mourn for him?

exhibits Caesar's blood-stained mantle,

> Through this the well-beloved Brutus stabb'd;

implies the conspirator's motives were personal,

> What private griefs they have, alas, I know not,
> that made them do it:

assures the audience he, Antony, is a guileless man,

> I am no orator, as Brutus is:
> But, as you know me all, a plain blunt man,

and, to cap his case, alleges Caesar's will leaves his property to public uses,

> To every Roman citizen he gives,
> To every several man, seventy-five drachmas.

This persuades the mob; they troop off ready to avenge Caesar. Incidentally, by saying over and over again, "But Brutus is an honorable man," Antony raises the issue of the conspirator's honor which, otherwise, would not be in question.

EXAMPLE. Peter is running for city coroner against an opponent who is a recent comer to the town. Peter addresses his audience, "I was born in this town and have lived here all my life. I went to Abraham Lincoln school, and probably some of you still haven't forgotten the time I struck out in the tenth inning of the Medfield game."

COMMENT. Peter appeals *ad populum* by stirring up the home-folks' prejudice. Long familiarity with a locality is a qualification for some offices, none at all for the duties of a coroner.

EXAMPLE. A milkman is soliciting orders for a small dairy. "The 'big three' dairies do 80 per cent of the business in this town while the small ones like ours get along on the remaining 20 per cent. I certainly appreciate everyone who helps give the little fellow a chance around here."

COMMENT. This is *ad populum* to anti-monopoly or pro-little businessman sentiment.

EXAMPLE. A soap box orator exclaims, "Those high priests of finance, the brokers, bankers and corporate directors of Wall Street, have only one thing in their hearts—the sacred dividend check!"

COMMENT. This appeal to popular passions is of the kind commonly known as "name calling." The device is stock in trade for demagogues. The essence of name calling is relying on prejudicial terminology (see #13) to evoke popular passion—"high priests of finance," "Wall Street," "The sacred dividend check." Inflection of the voice or a context of epithet can make a name like "Wall Street" into a term of abuse.

Appeals to personal self-interest are on the same level as appeals to popular passion. We notice how Mark Antony's funeral oration played on the mob's sense of loyalty, on the feeling that personal motives are out of place in state affairs, on faith in those who lack guile; yet it was holding out seventy-five drachmas "to every several man" which climaxed the scene. Personal self-interest or the appeal *ad personam* is a simple fallacy, the country cousin of *ad populum*.

EXAMPLE. Peter is talking to his friend Paul, "I'd advise you not to oppose the new Building Code, not vocally at least. The contractors are behind it, and you've got a lumber yard to keep out of the red. Just a tip to tell you what's good for you."

COMMENT. Peter shows adroitness in getting at Paul's self-interest. Sometimes personal reasons will overweigh a thousand sound arguments.

19 · *Damning the Origin:* "consider the source"

The opposite of regarding argument as established through an appeal to authority (see #15), is the so-called fallacy of origin, that is, rejecting an argument on account of its undesirable source. The force of an argument does not lie in the nature of the source which advances it. Plato makes this point in one of his dialogues, the *Phaedrus*. Here Plato depicts Socrates as illustrating an argument by inventing a little myth about ancient Egypt, whereupon Phaedrus replies by remarking that Socrates could, of course, invent tales about Egypt or any other place he chose. Socrates then answers the implied criticism by inventing still another myth.

> There was a tradition in the temple of Dodona that oaks first gave prophetic utterances. The men of old, unlike in their simplicity to young philosophy, deemed that if they heard the truth even from 'oak or rock,' it was enough for them; whereas you seem to consider not whether a thing is or is not true, but who the speaker is and from what country the tale comes.
>
> Plato, *The Phaedrus*

Socrates' rebuke is justified. It is true that we want to take into account the reliability of a man before adopting some view of his or before believing without other warrant something he tells us. But even a notorious liar or a man strongly motivated by self-interest can on occasion tell the truth. Of the millions of sentences uttered by Hitler, it would be remarkable if all were false—great numbers of the sentences in *Mein Kampf*, for instance, are true. Our disgust with Hitler does not relieve us from considering any true statements that he made or any sound argument that he advanced. Socrates is reminding us that what we should want to know about a statement is whether or not it is true, and that it is irrelevant where the statement originates, whether in a tree or a rock—or a myth for that matter.

EXAMPLE. A registered lobbyist for a group of lumber interests in the Northwest urges passage of a bill which would open a portion of Olympic National Park for logging by private companies. The following comment appears in the letter column of a local paper, "This town should resist the assault on the National

Park system which lobbyists for the lumber interests are trying to put across to their own economic advantage."

COMMENT. It may be in the national interest to reduce, maintain, or extend the limits of Olympic National Park. The fact that the plan is backed by a source whose strong economic interest provides an obvious reason for anticipating bias does not justify dismissing the proposal without enquiry into its merits.

EXAMPLE. Paul declares, "Though I agree with the opinion that Prohibition didn't work well when it was tried, it does seem to me that our present system of liquor control is inadequate. I favor outlawing hard liquor entirely, while permitting the sale and consumption of beer and wine." To this Peter rejoins, "This is a strange thing for you to be saying over a whiskey sour, Paul. Perhaps you don't realize that the quip, 'Do as I say, not as I do' gets its point because of feeble arguments like yours."

COMMENT. This example is a special sort of attack on origin (it has the classical name *tu quoque*). Instead of saying in such cases, "consider the source," the speaker says, in effect, "*You* believe that?" as if the position involved an inconsistency. Yet it is not necessarily inconsistent for a Republican to advocate public ownership, a Southerner integration, a doctor socialized medicine, a married clergyman celibacy. If an opponent upholds the expected position, you discredit him for special pleading (see #26); if the unexpected position, you laugh at him for inconsistency. *You* are in the comfortable position of saying "Damned if you do, and damned if you don't."

EXAMPLE. An address at a town meeting, "I believe in looking a gift horse in the mouth. Here we have the largest landowner in town offering to donate a site for the new high school. Let's choose our own site and pay a fair price for it."

COMMENT. The speaker refuses to *look* his gift horse in the mouth. He condemns the horse before he discovers anything wrong with it.

EXAMPLE. Overheard after a lecture: "I listened with interest to what Mr. Thomas has to say about the social policy for integration in the school system. But, I ask, has Mr. Thomas ever lived in Georgia? No, not in Georgia nor for that matter anywhere else in the South."

COMMENT. This line of argument suggests that lacking a particular experience somehow disqualifies any opinions advanced by the source. It is certainly no fallacy to bring out the qualifications or extent of experience possessed by one who advances opinions, for these bear on the source's standing as an authority (see #15). But to allege lack of qualifications with the innuendo that this disposes of the testimony is to commit the fallacy of origin.

20 · *Personal Attacks: "ad hominem"*

Damning an opponent is a common and odious method of damning the source (see #19). Personal attacks are effective because it is difficult to credit a man who has been tarred and feathered with obloquy. There is no argument easier to construct or harder to combat than character assassination, and this may be the reason personal attacks are so commonly on the lips of ignorance and demagogy. The armory of personal abuse is inexhaustible: nobody finds it easy to forget the doubts engendered when a man is represented as being dishonest, cowardly, crafty, greedy, perverted, conceited, incompetent, arrogant.

How, then, can one take account of the character and motives of parties to an argument without falling into fallacy? Personal considerations are certainly relevant for judging the reliability of a man, his willingness to tell the truth. If judgment of a man holds him unreliable, then his statements are rightly suspect. But there is a difference between "suspect" and "false." And there is a difference between taking into account the reliability of a witness and blindly assuming that personalities dispose of issues.

EXAMPLE. An alderman is indicted for payroll padding. Interviewed by a newspaper, he declares, "Everybody knows that Jones dug up this charge and that he has been out to get me for a long time. But I'm not worried. The people won't forget that I've been plugging for better schools and parks, while Jones's great public service to date was in getting mixed up in that Sunnyacre real estate scandal."

COMMENT. The alderman is resorting to personalities to becloud the issue. He does this positively by reminding us of his own alleged public service and negatively by discrediting Jones with allegations of bad motives and of involvement in a scandal. Whether true or false, none of these answer the charge.

EXAMPLE. Witness Paul: "My objection to the proposed legislation is that it sanctions depriving a person of his job without informing the person concerned of the nature or source of the evidence against him. Under these conditions there is no proper chance to answer the charges."

Senator Peter: "You are a member of the American Civil Liberties Union, which defends Communists?"

Witness Paul: "I do belong to that organization."

Senator Peter: "And you expect this committee to give weight to your testimony?"

COMMENT. There is no reason to suppose membership in the American Civil Liberties Union has any bearing on the individual's willingness or capacity to tell the truth. Clearly, Senator Peter's technique is to tar both Witness Paul and the American Civil Liberties Union with the brush "defends Communists"—an action expected to evoke general disapproval. The example, incidentally, also illustrates the trick of the half-truth. The statement "The American Civil Liberties Union defends Communists" is true—so far as it goes. But the Civil Liberties Union does not defend Communists as Communists, and it also defends on principle Republicans, Democrats, persons seeking to become naturalized citizens, or anyone else whose case presents an important civil liberties issue under our Constitution. Senator Peter has dropped consideration of the issue to indulge in the type of attack which newspapers characterize as the "smear" technique.

EXAMPLE. A foreman is fired by the XYZ Canning Co. He gives a newspaper interview charging unfair labor practices in the cannery. A cannery official declares, "The foreman is sore about being fired. He is a troublemaker and was once convicted of embezzlement."

COMMENT. The reference to the foreman as a "troublemaker" can be dismissed as a vague personal charge designed to create prejudice. His alleged spite and previous dishonesty bear on his reliability in telling the truth. This should be considered as character evidence; such evidence can justify not accepting his story without further confirmation. Notice that the idea of "not accepting" is not equivalent to "rejecting." After all, the foreman may be telling the truth even if he is a vindictive rogue. The problem is, then, to find out whether the unreliable foreman was telling the truth on this occasion. This can only be done by seeking more evidence about the facts. Those who adopt the simple solution of reasoning to themselves, "The foreman is a rascal, so we will disregard everything he says," are the victims of prejudice.

It might be remarked that lawyers call this the "bad man" argument. Juries seem inclined to believe that if a defendant has a previous criminal record he must be guilty of the present charge. The fact of previous conviction can be brought out legally only if the defendant testifies in his own behalf, when it becomes admissible as "character evidence." Because of the *bad man* possibilities, counsel sometimes decide not to allow a defendant of unsavory record to take the stand in his own defense.

21 · *Forestalling Disagreement*

The fallacy here lies in the attempt to make an opponent or an audience unwilling to meet the argument. Adults usually have learned to avoid needless quarrels and to steer clear of embarrassment. So they develop skill in phrasing their ideas in ways that will forestall disagreement, and in turn are silenced by the implied threat contained in assertions that are phrased to make disagreement embarrassing. Many expressions such as "it is obvious," "everybody knows," "clearly," "of course," "as any one can see," serve the double purpose of assuring the audience that it is not necessary to think about the problem and cowing those with the temerity not to go along. One who protests, "It isn't obvious to me!" runs the danger of appearing ignorant or boorish. Other means for forestalling disagreement are flattery of the audience ("I don't need to tell an intelligent group like this . . ."), appeals to the desire to be agreeable ("I believe everyone will agree that . . ."), appeals to the desire to be respectable ("Every decent American wants . . ."), and so on. Forestalling disagreement ranges from mild devices calculated to make agreement easy ("Of course we all believe . . .") to highly prejudicial assertions to intimidate opposition ("Only a muddled headed person would suggest . . ."). They are characteristically question begging (see #49).

EXAMPLE. "It is obvious," argues Peter, "that unless scientific research is subsidized, the whole country will suffer."

COMMENT. Whether or not "the whole country will suffer" is what Peter should be busy trying to prove. "It is obvious" is a mild attempt to forestall disagreement.

EXAMPLE. A teacher observes to his class, "Even a freshman realizes that great artists are not necessarily good draftsmen."

COMMENT. Further discussion is all but precluded here.

EXAMPLE. The Governor addresses the state legislature: "The state budget this year is the largest ever submitted to the legislature of this state. There are, as always, items and details in it of which I do not approve. No doubt some of you will find other items and other details of which you disapprove. Yet the keen sense of responsibility which has been so evident in this legislature is a guarantee to the people of this state that the needs provided for by this budget will be met."

COMMENT. Flattery seems to be the chief ingredient of the Governor's approach. The suggestion that the legislature's "sense of responsibility" assures passage of the budget is an attempt to forestall opposition to its provisions. Even this flattery seems designed to intimidate.

22 ◦ *Creating Misgivings:* "where there's smoke there's fire"

The lingering suspicion which follows on unfounded charges of immorality, corruption, or disloyalty is notoriously hard to clear away. Character assassination is probably the most powerful use made of this fallacy. Those close to a man who has lived down such a charge may be able, through their knowledge of the facts, to hold that man in undiminished regard. Others, long after they have forgotten the nature of the charge, to say nothing of whether or not it was substantiated, tend to retain lingering suspicions. Maybe they had better not rely on Paul because of that funny business back in—was it the election year? Yet what they ought to be remembering is the fellow Peter, who made the damaging allegations against Paul without impressive proof.

It is a paradoxical thing that the more wild and damaging the charges, the more likely they are to be believed. People seem to reason that nobody would say such a terrible thing unless it were true, partially at least. Hitler made a famous analysis of this phenomenon when he wrote,

> . . . in the size of the lie there is a certain factor of credibility, since the broad mass of the people will be more easily corrupted in the depths of their hearts than they will be consciously and intentionally evil. Consequently, with the primitive simplicity of their feeling they fall victim more easily to a big lie than to a small one, since they themselves occasionally lie in small matters but they would be ashamed to tell great lies. Such a falsehood will not enter their minds, and they will also not be able to imagine others asserting the great boldness of the most infamous misrepresentation. And even with the explanation of the matter, they long hesitate and vacillate and accept at least some ground as true; consequently, from the most bold lie something will remain. . . .
>
> Hitler, *Mein Kampf*

Hitler's "big lie" technique finds illustrations in the history of every nation. Instances from our own history are the fabrications, for example, by Allied propagandists, about Germans cutting off the hands of Belgian babies during World War I, by the Communists in making the "germ warfare" charges during the Korean War, and by those who labeled the Democratic Party as the "Party of Treason" during the heyday of McCarthyism. One extremely significant instance of the "big lie" in German history was the creation of the "stab in the back" myth to explain Germany's defeat in World War I. Actually, before the German home front crumbled the German army had failed in its last great offensive and there was no longer hope for military victory over the rapidly increasing Allied power. Yet misrepresentation of the facts, constantly reiterated, persuaded many Germans that their army had been undefeated. The creation of this historical myth during the post-war period was designed to restore the prestige of German military might and to provide a popular scapegoat by attributing defeat to demon groups—radicals, pacifists, defeatists.

The ultimate effect of lying makes interesting speculation. Hitler may well be right in arguing that the very boldness of the "big lie" gives it credibility, initially at least. But perhaps his own career fairly illustrates the shortsightedness of this sort of Machiavellianism. At least his repeatedly making promises which turned out to be "big lies" (For example, the Munich Pact and Hitler's assurance, "This is my last territorial demand in Europe.") finally

convinced millions of people—statesmen and householders alike—
that it was pointless to make agreements with Hitler. In other
words, confidence in communication broke down, and the conviction grew that further appeasement would lead only to further
aggressions. It was this conviction that turned Hitler's demand
for Danzig into a world war instead of another diplomatic con-
cession. The crude unscrupulousness of the "big lie" is apt to operate like a boomerang. Talleyrand might have dismissed the device
with his dictum, "It is worse than a crime, it is a mistake!"

EXAMPLE. A pastor is named in a paternity suit claiming support for an illegitimate child. Evidence shows that the woman and
the pastor both were guests at three social gatherings. Tests, however, establish that the accuser was blood type "O," the pastor
has type "A" and the child has type "B." Suit is dismissed after
uncontradicted testimony by an authority on eugenics that a child
of blood type "B" cannot be the offspring of parents with types
"O" and "A." In spite of being cleared of the paternity charge, the
pastor decides to seek a new congregation. He finds one only after
great difficulty.

COMMENT. The evidence clearing the pastor is as certain as
any that human beings can obtain. His accuser has patently in-
dulged in promiscuity and has wrongly—*probably* with intentional
falsehood—ascribed the paternity of her child. Yet a moral suspicion still lingers even, perhaps, in the minds of those who know
all details of the case. We have indicated this by italicizing "probably" above. What *were* the relations between the pastor and the
woman? Of course, he didn't happen to be the father, but. . . .

EXAMPLE. "They are saying around the City Hall that Mayor
Paul's cronies bought up a lot of land over there when they got
the tip that the freeway was going through." So confides gossiper
Peter to his neighbor.

COMMENT. If Peter's neighbor repeats this unsubstantiated
charge, he will be as guilty as Peter of rumor-mongering.

RATIONALIZATIONS AND LIP SERVICE

A wrestler does not rely wholly upon his own strength; he seeks
to take unexpected advantage of the movements of his opponent

so that the opponent's muscles contribute to his own downfall. A sudden tug on the arm provokes resistance, and the wrestler then throws his weight in the same direction. An argument is sometimes like this; one party to it may pull one way when his intent is to go somewhere else. We have chosen the heading "Rationalizations and Lip Service" to describe some of these feints. They are proposals which utilize the strength of others to throw them off balance. But, unlike the wrestler who is conscious of what he is doing, sometimes the speaker falls for his own deceptions.

Rationalization is the common human failing of offering to oneself or others some "good" reason in support of what one actually chooses to do or believe for another and perhaps discreditable reason. Nothing is more natural in taking one side of a case than to make the case one-sided. Though people are sometimes aware of their own rationalizations, more often they are not.

Lip service, the last fallacy under this particular division, is the fault of paying verbal homage to one thing while actually doing or advocating something quite different. The verbal acknowledgment smooths the way while the speaker heads for a different goal. Let us now take a closer look at some of the common rationalizations.

23 · *Self-righteousness*

Everyone in degree believes in the worth and justice of his own motives and interests. No one can view his own interests with perfect fairness; no one can even be certain of his own deepest motives. Yet a thoughtful man can be aware that his thinking may be beset with "secret faults." Hard as it is to avoid such faults, one can at least realize that righteous intentions do not attest to truth, and that neither interest nor motives have any necessary relation to the justice of a case. One may be right in a contention which accords perfectly with his desires and interests—or he may be wrong. And one can do the right thing for the wrong reasons: one can be selfish or bigoted and yet, at the same time, act correctly. We have already pointed out the fallacy of disposing of a proposition on the ground that its proponents are unreliable or actuated by bad motives (see #19). Here we deal with the error of confusing self-interest or good intentions with justice and truth.

EXAMPLE. A dictator addresses a vast audience: "We have done all that we can to keep the peace despite perfidy and insolent provocation. This morning I ordered our army to march on foreign soil, and, God willing, we will right the wrongs which we have too long endured. Our hands are clean. Our aim is justice."

COMMENT. The dictator appeals to the audience's willingness to believe in the justice and nobility of their own cause. Practically every modern war exhibits millions of people convinced of the rightness of the cause which coincides with their self-interest or what they are persuaded to believe is their self-interest. The spectacle is a tribute to cultural conditioning, the efficiency of distorting the news, and the human weakness for assuming that one's own motives and interests must be noble and just.

24 · *Finding the "Good" Reason*

Consider the commonplace excuse, "Sorry to be late. The five o'clock rush held me up." Here the speaker is offering a respectable minor premise from which it is possible to infer a syllogism (see #40) which will excuse the tardiness. The argument runs:

If a person is delayed, he will be excusably late.
I was delayed in the five o'clock rush.
Therefore, I am excusably late.

Suggesting a fact which implies the conclusions desired is a face-saving way to make an excuse. If you are not minded to accept the excuse, you may think up a different set of premises. For instance:

A person taking care to be on time will anticipate foreseeable delays.
The five o'clock rush is a foreseeable delay.
Therefore, this person did not take care to be on time.

"Finding the 'good' reason" is the process of selecting a fact which is creditable or, at least, not discreditable, and proposing it as the explanation for one's actions.

EXAMPLE. A student explains his failure in chemistry. "If you are a good parrot you can crack that course for an 'A.' I can't stand sheer memory courses."

COMMENT. There are lots of possible explanations for the student's failure. Maybe he does not study, maybe the course is too advanced for his background, perhaps the instruction is obscure, perhaps the student is dull; it is quite possible that he is uninterested in the subject so that his mind does not focus on it when he is "studying." Very likely the explanation of his failure involves several of these factors. For the purposes of rationalization, the student wants a reason which will be respectable. Thus, he presents this argument:

Chemistry is a sheer memory course.
I "can't stand" (i.e., do not learn the material in) a sheer memory course.
Therefore, I do not learn chemistry.

We are, of course, free to disagree with either or both of these premises.

25 · *Wishful Thinking*

Self-interest often leads us to refuse to look for evidence that we don't want to face. Ostrich-like, we ignore the facts. On wishful thinking we build false expectations. When these are disappointed, we may have a rude awakening.

EXAMPLE. On a balmy spring day Salesman Peter wearies of soliciting prospects. "There are lots of good contacts to make at the golf links, and besides I need a rest," reflects Peter. He takes the afternoon off.

COMMENT. Let Peter not wonder if his sales drop.

EXAMPLE. Caesar relates in his *Commentaries* how a Gallic tribe accepted a wild rumor to the effect that the Roman army had been destroyed and how they poured down pell mell on the Roman camp. "People believe what they want to believe," noted Caesar.

COMMENT. Rationalizing isn't new. It was the Gauls who met destruction.

26 · *Special Pleading:* "having it both ways"

When scientists of the American Cancer Society presented evidence strongly linking cigarette smoking with lung cancer, many smokers became uneasy. Then other research organizations argued that the conclusions were not proved, and smokers were supposed to be reassured. But some noticed that the reassurance came from laboratories supported by the tobacco interests. Now it certainly does not follow that arguments favoring the use of cigarettes are automatically wrong because those making them stand to gain by the sale of tobacco. To suppose so is to fall into the fallacy of origin (# 19). Yet such arguments become suspect. They seem likely cases of one-sided pleading.

One-sided pleading becomes special pleading when you "have it both ways." You find the reasons where your advantage lies, but refuse to apply the same principle to yourself that you apply to others. Salesmen, lawyers, debaters are not the only people ever guilty of rationalizing in this way. Scientists, educators, statesmen —in fact anybody who has something to gain or who has merely warmed to his argument—can be found on occasion ignoring or twisting the facts to his own advantage.

EXAMPLE. A realtor shows a friend a large parking lot which he has recently acquired to accommodate the cars of his salesmen. "It is a good investment," he declares. "Nothing I could have done would have saved more time and annoyance for my employees." Shortly thereafter the City purchases land for a parking lot to accommodate municipal employees. The land values are comparable and the parking facilities equally congested in the two areas. "Another instance of extravagance in the City Hall," protests the realtor.

COMMENT. Unless the realtor can point out significant differences between the two situations, what is a "good investment" for one employer will hardly be "extravagant" for another.

EXAMPLE. Geopolitician Pietro writes: "Though Nice was lost to France in 1860, the historic claim of Italy to this city remains bright in the hearts of Italians. No true Italian can forget Garibaldi's protest against this annexation: 'You have made me a stranger in the land of my birth!'" Later, Pietro is discussing Italy's possession of the South Tyrol, a German-speaking area annexed by Italy after World War I. "Only in the crucible of war did our country earn her natural frontier on the Brenner Pass. Geography must forever ratify Italy's claim to this land."

COMMENT. Pietro's claims manifest the desire to have it both ways, a desire characteristic enough of those advancing historic, ethnic or geographical claims to suit the convenience of their own nations. Pietro's shift of grounds from a historical to a geographical basis reveals the special pleading of his contentions.

27 · *Lip Service*

All of us are more or less restrained by the taboos current in our particular society, in our culture. Perhaps this is fortunate since it promotes the stability of social institutions and makes for cultural unity. At any rate, the pressure which society exerts to make individuals conform to its beliefs and ideals is generally sufficient to prevent all but occasional individuals from openly repudiating the prevailing notions. Examples may be found in any culture. The principles of orthodox Marxism have been so enshrined in the Soviet Union that Lenin and his successors have constantly made obeisance to Marx even though departing widely from his notions. In America, almost every group renders homage to the ideals of the U. S. Constitution, although it is quite clear that neither the communist, neo-fascist nor superpatriotic elements actually uphold the civil liberties essential to the plan of government which the Constitution provides. In American culture it takes a hardy individualist to express dissent from the principles of Christian ethics or to idealize war. One may, without evoking any intolerable hostility, advocate or do all sorts of things inconsistent with Christian ethics or continued peace; only open acknowledgment of the consequences of one's acts is apt to bring immediate public repudiation. Consequently, individuals who find themselves opposed to some cultural norm often see the wisdom of giving lip service to it. In fact, a person may render lip service to an accepted ideal of his group without even realizing that he is constrained in his belief. For instance, an individual may support an ideal such as racial equality without ever questioning the depth of his belief until one day he is called upon to put it into public practice. Sometimes lip service is a smoke screen consciously created, as with the person who proclaims his support of sexual taboos which he clandestinely violates. Such a person has made the passage from cowardly lip service to flagrant hypocrisy. It is not a difficult passage.

As is the case with much faulty reasoning, lip service often goes unnoticed because it is so hidden in verbiage that the announced ideal and the inconsistent behavior are not exposed to sharp contrast. Or time may obscure the fact that an individual's deeds do not match his words. At any rate, the majority of mankind on occasion, intentionally or otherwise, say one thing and do another.

The extent to which even very good people fall short of their professed standards of behavior is brought out forcibly in a well known passage from J. S. Mill's *On Liberty*:

> All Christians believe that the blessed are the poor and humble, and those who are ill-used by the world; that it is easier for a camel to pass through the eye of a needle than for a rich man to enter the kingdom of heaven; that they should judge not, lest they be judged; that they should swear not at all; that they should love their neighbour as themselves; that if one take their cloak, they should give him their coat also; that they should take no thought for the morrow; that if they would be perfect they should sell all that they have and give it to the poor. They are not insincere when they say that they believe these things. They do believe them, as people believe what they have always heard lauded and never discussed. But in the sense of that living belief which regulates conduct, they believe these doctrines just up to the point to which it is usual to act upon them.

EXAMPLE. Peter is giving a speech to the Independent Farmer's Association. "Our country has grown great under the system of free private enterprise. We are proud of the industry and initiative of the millions of individuals who have worked out their own destinies under our flag. Free enterprise has built up our nation and will continue to build it up." After this introduction, Peter devotes the main part of his speech to advocating government subsidies for wheat based on a system of price and acreage controls.

COMMENT. Peter draws attention to his belief in free private enterprise. Then, cuckoo like, he lays a plan which hatches into a very different kind of bird. Subsidies and government controls, whatever their form or merit, are not applications of free private enterprise.

EXAMPLE. Address to a Veterans' Organization: "Democracy must be alert against government by special interest and pressure groups. The legislator should listen to the farmer, the businessman, the veteran—but he must *decide* for the good of all." The speaker goes on to explain how he is supporting a bill that greatly extends benefits for veterans. "Your Congressman won't be against this bill if he gets a lot of letters from you!"

COMMENT. Though it is fashionable to deprecate "special interests and pressure groups," few speakers can resist the temptation to appeal to such groups whenever opportunity offers and the question concerns their own interests.

BIASED MISCONSTRUCTIONS

The previous section dealt with fallacies that are primarily self-deceptions, and this section will add another group of the same sort. If a man rationalizes to his own advantage, he may incidentally beguile others into seeing things his way, but the principle operating to produce errors in his arguments is that he has already deceived himself. In the present group also there is a psychological precondition or bias on the part of the speaker, by which he genuinely deceives himself. If he deceives others, he does so incidentally.

The man who refuses to examine evidence against his friend because he "knows" his friend is honest, who praises the "industry" of the ants, who complains at the absence of ambition amongst a tribe of Indians, who gambles foolishly on mistaken notions of odds—this is the man who forgets that circumstances alter cases. He gets hold of some quite intelligible concept and brashly misapplies it to situations it was never designed to cover. These misconstructions are interesting chiefly as illustrations of the protean ways bias can disguise itself.

28 · *Apriorism:* "invincible ignorance"

Closing one's eyes to evidence alleged against something one believes in, such as the honesty of a friend, is frequently described as an attempt to deduce facts from principles, instead of inducing principles from facts. Reasoning *a priori,* "in advance" of the facts, is regarded as a fallacy. When Galileo invited learned men of his time to view the moons of Jupiter through his telescope, some refused on the grounds that, if they saw anything, it would be an illusion, no doubt diabolical, since the number of the heavenly bodies had already been fixed with finality by astronomy. This is the notorious text-book example. Let us first consider a rather ordinary case, also related to science.

My friend is ill. Urged to see a doctor, he waves aside the suggestion declaring, "Medicine is an art, not a science. It's a hodge-podge of theory and specific remedies." Now it is true that medicine as a whole is not a science in the sense in which physics as a whole is a science. Yet many medical facts are scientifically established with a reliability approaching that of physics. Diagnosis is frequently very confident and treatment successful. My friend seems to be deducing a distrust of medicine from a definition of "science." The definition of a term cannot affect the nature of the facts; all that one can deduce from a definition of "science" that excludes medicine is that medicine is not a "science" as defined. This has nothing obvious to do with whether or not one should see the doctor.

Yet isn't it likely that what my friend is doing is merely rationalizing a disinclination to seek medical advice? This disinclination may arise from entirely other grounds. But even supposing that he is standing vigorously on principle, what is so wrong with standing on principle? If I refuse to spend an evening watching TV on the principle that TV is a waste of time, I might on a given occasion miss out on a first-class program. Does not that lay me open to a charge of deducing facts from cast-iron principles? Yet a man must be allowed to act on some simplifying principles in his life. My friend avoids medicine as long as he can. I turn my back on TV. My wife refuses to study logic on the principle that it is dull. Her brother refuses to travel on the principle that tourists always get overcharged.

At the worst, some of these principles seem to be merely rather broad and illiberal. As such, arguments based on them can be dismissed as faulty generalizations, rationalizations, or irrelevancies.

The case of the learned men who refused to look at the moons of Jupiter seems more important. What is the nature of their difficulty? The science of astronomy, at that time Ptolemaic and Aristotelian, allowed no provision for the discovery of new planets, and moons are planets. Should the astronomers have overthrown their science at the behest of a crank with a gadget? The telescope had just been invented, and optics was not at all well understood. Nobody in Galileo's day could have provided a very clear explanation of how a telescope works. Cautious men were in effect being asked to invest enormous intellectual capital in what might very well seem a mere conjurer's apparatus. It is rather as if someone were to ask me to invest $1000 in a perpetual motion machine; I do not understand the novel theory of the device, and I don't propose to take the time to learn about it. The analogy is not accurate, for the situation with Galileo is even worse, but it will do. Can I be accused of apriorism when I "deduce" from the laws of classical physics that the machine cannot work? Why not? After all, I am being asked to question these very principles, and I refuse "in advance" to examine the facts.

Whenever in science or ordinary life people predict from principles that something will or will not occur, they are in a sense "deducing" facts in advance. It is hard to see where a line can be drawn between what is called apriorism and ordinary prediction.

There does remain, nonetheless, a cast of mind which seems peculiarly closed to evidence. When confronted with such a mind, one feels helpless, for no amount of evidence seems to be clinching. Frequently the facts are simply ignored or brushed aside as somehow deceptive, and the principles are reaffirmed in unshakable conviction. One seems confronted with what has been called "invincible ignorance." It is this approach to evidence that offends persons with a more empirical cast of mind. Empiricists are characteristically ready to throw out principles that don't fit neatly with the evidence. They regard principles as *a posteriori* expedients (derived "from after" the facts) rather than absolute charters of truth. Nevertheless, philosophers have spun out many different worlds from such absolute principles. These worlds are often beautiful and compelling, but as they differ among themselves, they cannot all be true, and few have the remotest similarity to the cosmology of modern science.

Our examples are intended to illustrate the cast of mind that clings with blind certainty to principles, even in the teeth of the facts. We do not suppose that there is a *use* of principle that is apriorist in itself.

EXAMPLE. Mrs. Peter is told that a ten-year program of introducing fluoridation into the water supply demonstrates that decay in the teeth of grammar school children fell off 60%, as compared to the school group immediately prior to the introduction of the fluoride. "Well," rejoins Mrs. Peter, "I'm still against the program because I am opposed to experimentation with human beings, children especially."

COMMENT. If ever it was sound to generalize that innovations in public health were as apt to be injurious as beneficial to health, this generalization itself would be subject to continual reassessment as man's endeavors to control environment become guided by improved techniques and increased knowledge. Mrs. Peter evidently chooses to reject out of hand such innovations as "experiments." Perhaps her mother objected to vaccination.

EXAMPLE. "Government regulation is a noose around the neck of initiative, and I'm against having any more of it than we have to. So when the state sets out to prescribe uniform accounting methods for business, I am not even interested in hearing the reasons."

COMMENT. The "noose" is the gathering together of a wide range of instances, branding them indiscriminately "GI" for "government interference," and threatening to shoot as a rustler anybody daring to attempt rescuing one calf or another from the corral. "I am not even interested in hearing the reasons." Here speaks the apriorist mind.

EXAMPLE. A union member addresses a meeting of his local. "Friends and brothers, the object of the company is to make money, and the way to make the most money is to pay low wages. The only way we are going to get any concessions is by fighting for them. The idea of negotiating on a new contract for three weeks more is just so much time wasted. Thank you."

COMMENT. Past experience in dealing with the company in question might give more or less support to the speaker's view. But no such evidence is cited; rather the opinion of the company seems to be derived from a general principle concerning employers, that their object is to make money and, hence, to depress wages. Such a speaker is almost impossible to reason with. Down comes the principle, and that settles it. The union member has managed to cast his thought into an unfortunate mold: the cast-iron mold of apriorist principle.

29 · *Personification*

Man projects himself into nature: animism is found everywhere in the world. Primitive peoples almost universally attribute human characteristics to natural phenomena. Storms are conceived of as angry gods, perhaps gods that can be propitiated. This leads to ceremonies which give the feeling of dealing with a recalcitrant nature. At the same time, since nature is made over in man's image, man is able to feel the security of kinship. Nature becomes humanized, she can be dealt with, understood. Events on Earth cease to be pitiless and inexorable; they respond to the will of gods, who also exhibit all the passions from anger to love. So one may make his way through life's dangers by staying on the right side of the gods, propitiating them when they seem displeased, playing one god against another, seeking their help against enemies (who need no personifying) or against illness which is usually conceived as possession by spirits or devils. By animism man escapes his aloneness in an indifferent world.

Allegedly civilized people differ from primitive men in projecting themselves into nature chiefly in the degree to which they believe in their personifications. Children people the dark with terrors, and they build castles in the clouds. Still, the child who sees a dreadful thing in the ink-blot is not much different from the adult who sees a menace in the forces of nature (the "pathetic fallacy") or endless conspiracy in the hearts of men ("paranoia"). There are less dramatic forms of projection. If we interpret the activities of ants, say, in terms of concepts derived from human society, we are misapplying the concepts in a fanciful way. The nature-lover who praises the "industry" of the ants, or complains of the "cruelty" of weasels, the "matriarchy" in a beehive or the "neglect of maternal obligations" of the cuckoo, is either playful or foolish. Strictly, "animism" refers to the primitive belief that rocks, trees, etc., have independent life and soul, but the term currently applies to a more general projection of soul into nature: like man, the world and its parts live, feel, strive.

Striving, motivation, purpose, desire are human traits. It is risky to attribute them to other creatures, however much they may at times seem to behave like people. And it is folly to read a purpose into inanimate configurations. If an observer sees a design in, say, the constellations of stars, this is no evidence that it was *designed* to be there.

EXAMPLE. A novelist writes, "Hans' wife thought of the thing she must tell Hans. Could Hans ever forgive her? The money was so hard earned, so hard saved. And now it was gone. Hans would roar through the old house like a bull. He would glower and stamp, as he did when his temper, that unpredictable temper of his, was fully aroused. He had never yet struck her, but now she trembled and covered her face with her hands as an image, a sort of day-nightmare, passed before her eyes: Hans, his great hand raised about to strike. With an effort she attempted possession of herself. She began to draw the drapes in the big room, against the gathering night. A strong wind had sprung up, the trees lashed against the palings. Black clouds gathered, like the curtain of a tragedy, across the evening gloom."

COMMENT. After Hans had forgiven his wife for her extravagance, or whatever it was, the reader should not be surprised to learn that little fleecy clouds whisp across the clean, fresh-washed blue of the morning sky, and little happy lights glisten on the clear puddles in the garden. Only a sentimentalist will suppose that the evening's storm and the morning's clearing "reflect" in real life the passions and joys of people in their houses. Though novelists must be allowed to get their effects where they can find them, even in literature the suggestion invoked by the novelist is a tiresome cliché, and critics complain of its abuse under the label "the pathetic fallacy." But it would never have become a cliché in literature unless it had its roots somewhere in the feelings of men.

No critic would ever complain of the storm in *King Lear,* and far from complaining of the moors in *Return of the Native,* critics have said of them that they are the protagonist, for the moors dominate the lives of the characters. The same storm that might seem to reflect her troubled spirit to Hans' wife, might seem a fitting accompaniment to someone starting out on high adventure, full of excitement and imagined triumph.

In our society, animism is not so much a question of belief as one of mood. The effects of nature are not, for us, whipped up by the Moon Goddess or the Furies. But they are still effects.

30 · *Cultural Bias*

It is hard to avoid judging others by ourselves. It is especially hard to be tolerant of the customs or beliefs of other groups, classes, cultures, when they run counter to our own. All of us are molded by our social life until we become its creatures; we mistakenly take custom for human nature. "Cultural fallacy" is the name anthropologists give to the misapplying of the values of one culture to another. Ruth Benedict showed in her *Patterns of Culture* that so fundamental to western culture is a sort of social ambition or aggressiveness that it is hard even to find means of explaining these traits to the Pueblo Indians, whose culture discourages such motivation. Cultural bias is allied to many sorts of social prejudice, and its name can conveniently cover them all.

Personification is taking man as the measure of all things. The cultural fallacy is taking one's group as the measure of all men. Both involve a pouring of new wine into old measures. The measure is often a moral or aesthetic judgment. In the case of the cultural fallacy, sometimes people find the foreign to be "alien" in the pejorative sense; that is, they regard it as bad or ugly or both. At other times, they more charitably find it "exotic" or "quaint," that is, novel and interesting in its appearance but not fundamentally different: "We do it this way. They do it that way. That's all." Both reactions reflect a particular "pattern of culture." Both judge. The one frankly accuses. Though the other attempts to excuse, it excuses on the ground that what is different is only superficially so: one's own pattern is somehow still basic.

Now some cultural patterns may indeed be basic, as where two differing rituals serve the identical cultural function. Whether a swain courts his choice with a box of chocolates or with a handful of raw fish is probably an economic accident. Moreover, some cultural traits to be found in the world, indeed, in our own culture, *are* bad or ugly. When Bertrand Russell remarks that we cannot *know* it is bad to enjoy the infliction of cruelty, since science cannot prove it bad, he seems to lean over into cultural relativism—the opposite of the cultural fallacy. If science can show that the enjoyment of cruelty is psychotic in an individual or a culture, then that would seem reason enough to call it bad wherever it occurs. Psychosis is self-defeating and cannot consistently be encouraged or permitted, if survival is a goal.

There is no occasion to despair of a knowledge of morality, or to relegate morality to an area of mere feeling, in order to account for the fact that cultural patterns exhibit differing moral codes as well as mere differences in custom or etiquette. It is, in fact, a truly scientific knowledge of morality that teaches us that what might be good in relation to our culture may be good or bad or indifferent relative to other cultures. Yet some things, indeed, must earn the same moral judgment wherever they occur, though these are apt to be fewer than most people think. It will require a profound study to understand this complex planet—well beyond the capacity of any one man. Yet it is not beyond the power of every responsible person to refrain from judging the practices of other ethnic, religious, occupational, or class groups, by the principles of one's own little place in the world. The chances are that, far from being the basic principles of human conduct, these reflect only the most parochial or transitory prejudices.

EXAMPLE. An American soldier, returning from Korea, praised the endurance and courage of the Koreans. Then he complained that the whole country "stank" from the "incredible" methods of fertilizing the rice fields, and he added, "Even the food of these gooks stinks."

COMMENT. Courage and endurance are praiseworthy traits in most cultures, perhaps in all, and the soldier's praise of the Koreans, who prize them highly, is deserved. When the soldier speaks of the use of human excrement as an "incredible" method of fertilizing, he shows only his ignorance, since vast areas of the world employ this method. It is true that *Kimch'i* "stinks." So do many western herbs and cheeses—consider limberger. The word "gook" has become a name of contempt; it is an offense, not only to the Korean people, but to all men of decent feeling. Incidentally, the name arose innocently enough, for it is close to the way the Korean people refer to themselves: their word for "person," occurring in many names, is *"Kuk."*

EXAMPLE. Frenchman Pierre returns to Paris. "L'Amerique! Une telle experience! Why, they boo the umpire at their games and have a 'drum majorette' parade the stage when they are nominating the President! I'd rather lose half our empire than have people chew gum in my face."

EXAMPLE. Hero Peter returns to New York. "Yes, I got the Croix de Guerre complete with a manly kiss. You bet I blushed!"

COMMENT. When the cultural bias impedes understanding between cultures so closely related as those of contemporary France and the United States, no wonder that some practices in distant or primitive cultures seem, not merely strange, but contrary to good morals or even to human nature.

EXAMPLE. Northern travelers often return from the South complaining of the indolence, ignorance, racial attitudes, and general backwardness of certain areas. Typical comments include "They're still trying to live in the antebellum days." "Even their language reflects their backwardness; they drawl their words and drag their feet." "Jim Crow is simply insufferable."

COMMENT. These remarks are as intolerant as Jim Crow. Some of the areas of the South are, indeed, economically backward—through little fault of their own, as people don't willingly choose pellagra and substandard housing. Jim Crow is indeed intolerable, but the Supreme Court itself has recognized that the process of non-segregation involves vast complexities and difficulties and requires only that it be achieved in a reasonable time. As to the way of speaking, it reflects ordinary dialectical or regional differences. These same travelers, if they go to England, probably come home imitating the oh-so-funny "veddy, veddy" British pronunciations.

31 · *The Gambler's Mistake*

"If the chances of a coin coming tails are exactly one in two, and we have just had a run of nine straight heads, what are the chances of heads coming up the next throw?" "Let me have a pencil." "You don't need to calculate. The chances are one in two." "You mean that it is one in two to have ten straight heads?" "No, the chances of that are less than one in a thousand."

There is no contradiction here. The gambler who bets his fortune that the next throw will be tails has an even chance of losing it. The series of heads has no effect at all on the next throw. If *in advance* he had bet against ten consecutive throws, he probably would have collected his bet; it would be a sound investment to give odds of several hundred to one. This fallacy has been discussed ever since the invention of roulette and the consequent discovery of probability theory by Pascal. But perhaps the little dialogue above brings out all that is important to remark here.

There is a variation of the gambler's fallacy consisting of the failure to realize that a slight possibility is, nevertheless, still a possibility. This is a sort of failure of imagination. Of course, a man directs his main efforts to meeting those conditions which seem most probable, but, in important matters, he should not dismiss the improbable. The unlikely may be what actually happens.

EXAMPLE. When the presence of unidentified aircraft in the vicinity of the Hawaiian Islands was indicated by radar on the morning of December 7, 1941, the officer in charge disregarded the evidence on the grounds that hostile planes could not be anywhere near.

COMMENT. Great generals have won battles by outwitting less imaginative opponents whose preparations were limited to taking care of only what was likely to happen. Washington's crossing the Delaware to capture the Hessians is an instance, from American history, of taking advantage of this. History affords hundreds of similar examples. Poor generals lapse into this fallacy; great ones use it by consciously outimagining their opponents.

EXAMPLE. Peter excuses his marrying again after his fifth divorce by saying, "Statistics show that at least half of American marriages are happy. My luck is bound to change this time."

COMMENT. Even if the chances were nine out of ten, he would be *bound* to do nothing at all. He might still have bad "luck" in his choice of brides. As a matter of fact, if the statistics Peter quotes are correct, he still has about an even chance of needing another divorce. A likely explanation for Peter's persistent bad luck is a character flaw that bars him from achieving a happy home life—no matter what the general statistics reveal. Unlike the tossed coin which has no ties with the past, Peter's matrimonial problems surely have.

DIVERSIONS

To make a diversion is to lead discussion away from the issues by directing it elsewhere. There are many devices for doing this: resorting to humor, bringing up irrelevant material, interrupting thought with trivial protests or questions, appealing to pathetic circumstances. There is no complete defense against diversions. Their function is to make the audience forget the point or become unwilling to consider it. After a successful diversion the audience may find it tedious to get back to business. To be sure, audiences generally do have a sense of fair play which demands that individuals be given a hearing, and people may resent a diversion if they recognize it as such; so sometimes it is effective to expose a diversion and then appeal for orderly discussion. Diversions, like almost all other fallacies, occur also in writings and speeches where no party is responsible to answer and where the alertness of the audience or reader is the only guard.

As an introduction to the general problem of diversion, we will examine Hitler's use of this device in one of his great speeches, that delivered at the Industry Club in Dusseldorf on January 27, 1932. This was a year before the Nazi Revolution, and, though Hitler was facing a rather skeptical audience of industrial leaders of the Ruhr area, the speech is credited with winning substantial support for National Socialism from among these leaders. Hitler began with a feeling that the audience shared with him, dilating on the nationalistic and anticommunistic nature of his movement. Judging from the record of applause, this approach impressed the audience considerably. Then he proceeded to defend his antidemocratic objective as follows:

> If anyone today wishes to fling at me as a National Socialist the gravest possible accusation, he says: "You want to force a decision in Germany by violence, and we are bound to protest against this. You want one day to annihilate your political opponents in Germany. But we base our stand on the constitution, and we are bound to guarantee to all parties the right to exist." I have only one answer to this. Translated into practice it means: you have a military company and you have to lead that company against the enemy. But within the company there is complete liberty to form a coalition. [laughter] Fifty per cent of the com-

pany have formed a coalition on the basis of love of the Fatherland and of protection of the Fatherland. The other fifty per cent
have formed a coalition on the basis of pacifism; they reject war
on principle; they demand that freedom of conscience should be
inviolate; and they declare that to be the highest, the sole good
which we possess today. [laughter]

Let us look carefully at the diversionary technique used. Hitler
begins by bringing up what he himself terms "the gravest possible
accusation," namely, the Nazi resort to violence in order to establish
a dictatorship. He answers this serious charge with ridicule. There
is a topical joke in "liberty to form a coalition," a reference to
cabinets formed by coalitions of several parties, an unpopular
feature of government under the Weimar constitution. Thus, the
fanciful notion of a military company directed by a miscellaneous
assortment of politicians is advanced to present a ludicrous picture
to the German audience. But the problems of leading a small army
unit and administering a government are not analogous (see #4),
and, in any event, reference to coalition government is obscurantist
since dictatorship is not a necessary alternative.

Hitler proceeds to heighten the grotesqueness of the image of a
coalition commanding a small military unit by fancying its elements
incompatible—half patriots and half pacifists. This draws a second
laugh and opens the way for a further diversion (not quoted)
whereby Hitler proceeds with a violent attack on toleration of
pacifism, an unpopular minority idea and hence a convenient straw-
man. Thereafter the speech continues without ever taking up the
charge of overthrowing democracy. Indeed, if this crucial accusation had been treated in a thoughtful way, it might well have
raised doubts and made this particular audience ponder.

32 · *Humor and Ridicule:* "lost in the laugh"

Continuous humor sometimes is diversionary. Sarcasm, parody,
mimicry—all the various forms of ridicule—are impertinent in-
trusions in argument. Yet heaven help the man incapable of laughing where the occasion warrants. As audience members we will
wish to enjoy any good sallies—and then to scrutinize the argument.

EXAMPLE. "My opponent's position reminds me of a story . . ."
COMMENT. Let us hope the story is a good one. If so, we will

be entertained and *then* we may return to reason. If the story is irrelevant, then it is an impudent diversion, and if the story has a point which allegedly applies to the issue, then we will have to consider whether it does in fact apply.

EXAMPLE. In a college debate on public development of power, one speaker got a ludicrous effect by talking about the "dam sites."
COMMENT. It would be crude punditing to punish a punster. But continuous humor is sometimes an ally against thinking.

EXAMPLE. Clemenceau is said to have once remarked, "Fourteen points, fourteen points! Why the Lord Almighty had only ten!"
COMMENT. The quip deserves a laugh, but it is not an innocent intrusion on the discussion. It seeks, by belittling Wilson's program, to put the audience into an unreceptive mood.

EXAMPLE. In the course of a parliamentary debate the young Disraeli was once heckled with cries of "Jew! Jew!" He responded: "My people were kings and princes, when yours were galley slaves."
NO COMMENT.

EXAMPLE. When Darwin's *Origin of Species* set the world to debating the theory of evolution, Bishop Wilberforce and Thomas Huxley appeared together in a public discussion of the topic. The bishop made a skillful speech without seriously examining the scientific evidence. "Then, turning to his antagonist with a smiling insolence, he begged to know, was it through his grandfather or his grandmother that he claimed his descent from a monkey?"
COMMENT. Huxley is reported to have arisen slowly and deliberately. "I asserted, and I repeat, that a man has no reason to be ashamed of having an ape for his grandfather. If there were an ancestor whom I should feel shame in recalling, it would be a *man,* a man of restless and versatile intellect, who, not content with an equivocal (*sic*) success in his own sphere of activity, plunges into scientific questions with which he has no real acquaintance, only to obscure them by an aimless rhetoric, and distract the attention of his hearers from the real point at issue by eloquent digressions, and skilled appeals to religious prejudice."
[The description of Wilberforce's conduct is taken from "A Grandmother's Tales," *Macmillan's Magazine*, vol. 78, p. 433; Huxley's retort is quoted from Woodbridge Riley, *From Myth to Reason*,

p. 316. Very likely none of the several versions of this celebrated incident are wholly accurate.]

33 · *Demand for Special Consideration*

Is there a man with soul so dead that he has never succumbed to an irrelevant appeal to pathos, sentimentality, human sympathy? Drawing attention to pathetic circumstances is an age-old refuge of individuals in difficulty—it is the most obvious form of demanding special consideration. This demand particularly recommends itself to unscrupulous pleaders, since it works by taking advantage of the audience's feelings of decency and common humanity.

EXAMPLE. Paul is on trial for a murder committed in California. His lawyer, Peter, points out to the jury that Paul is a veteran with several decorations, that he has a wife and six children, and that he is the sole support of his aged mother.

COMMENT. "Murder is the unlawful killing of a human being, with malice aforethought." *Penal Code of California,* section 187.

EXAMPLE. A student approaches his teacher at the end of the term: "My grade in this course will probably decide whether or not I can get into dental school."

COMMENT. Fortunately for the peace of mind of teachers, academic records are a matter of numerous independent grades to which no single instructor ordinarily contributes a decisive share. In any event, grades measure a student's accomplishment, not his needs.

34 · *Clamorous Insistence on Irrelevancies:* "red herring"

One way of hiding the weakness of a position is to draw noisy and insistent attention to a side-issue. The side-issue may be the character of an opponent, who is damned vigorously while the argument gets lost in personalities (see #20). Or it may be some movement or group that serves as a whipping post. This, the red-herring technique, is the tactic of the familiar speaker who, instead of meeting the real question, turns his talk into an attack on international communism, or Wall Street, or whatever else will deflect the attention of the audience. Such speakers often lose all sense of proportion, they pettifog, they make much of little and little of much. They talk of anything except the issue, at great length, with much noise and sawing of the air. We all are addicted to this fallacy. It is, of necessity, the patron saint of those being overwhelmed in argument.

EXAMPLE. Accused of having misbid his hand, Mr. Peter points out that his partner is always picking on him. "How can I play good bridge when nothing I do pleases you?" he complains.

COMMENT. A relatively innocent side-issue. Moreover, there is a flavor of justice in the complaint; it *is* hard to think well while being constantly criticized. Notice, however, that Peter merely defends himself, not his bid.

EXAMPLE. In an article entitled *Does Retroactive Punishment Endanger Civil Liberty?* a jurist writes in a Nazi law review: "Shocking though the concept of retroactive punishment may be to the liberal concept of justice, it must be recognized on occasion that such punishment is both necessary and right: otherwise clearly immoral acts will go unpunished. For example, in 1902 a certain individual who completed a phone call with a lead slug was brought to trial but had to be acquitted since this act did not amount to theft or to any other offense for which a penalty was then prescribed. When such loopholes exist, retroactive punishment is needed to vindicate the law."

COMMENT. This is a phantom issue. Crime in any nation is a phenomenon with an annual volume of thousands or even hundreds of thousands of cases. From a criminological point of view it is not a problem when an occasional instance of anti-social conduct goes unpunished, though from a moral point of view it is repugnant. In any event, the great cause of escape from legal punishment is not the occasional loophole in law, but the difficulties of apprehension of criminals and proof of their guilt. Though occasional loopholes are bound to occur, appropriate legislation is readily available to close them for the future. To cure the evil of one or a few rogues going unscathed by granting the state the power of retroactive punishment, a power notoriously open to abuse, is to apply a violent remedy to a slight malaise.

35 · *Pointing to Another Wrong*

Though many give lip service to the adage "Two wrongs do not make a right," few are not tempted to mitigate blame for wrongs on one side by citing those on the other. Justice seems to demand that that one who complains of wrong-doing should himself have "clean hands." Powerful advantage can be taken of this feeling to turn away attention from charges that are difficult to answer, by showing that the accuser himself is guilty of misconduct. This device is an effective rejoinder in controversy since it both deflects attention from the original grievance and creates sympathy for the accused party. And in the practical affairs of life a sort of rule-of-the-game approach is often adopted so that the misdeeds of one side are set over against those of the other. Yet even when the countercharges are deserved, all that is demonstrated is that *neither* side is right when both are wrong. Recently, when certain teams in a big football conference were found guilty of paying their players, moderate penalties were assessed against these teams. Some sports writers and alumni opposed the penalties, alleging that other teams in the conference were equally guilty of the forbidden practices. If these allegations were substantiated, then the other schools should have received equal penalties; justice certainly demands equal treatment for all. But the apologists were by no means urging the imposition of further penalties, but rather the suspension of the penalties already imposed. As in this instance, the citation of other wrongs is at its best a generously motivated confusion of the issue. At worst, crimes can be condoned and criminals excused or even praised because others have committed crimes against them.

Sometimes man's propensity for revenge creates a sort of tradition which bedevils human relations by piling wrong upon wrong for decades or even centuries. Thus individuals have their vendettas while whole peoples nourish traditional hostilities on a diet of past grievances. The historical animosities between England and Ireland, France and Germany, Russia and Turkey, Japan and Korea, of colonial areas throughout the world and their former colonial governors—all these provide instances in which old grievances remain living forces dominating present relationships.

EXAMPLE. Pointing out that Breslau had been a German city for over five hundred years before 1945, a debater maintains that the action of driving the German inhabitants out of the city at the conclusion of World War II was a great injustice to the people concerned. His opponent replies, "I don't see that it was wrong. After all, when the Germans had the upper hand in Warsaw, we all know how they behaved."

COMMENT. The question raised is whether the German inhabitants of Breslau were treated justly. No amount of past injustice has any relation to this problem. In fact, the more moral indignation the speaker feels against Hitler's brutal creation of "living space" by the sword, the more sympathetic one might expect him to feel toward victims of similar treatment anywhere, even in Germany. The opposition argument amounts to this: "Injustice has been done in the past to Poles living in Warsaw; therefore, I favor a further act of injustice to Germans living in Breslau."

EXAMPLE. Paul: "Why are you late, friend Peter?"

Peter: "Huh? Since you failed to show up at all on Friday night, you live in a glass house, Paul. You really shouldn't throw stones."

COMMENT. The moral of the glass house adage is nonsense. There is also an *ad hominem* appeal here (see #20).

EXAMPLE. Paul: "Liberty USSR style is a travesty on individual freedom. Free speech does not exist, voting is a farcical ratification of official candidates, to strike is punishable as treason, the slightest opposition is dealt with by the secret police and the slave labor camp."

Peter: "I don't think it behooves us to criticize other nations in view of our racial discrimination and the way legislative investigations are carried on in this country."

COMMENT. Paul advances the proposition "Liberty USSR style is a travesty on individual freedom" and brings forth certain supporting facts. Peter ignores the supporting facts; instead he alleges other wrongs. Peter's argument, called by Arthur Koestler the "soul searching fallacy," should not be permitted to hamstring thought or action. Saints and sinners alike have a right to rational criticism, and the thief confined in his cell may justly complain when his watch has been stolen.

EXAMPLE. Francis Bacon, the great English philosopher, served as Lord Chancellor under James I. In 1621 he was convicted of accepting bribes in chancery suits. All his biographers have pointed to the wide-spread practice of the jurists of the day of accepting "presents" from contending parties.

COMMENT. A climate of opinion condoning practices that are recognized as immoral does tend to mitigate the culpability of an individual who is merely doing what everybody else does. The evidence offered by Bacon's biographers is relevant for assessing the grievousness of the crimes for which Bacon was convicted. Yet it is significant that Bacon himself did not rely on the prevalence of the practice when arguing in his own behalf. He said simply, "I do plainly and ingenuously confess that I am guilty of corruption, and do renounce all defense. I beseech your Lordships to be merciful to a broken reed."

36 · The Wicked Alternative

There is a legitimate form of argument which defends one thing by attacking its opposite. If a speaker can prove that heavy consumption of alcohol is harmful, he gains support for the thesis that temperance is beneficial, provided that he can show that temperance is the opposite of excess and if we allow that it is beneficial to avoid the harmful.

It is clearly irrelevant to support A by denouncing B, unless B is the opposite of A. Yet people often do this. They praise San Francisco by running down Los Angeles, just as if allowing a merit to one city would involve disloyalty to the other. They seek to win admiration for so-called serious or classical music by sneering at so-called folk or popular kinds of music. If they are in the other camp, they call classical music "long hair" or "high brow." It must not be supposed that all occurrences of this common fallacy are as lightweight as these instances.

EXAMPLE. A famous modern poet, in an essay on "poetic truth," sought to establish his claims for the importance to our culture of the poet's vision and insight. He soon ran out of instances to praise, so turned his rhetoric to an intemperate attack on "positivism," and "the substitute truths of science," which, he said, lead only to "goof pills," to the vivisection and "torture" of dumb animals, and to "the mushroom cloud of death."

COMMENT. What this poet should be doing is making clear what distinction he intends to draw between "scientific truth" and "poetic truth." Attacks on selected instances of scientific practice that elicit his disapproval are irrelevant unless it can be shown (a) that this practice is typical of the application of scientific truths, and (b) that this truth is so related logically to poetic truth that the disadvantages of the one are the advantages of the other.

EXAMPLE. Peter writes an article attacking the British system of socialized medicine. He concludes, "The difficulties experienced under the National Health Service in Britain should confirm the opinion that the organization of the medical profession in America is satisfactory."

COMMENT. Peter is right in assuming that British experience with socialized medicine can be applied by analogy to the United States (see #4). If the British system has not worked well, then a system similar to it would not be likely to succeed in this country. But a pointing out of shortcomings in the British system does not establish the affirmative merits of medical organization in America unless it can be shown that the American system is the opposite of the British plan.

37 · *Nothing but Objections*

In the complexity of affairs there are few designs or proposals so well considered that objections cannot be raised to them. A man must often choose the lesser of evils and try, if he will accomplish anything at all, to dedicate himself to a course of action in spite of grave misgivings.

Why choose the lesser evil? Why not, in such cases, reject all proposals? The answer is that sometimes there is no escape from choice; to fail to decide is to "decide by default." Suppose there is a bond issue before the electorate and today is polling day. You know that the conditions the bond issue is designed to remedy are, as you say, intolerable, but you also know that many objections are raised against the proposed remedy. Now in your community a bond issue must receive two-thirds of the votes to pass. It is clear that if you cannot make up your mind to vote for the issue, though you do not vote against it (leaving the spaces blank), you in effect help defeat it.

In the homely case it is clear that often a man who cannot make up his mind ends in making a "decision by default." People say, "Peter could not decide to accept the invitation until it was too late"; in effect he decided not to accept it. "When the inflation began, Peter could not make up his mind whether to invest in stock or in a piece of real estate; his money is still in the bank." The inability to decide between two becomes a decision against both. We have already remarked on the donkey that starved to death when placed at an equal distance between two bundles of hay (p. 49).

Sometimes an opponent to a measure will take account of this incapacity of some persons to decide for a plan of action when they have misgivings, and will exploit it by raising continuous objections until the defeat of the proposal is assured. There is here the fallacy of objections. One can find objections to almost any plan—the fallacy is failing to weigh in the balance the objections to the alternatives. It is apparent that this is a fallacy of the audience; it is they who must decide and who fail to weigh the counter-objections.

This fallacy was first analyzed at length by Richard Whately, well over a hundred years ago, who summarized, "There never was, or will be, any plan executed or proposed, against which strong and even unanswerable objections may not be urged; so that unless the opposite objections be set up in the balance on the other side, we can never advance a step."

EXAMPLE. In late 1953 the Administration proposed a "new look" for defense, based on the potentiality of "massive retaliation." Many persons objected that concentration on the building of a long-range airforce might leave the nation unable to resist "new Koreas."

COMMENT. Without going into the merits of this controversy, we can easily see that no matter what course the Administration might have taken, very serious objections could be raised to it. Yet to allow things to go on in the old way of "balanced forces" and enormous expenditures would itself constitute a decision of the gravest sort. There is no suggestion in this example that all those who opposed the concept of massive retaliation were exploiting people's propensity to commit the fallacy of objections. But the public discussion was marred by the fact that numbers of speakers and writers failed to weigh the admitted difficulties of this concept against those of the practical alternatives.

EXAMPLE. Swain Peter, courting Hortense, delayed and delayed the decision to propose marriage. He saw all sorts of difficulties—too little money, doubts about his compatibility with Hortense, fears of having his suit rejected—and found himself simply unable to propose. Hortense waited with patience for a long time. She's now married to Paul.

COMMENT. Peter is just as much a bachelor today as if he had decided definitely *not* to propose.

38 · *Impossible Conditions:* "the call for perfection"

This maneuver is related to the fallacy of objections (#37). In a discussion concerned with reducing theft in a locker room, all would recognize the suggestion, "If men were taught to be honest, we would need no locks" as a mere idle observation. In less obvious situations the contention that mankind should first be changed or perfected in one way or another may be successfully interposed to dull the blade of action.

EXAMPLE. Every time in recent years that an administration has proposed a legislative program for extending the benefits of social security, the proposal has met with a determined opposition. Among other objections advanced, one can usually encounter some form of the following:

"We must pause to re-examine the whole philosophy of this movement. Americans are constantly being urged to attack poverty and insecurity by extending government help or raising wages again or enlarging the scope of benefits. Man does not live by bread alone. If we suffer from domestic insecurity, it comes from the spiritual poverty of our people and our lack of faith in ourselves. The crying need for our age is not the patching up of our institutions, but a reform of the human heart."

COMMENT. Moral improvement of man is worthy of constant seeking. Yet if social action in this world had to wait upon "a reform of the human heart," the practical solution of problems would come to a dead stop until the millennium.

EXAMPLE. Student Peter reads the Supreme Court decision declaring unconstitutional racial segregation in public schools. "Well," says Peter to his roommate, "I am sure that most people are aware that this problem must be overcome in the United States. But I'd think the court would realize racial discrimination cannot be ended by operation of law. People will have to change their attitudes, and then the segregation problem will settle itself."

COMMENT. There are two things to notice about Peter's argument. First, it is a call for perfection as a prerequisite to action. Second, Peter indulges in an oversimplification, thereby creating a straw man which he proceeds to knock over as if this were impressive argument. Few people, certainly not the Supreme Court justices, think that a legal opinion or any other simple remedy will solve the problem of discrimination. So when Peter declares "racial discrimination cannot be stopped by operation of law," he is asserting what no one denies. That is, Peter's statement is obviously true, assuming he means "stopped *solely* by operation of law," which is what he must mean in order to put bones in his straw man. If Peter had said "racial discrimination cannot be stopped *at all* by operation of law," he would raise a real issue. His oversimplification avoids this issue. What he should be discussing, apart from the legal soundness of the decision, is whether or not law is a *partial* remedy for racial discrimination.

39 · *Abandonment of Discussion*

Refusal to carry on argument is so palpably *not* an argument that one might question the necessity of identifying this action as a fallacy. In its crudest form—where Peter stops talking and begins to pummel his opponent over the head—no one can fail to realize that reasoning is at an end. The fact, however, is not always evident when discussion is abandoned verbally. Refusal to argue a matter may take the form of claiming that discussion is unnecessary, irreverent, indecent, immoral, or unpatriotic, and the like, or it may be by resorting to abuse. Personal attacks against an opponent's physical appearance, dress or mannerisms will succeed only where the vulgarity of the audience permits. Abandonment of discussion by these means is often combined with fallacies of the red herring, of ridicule, or of origin.

EXAMPLE. Paul remarks, "It is a sort of false chivalry that tells us not to speak ill of the dead. After all, we need not fear harming the dead: it is toward the living that our tongue should be charitable." Peter, shocked by what he considers Paul's irreverence, replies sternly, "Paul, you lack respect even for death itself."

COMMENT. Paul is challenging a generally accepted custom of our culture. Peter's rebuke amounts to abandonment of discussion since he makes no attempt to examine the soundness of the cultural attitude or of Paul's observation. Peter's comment illustrates the devices of implying that an opponent's position is scandalously beneath notice.

EXAMPLE. Paul, a resident of A-town, is comparing the city planning and zoning development of A-town and B-ville. He concludes, "B-ville, without any particular natural advantages, has been made into a more pleasant place to live than we have achieved here." Peter jeers, "Why, Paul, I suggest you move right over to B-ville."

COMMENT. Maybe an effective silencing of the critic, but not of the criticism.

EXAMPLE. Dr. Johnson, after hearing Bishop Berkeley expound his view that there is no material substance, was asked by friends what he thought of Berkeley's idealism. The great man replied by kicking a stone.

COMMENT. Johnson's refutation of Berkeley, a form of refusing to discuss the "absurd," is jestingly referred to by philosophers as the invention of a new fallacy, the appeal *ad lapidem* (to the stone).

PART III

Logical Fallacies

T HE MISTAKES and tricks in argument, so common in the markets
and parliaments of every-day life, are of small interest to the
logician. The logician might allow that faulty generalization, wishful thinking, etc., are *sources* of error in discussion. On the analogy
of a manufacturing process (p. 4), he would perhaps admit that
if inadequate materials or human aberration lead people to maintain
false premises, they should hardly be surprised when their conclusions are unreliable. But the logician has as his only concern with
fallacy the avoidance of error in the *processes* of argument. He is
ceaselessly watchful for breakdowns in the functioning of processes
designed to produce valid conclusions. As to the premises from which
the conclusions are drawn, he merely assumes them true or false
for the purposes of his demonstrations. The logician, as logician,
does not care at all what fallacies might have entered into the
formulation of the factual premises he is borrowing. As an ordinary
man, he may be tremendously concerned, like the rest of us, for on
the truth of some moral or political premises may hang the happiness
and even the future of the race. But in logic, taken in isolation,
the problem of error is a formal problem, quite like mistakes in
mathematical proofs. Such mistakes are of great importance, nonetheless, and if they are not avoided, the most vigilant care in safe-
guarding the purity of the premises will be wasted, since the conclusion will be contaminated. The history of reason, since the invention long ago of logic, is in part the history of guaranteeing the
purity of the processes of argument.

Two of the most important notions in the history of reason are
logical truth and *validity*. The elements of these notions must be
understood before there can be any profitable discussion of the

processes of argument. Though they have been prominent in analysis since the days of Greece, recent decades have seen great progress in the understanding of them. The subject still bristles with difficulty for logicians and mathematicians. Yet the elements perhaps can be explained with sufficient clarity for the present purpose.

LOGICAL TRUTH

There are two kinds of true sentences in discourse. One kind is empirical, which is to say, derived from experience. This is what people most often mean when they say that something is true or is a fact. When someone says, for instance, "It is almost four o'clock," the kind of truth involved is empirical: the sentence states a fact or not, depending on the time. All scientific observations and historical statements have this kind of truth or falsity. "The hyena belongs to a species somewhere between dogs and cats." "It was in the Ford Theatre that Abraham Lincoln was assassinated." "The narrator in *Moby Dick* calls himself Ishmael." "I was driving sixty miles an hour in a twenty-mile zone." There are sometimes great difficulties in ascertaining the truth of empirical sentences or even in understanding what it means to say of such sentences that they are true. Some of these difficulties have been explored in the section on material fallacies. But it can be seen already that where one is content with the truth of such sentences, one can employ them as premises in argument. For the present, we are concerned with the second kind of true sentences, those that are *logically* true.

Of logically true sentences there are simple varieties that most people are already familiar with. Consider the following sentence, "If today is Tuesday, then today is not not Tuesday." This sentence is true on Wednesday or any other day as well as on Tuesday. "If today is not Tuesday, then it is not not not Tuesday." Thus if there is no negative in the *if*-clause, any number of true sentences can be made out of the whole conditional by adding even numbers of *nots* to the *then*-clause. And where there is a negative in the *if*-clause, one can know that the whole conditional is true if there is an odd number of *nots* in the *then*-clause, no matter how large a number. These sentences are true because of the way "if-then" and "not" are used in English. "If *a*, then not not *a*" is always true; in fact, logicians say it is "trivially" true. No matter what sentence, including a false sentence, one substitutes for *a*, the complex sentence in this case will be true. It is trivial because nobody learns anything about the world of fact from such a sentence.

"If he's an uncle, he's a male" is also trivially true, not only because of the syntax of "if-then," but because of the meanings of "uncle" and "male." "If it is red, it is colored" is likewise true because of the meaning of "red" and "colored." Such sentences explore the semantics of a language for connections and implications between the meanings of the various terms. They may give information about the language in the sense of making evident those relations not previously clear, but they give no other information. Arithmetic in a similar way makes clear the relations among numbers. David Hume, the first to understand well the distinction between empirical and logical truth, gives the example "three times five is equal to the half of thirty." The truth of this proposition, he says, can be ascertained without assuming any knowledge of the world of fact; it is known to be true by reasoning alone—to *deny* it implies a contradiction. Let us try to deny it, that is, assume that it is false:

Assuming, $3 \times 5 \neq \dfrac{30}{2}$

Then, $5 + 5 + 5 \neq 15$

Or, $15 \neq 15$

The above contradiction, saying that fifteen does not equal fifteen, is implicit in the meanings of the various numbers and in the use of the signs for division, addition, etc. To deny that three times five is the half of thirty involves denying that fifteen equals fifteen. This is a contradiction, since it is prerequisite for intelligible discourse that a term be taken in the same sense whenever it occurs in the same context—that it be identical with itself. Such mathematical propositions, Hume says, are true by *necessity*, since one cannot assert them false without contradiction, in fact, cannot even imagine them false.

There is a third variety of true sentences which logicians frequently speak of, "true by definition." There are all sorts of definitions, but it is not the truth *of* the definitions that logicians have in mind. A dictionary definition can be a correct report of usage, and hence regarded as true like any other report, but this would be empirical truth, which logicians are not concerned with. Moreover, most of the other kinds of definition are not reports of usage.

In mathematics, for instance, where often one symbol is simply substituted for another by a process of definition, it would be meaningless to ask whether or not the definition is true. In general argument, persons often introduce a special definition of a term which may or may not conform very closely to ordinary usage —that is not the point of the definition. In such cases the definition is intended as a decision to use the term in a particular way for the duration of the argument. This is done, among other reasons, to control the ambiguity of ordinary usage. Clearly it is also meaningless here to ask if the definition is true. How can a decision be true or false? It can be kept to or overlooked. (It is a grievous fallacy in argument to take advantage of this convention, to define a term in one way and then slip over into conventional meanings—see p. 158.)

What logicians mean when they speak of "true by definition" is the status of a sentence which is implied as a logical consequence of a definition. Suppose in the course of an argument I define "extravagant" as "spending more than you earn." Then I demonstrate that my friend has consistently for years done just that. It follows that my friend is extravagant *as defined*. The sentence, "My friend is extravagant," granting the other premise about his spending, is true by definition. Like the other kinds of logical truth, definitional truth is also innocent of any factual substance —the only information it gives is that if you define a term in a certain way, then, the conditions of the definition being met, you can use the term.

These, then, are the three most important kinds of logically true sentences, true by definition, true by the meanings of words, true by the use of syntactical elements. They give no information about the world, but only about the use of language in reasonable discourse. It is this lack of material content that is referred to when it is said that such truth is tautological or trivial.

Not all logical truths are as obvious as "Mars is inhabitable or not." Many sentences in books of logic are true by analysis, as logicians say, but some of them provide the greatest difficulty in that analysis. In less rigorous fields, students are sometimes warned against tautologies. A student theme replete with them may be inane—of course, this is what teachers rightly protest—but at least it contains some certainly true sentences, since all tautologies are true.

VALIDITY

The reason for the importance of the notion of validity is connected with what has been said about logical truth. If an argument is valid and if the premises are true, then the conclusion must also be true. This "new" truth is also essentially empty of any new information about the world—it merely reformulates what was already expressed in the premises. It is a mere consequence of truths already stated—and sometimes, as in arithmetic, the truth of the premises themselves is merely logical, consisting of definitions, tautologies, and the like. The conclusion, however, may embody important novelty, and the mathematician feels himself possessed of a new truth indeed. The student of geometry who masters the Pythagorean theorem is often struck with the fact that this very complicated and unexpected result is a consequence of a chain of reasoning reaching back to a handful of postulates and axioms. If there were men of godlike intellect, as the French philosopher Laplace pointed out, they would immediately see all the possible consequences of whatever consistent set of postulates one could offer them. But men are not gods and thus are capable of surprise.

Moreover, people often wish to test the consequences of their premises without being in a position to say whether or not they are true. The "postulates" may not be obviously inconsistent, but if they are inconsistent, this will become evident as their consequences are explored. It is indifferent to logic whether or not the premises are well founded in experience. One can *assume* them true and explore the results. Similarly, in ordinary things, one need not wait for certain proof of some propositions before finding out what other propositions *would* be true, granting them. For instance, some astronomers have asserted that lichens probably grow on the planet Mars. Now lichens are a fungus living symbiotically with an alga. With this fact as a premise, it is easy to construct an argument proving that the cooperative phenomenon of symbiosis occurs on Mars, if one assumes other premises, including "There are lichens on Mars" to be true. Sometimes propositions are actually known to be false, but it would be interesting to see what would be the case, if only they were true. No language has succeeded in becoming an international language, neither Esperanto, nor Io, nor Basic English, but it is certainly legitimate to speculate on the consequences of the adoption of one or another of them. The results of such speculations may actually suggest the design of a practical course of action.

The process we have been describing is possible only because some propositions can be shown to entail other propositions. If one understands the notion of entailment in the sense that conclusions can be entailed by premises merely on the assumption that the premises are true, then he is getting close to understanding what is meant by speaking of *valid* arguments.

It is the validity of the argument that guarantees the production of true conclusions when they are entailed by true premises. Thus when a conclusion is derived from premises, we cannot know that it is true because of this fact, unless we know that the premises are true. What we can know in many well understood forms of proof—such as the syllogistic form, which will be examined in some detail—is whether or not the argument is valid in itself. If the conclusion necessarily follows, then the argument is valid; if it does not, then this is invalid. "If this is an omen, then it is also a portent. But it is an omen. Therefore, it is also a portent." There may be no such things as omens or portents, but the argument is valid.

We will not attempt to define "validity" in the abstract. Let us rather adopt the following rule: *An argument is valid if and only if to assert the premises true and the conclusion false involves a contradiction.* The notion of validity, it is seen, depends upon the notion of truth. Yet there is a sharp distinction between validity and truth.

All the cases we have been discussing can be shown to be consistent with this rule. The most important case occurs when the premises are in fact true. Here a new truth emerges, for the conclusion is necessarily true, by the rule. Most every-day arguments try to be of this sort. Another case is that of dubious premises assumed to be true for the sake of testing the validity of the argument. "If all the people in New York have purple eyebrows, then they do not believe in Baal. But all the people in New York do believe in Baal. Therefore, they do not have purple eyebrows." The premises are presumably false; it is unlikely that all the people in New York believe in Baal, or that, if they do, this is related to their not having purple eyebrows. Yet the conclusion follows from these premises. Moreover, this conclusion seems in fact true, though foolish. The truth of the conclusion must be independent of these premises, since they are false. This, then, is a case of a valid argument leading to a true conclusion from false premises. How is it seen that the argument is valid? By the rule, because the rule states only that the conclusion *could not* be false if the premises *were* true, and we can see that this is so in the example. What we do to see it is assume the premises true for the sake of the argument (as people say), and then observe if the conclusion *must* follow. This may be hard to do in an absurd case like the above; for this reason it is customary to show the shape of the argument by the use of a notation. A simple notation will show that the argument about the purple eyebrows has the shape: "If *a*, then not *b*, but *b*; therefore, not *a*." All arguments in this shape are valid. Let the student experiment with this shape 1) using true premises, and 2) using false premises leading to conclusions in fact false.

It is a fallacy, in a way the most fundamental fallacy, to confuse validity with truth. Persons are often convinced of the truth of a proposition because they can see that it follows rigorously from certain premises, while failing to notice that the premises are by no means certainly true. The Nazis convinced themselves that the Germans should rule the world by asserting (a) the master race should rule the world, and (b) the Germans were the master race.

It also happens that an argument seems sound to some people because the conclusion is acceptable and they are told that it derives from premises which they see to be true. I may reason (a) if I can afford to build my own home, I shall not have to go on paying rent, (b) but I can't afford to build my own home, (c) so I shall have to go on paying rent. The conclusion may be a true proposition and so may each of the premises, but the argument is still invalid, since the conclusion *could* be false, though the premises are true (see pp. 142 ff.). When this happens, the argument does, in a way, contain a statement that is false. This is the statement, implicit in the order of the propositions, or partially avowed in some such expression as "therefore" or "hence" or (as in the example) "so"—the statement that the conclusion follows. In valid arguments this implicit statement about the argument is true, in invalid arguments, false. Sometimes one finds this statement made explicitly: "it follows that," "Q.E.D.," "you have to admit that," and the like.

Let us turn now to a simple traditional example which applies what we are learning about the difference between valid and invalid argument. (The reason for using the letters "*M*," "*S*," and "*P*" will become apparent.)

	All *M* is *P*			All *P* is *M*
	All *S* is *M*			All *S* is *M*
so	All *S* is *P*		so	All *S* is *P*

The scheme on the left can be seen intuitively to be valid. That on the right seems to be a mistaken version of it. No matter what values we substitute for the letters, just as the formula on the left will result in a valid argument, mistaken formulas such as that on the right will result in an invalid argument. Valid: "All good students like to argue; all our freshmen are good students; so all our freshmen like to argue." Invalid: "All good students like to argue; all freshmen like to argue; so all freshmen are good students." Or another invalid case: "All loyal Americans are anti-communist; the American Only League are anti-communist; so the American Only League are loyal Americans." Suppose the premises perfectly true, the conclusion does not follow—the League might be fascist or in some other way both anti-communist and still not loyally American. Even if true also, the conclusion still does not follow.

The relationship between the propositions of a syllogism can be diagrammed by the use of circles to represent the classes involved. In the case of valid arguments there is no way to draw the circles to avoid showing the conclusion true. Take the simple form already given:

All *M* is *P*
All *S* is *M*
so   All *S* is *P*

The argument is revealed to be invalid if there is any place permitted by the statements made about the classes in the premises so that one can escape the position required by the conclusion. Let *P* represent the class of loyal Americans, *M* the class of anti-communists, and S the America Only League. Then the invalid example just cited outlines and diagrams as follows:

All *P* is *M*
All *S* is *M*

so   All *S* is *P*

The process is to take the premises as giving directions for the construction of circles. In a valid argument they *compel* the circles to show that the conclusion is inescapable. Circle diagrams are a sort of game in which one seeks to embarrass the contention that the conclusion follows. If one wins, then the argument is invalid. Let the reader invent arguments constructed according to the above valid and invalid examples. He will gain some insight into the notion that validity is a matter of structure, of form, not simply of the truth or falsity of the premises.

There are large numbers of valid forms of argument. In the discussion that follows we confine ourselves to the traditional forms. We choose to do this, as most of the formal fallacies have been discussed in the literature of the syllogism (a form of the syllogism is given at the left on p. 141). Moreover, as the use of the circles shows, the validity of the syllogism can be seen intuitively and thus does not require the elaboration of difficult formal systems.

Now there are theoretically as many formal fallacies as there are ways to argue invalidly, that is, to make mistakes in arguing from premises to conclusions. But our concern here is with commonly occurring and well recognized errors. Some of the logical fallacies were known to the ancients; philosophers in the Middle Ages were often adroit at detecting them. They persist, nevertheless, to our day, and every educated person should know the name and face of them.

40 · *The Undistributed Middle Term*

The scheme given at the left on page 141 is typical of the syllogism. For variety let us take a slightly different format of a valid syllogism, illustrate, schematize, and diagram it in circles:

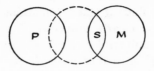

| No M is P | No raw fish is edible |
| Some S is M | Some Japanese dishes are raw fish |

so   Some S is not P So some Japanese dishes are not edible

It will be seen that in this traditional form of argument the con-clusion is entailed by two premises taken together. When the classes of raw fish, edible things, and Japanese dishes are related as the premises require, the conclusion is inescapable. Any argu-ment so constructed is valid. The circles show this clearly. The conclusion "Some Japanese dishes are not edible" is true *if* the premises given are true.

Note that both premises relate to the same subject matter. This means only that there is a concept common to both, M in the formula (*raw fish* in the example), which, once it has related the other two classes of the premises, disappears—it does not occur in the conclusion. This is called the "middle term" (hence "M"). The most important rule of the syllogism is that the middle term must be distributed—important because frequently violated. In the invalid examples about the freshmen and the American Only League, the middle term was not distributed; in letters, every rele-vant case of P and of S is accounted for, but not every case of M. We must make clear what it means to say that a term is distributed.

In the formulas on page 141 both premises and the conclusion are "All" propositions. These are called universal propositions, since they refer to the whole universe under discussion: "*All* men must die. *All* dictators are men. Therefore, *all* dictators (thank God!) must die." Since such propositions give information about every case, the terms ("men," "dictators") are said to be distributed. As in this example, the formula shows another characteristic. The propositions are affirmative; they make positive statements, or, better, they do not contain the words "no," "not," or their equiva-lents.

It is permissible to use negative premises, provided that only one occurs in any given syllogism. "No good Christian is selfish" dis-

tributes both terms, since it states something that every last good
Christian is not. It is clearly universal. There is another class of
proposition, the non-universal or particular proposition. "Some men
are not self-seeking" is evidently *both* particular *and* negative.
Particular premises do not distribute their first terms; simply from
the truth of "Some men are not self-seeking" we cannot know
whether or not "Some men are self-seeking" is also true: we *can*
know that "Some good Christians are selfish" is false merely from
the truth of "No good Christian is selfish." Like the case of the
negative premise, only one particular premise can occur in a given
syllogism. It follows that if this particular premise is also negative,
then the remaining premise must be both universal and affirmative.
"All aggressive types (*P*) are self-seeking (*M*); some men (*S*)
are not self-seeking (*M*); therefore, some men (*S*) are not aggressive types (*P*)."

Let us look at this last example.

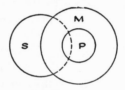

We see (1) there are two premises and a conclusion. This arrangement of sentences combines three terms in the following way:
(a) the subject ("*S*") of the conclusion "men" occurs in the minor
premise, and its predicate ("*P*") "aggressive types" in the major
premise. (This is all that is meant by calling these two propositions "major" and "minor" premises, that is, in order, the premises
containing the predicate and the subject of the conclusion. Which
premise comes first is immaterial.) (b) the middle term ("*M*")
"self-seeking" is distributed once: we know that no matter who the
self-seeking are they are not *some* men; (c) there is no term distributed in the conclusion which is not distributed in the premises:
"Aggressive types" is the only term distributed in the conclusion
(by the negative, as above). Since the subject of the conclusion
"men" is not distributed in the premises—it is particular—it may
not be, and is not, distributed in the conclusion; the conclusion
must be particular since the minor premise is particular. (2) We
also see that at least one of the premises is affirmative, and (3)
that since there is one negative premise, the conclusion is negative.

These observations can be briefed as rules. All valid syllogisms observe them. If a syllogism is invalid, it has violated one or more of them. They constitute the necessary and sufficient conditions for a valid syllogism.

1. The two premises and the conclusion must each contain only two terms, and the syllogism altogether three and only three terms. These three terms are so combined that no term will be distributed in the conclusion which is not distributed in the premises and that the middle term will be distributed at least once.
2. At least one of the premises must be affirmative and one universal.
3. If one of the premises is negative, the conclusion must be negative, if particular, then particular.

A syllogistic argument which violates any of these rules is invalid. We shall now try to see intuitively, with the help of examples, *why* this is so.

EXAMPLE. Peter argues. "All weapons ought to be abolished. All propaganda ought to be abolished, too. You can see that propaganda is a weapon."
COMMENT. Paul takes a sheet of paper and works out the argument, as follows:
S = propaganda, P = weapons, M = things that ought to be abolished. Thus,

All P is M

All S is M

so   All S is P

Paul says, "Your argument, Peter, is simply another example of the undistributed middle as found and diagramed on p. 142."

EXAMPLE. Peter tries again, "Well, I mean that propaganda is always a weapon and that some weapons are not safe in anybody's hands. So propaganda is not safe, either."
COMMENT. Paul applies the formulas again. In this argument, they are: S (subject of the conclusion) = propaganda; and P (predicate of the conclusion) = things safe in anybody's hands; M (middle term) = weapon(s).

All *S* is *M*
Some *M* is not *P*

so   Some *S* is not *P*

Paul shakes his head, "Just another undistributed middle."

EXAMPLE. "No proof exists that smoking causes tuberculosis. Some smokers do not get tuberculosis. So some smokers get tuberculosis from other causes."

COMMENT. This example is more complicated than the usual artificial examples employed in explanation. Peter's first premise seems to contain three terms, and so does the conclusion. But the classes might be stated in such a way that one of the terms would get absorbed. Even if this can be done, the argument is invalid because both premises are negative. Can the student see how other rules are violated?

EXAMPLE. "Some people get on my nerves; so some people better watch out!"

COMMENT. This is a truncated argument, called an enthymeme (see p. 3). It will depend on what proposition is supplied whether or not a valid argument results: "Some people get on my nerves; all those who get on my nerves had better watch out; so some people had better watch out!" Perfectly valid, if a little vapid. Note here that the major and minor premises are reversed. How is this demonstrated? (See p. 144.) Can the student invent any plausible major premise which would make the argument invalid?

EXAMPLE. That man Jones was a member of Stone Throwers, Inc., and *that* organization is a branch of the Hit-and-Runners. It's plain as the nose on my face that old Jones is a Hit-and-Runner.

COMMENT. Too bad, but valid. The ambiguity of the term "branch" and of the "er" formations (in Hit-and-Runner), like some "-ite" and "-ist" formations, are not problems related to formal logic (see #10).

EXAMPLE. Peter says, "I've heard that Jones voted for Schmidt. He must be a Democrat."

COMMENT. Another typical enthymeme. To make this enthymeme into a valid argument one would have to supply an unlikely major premise: "All those who voted for Schmidt were Democrats."

EXAMPLE. Scientist Smith belongs to the A.S.C., a scientific organization. Communists belong to the A.S.C. Therefore, Smith is a communist.

COMMENT. This is guilt by association. The argument seldom occurs so baldly. One begins by proving what perhaps is never denied, that Scientist Smith is a member of the A.S.C. Then one proves that Jones, Robinson and some other members of the A.S.C. are "communists." Finally, in a triumphant enthymeme, the speaker makes a gesture with his hands and leaves the audience to draw the conclusion. As the audience goes out, members can be heard to say to one another: "Think of an important scientist like Smith being a communist!" This conclusion is warranted only if association with communists makes Smith a communist himself.

41 · *Suppressed Quantification*

Let us look at this last example a little more closely. Notice that the major premise is "unquantified," that is, it is not stated whether every A.S.C. member is a communist or whether only some members are communists. The audience turned the proposition around, converted it, for the reason that it would be patently idiotic to say that all communists belong to this scientific organization—some of them are housewives or journalists. It would be true that *some* communists are A.S.C. members if all or some of the members are communists. Yet the speaker does not say "some." To do so might suggest a weakness of assertion. If the speaker does not quantify, the audience might be led to supply "only," *thus:* "Only communists belong to the A.S.C.," which is equivalent to "All members of the A.S.C. are communists." Now if the speaker wants the audience to supply "only," why does he not say it himself? Presumably because the statement would be false, and somebody might easily expose it as false. Though the speaker refrains from saying "only," the audience can still uncritically supply it, and the point is won for propaganda—and lost to reason.

It is a fallacy to exploit this ambiguity of the English language or to be taken in by it. "Women are able to endure more than men." All women, or some of them? "Children are cruel." Inevitably? Occasionally? Characteristically? "We live lives of quiet des-

peration." Most of us some of the time? All of us most of the time?
Some of us some . . . ? "We" Americans? "We" moderns? "We"
humans? "We" sensitive, civilized people?

The handbooks treat this fallacy often as one of improper generalizing, and in conversation sophisticated persons often warn
against making broad observations about women and life. All of
this is well intended, but it seems to miss the point. It assumes that
occurrences of this fallacy are taken to mean *all*, where their in-
sidiousness lies in their ambiguity in respect to *all* and *some*.

The audience can escape from the snare of a speaker who wants
them uncritically to supply "all" or "only" by actually supplying
these terms in a very critical, conscious way. And speakers can
avoid becoming the first victims of their own rhetoric or victimizing
others, by asking themselves precisely what they want to say by
such a sentence as "Communists are members of the A.S.C." If
they do mean only Communists are members, they can say this
and get a valid argument. If they mean that seven members of the
board of directors are members also of the Communist Party, they
can say so. And if they feel that is a very high percentage, they
can say that, too. Similarly, in the case of "Children are cruel,"
one can ask himself whether he means perhaps that children characteristically tend to be cruel in certain situations. If this is what
he means, he can specify the situations. Such discussion may not
be compressed and neatly aphoristic, but what one says may increase the store of knowledge instead of nonsense.

EXAMPLE. Comic books are the literature of the young. And
what a literature! They show cruelty disguised as virtue, virtue
exposed as foolishness, stupidity and vulgarity enthroned as the
normal and sane. They have dug themselves so solidly into the
culture of our children that, to succeed, radio and television programs must mimic them in crudity and nervous excitement. Sunday schools have to tell the living story of the Bible in colored
pictures wretchedly printed on pulp paper, and in installments . . .

COMMENT. Let the student translate this bit of rhetoric into
perhaps less epigrammatic but more rational prose.

42 · *False Conversion of Propositions*

The example about the Communists and the A.S.C., if we may labor it, also illustrates another important fallacy. We remarked above (p. 147) that "Only Communists are members of the A.S.C." can be translated into "All members of the A.S.C. are Communists," presumably a false sentence. If it were true, the speaker would certainly have said it, and with emphasis, rather than using the trick of leaving it to his audience to supply the "only." But the point we wish now to make is that frequently unsound syllogisms succeed in escaping detection because the audience is prone to "convert," that is turn around, one of the premises in a way to make tenable its relation to the other premise and, hence, to the conclusion. It is sometimes difficult, in following or advancing an argument, to bear in mind just how true propositions can be validly converted and still make the same assertion. Perhaps some of the time speakers take advantage of the ambiguous English usage discussed in the last section ("Children are cruel") in order to avoid thinking out just how they are entitled to convert some proposition they know to be true, without intending to commit the fallacy of suppressed quantification. In this way they will at least avoid the fallacy of false conversion.

This is the fallacy of getting the turning-about process wrong, so that, though one starts with a true proposition, he ends up with one that does not follow. In a simple case, it is easy to see the kind of mistake one should avoid. Only a very small child, learning that dogs are furry animals, will regard all furry animals as dogs, and say, "Doggie!" when he sees a cat or a pony. "All dogs are furry animals" converts into "*Some* furry animals are dogs." All S is P converts to Some P is S, or Only P is S.

Particular affirmative propositions also have their valid and invalid conversions. These, however, convert directly, as one can see intuitively. Some S is P converts to Some P is S. (See next page.)

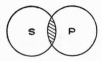

This is as good as we can get with the universal propositions in respect to "some." But notice, one cannot here say "only." "Some great sinners became great saints." With an adjustment of the tenses of the verbs, this converts to "Some of those who became saints had been great sinners," but not (alas!) to "Only those who became saints had been great sinners."

The negative universal propositions also convert directly. No S is P converts to No P is S.

But one is not apt to fail to notice this. "No lips that have touched wine shall ever touch mine," seems perfectly clear no matter whose lips we start with: "No lips of mine . . ."

The remaining case, the particular negative, is ticklish. "Some students are not interested in politics" does not assert that some people other than students *are* interested (though, of course, this is true). It does not even assert that anybody else is also not interested in politics, that is, that the class of those not interested in politics has members other than students. Nor does it assert that some students *are* interested; it is the temptation to make this last supposition that is dangerous here.

The temptation is to fill in the dotted lines. Here the temptation will occur in the simple case (for everybody knows from other sources that some students are in fact interested). In the case of more difficult formulations, one will perhaps be more careful. "Some stars cannot forever maintain their stability. They explode into novae." One would hesitate to convert here and say that some stars *can* remain stable, for it is easy to see that this statement involves a long-range prediction in a very technical matter, indeed.

This kind of proposition also converts directly, but (as the diagram shows), one must be careful of the *not*, keeping it always with the same term. "Some S is not P converts to "Some Not-P is

S." Thus there is a second source of error here. "Some disloyal Americans are not communists." False conversion: "Some communists are not disloyal Americans." This remains to be discovered, if true, from other evidence. It does not follow from the obvious truth of the first proposition. All that follows is that some people other than communists are disloyal Americans.

The fallacy of false conversion consists in making an illicit conversion of any of these four kinds of propositions. Let us gather in one place the permissible conversions:

1. All *S* is *P*   converts to Some *P* is *S* or only *P* is *S*
2. Some *S* is *P*   converts to Some *P* is *S*
3. No *S* is *P*   converts to No *P* is *S*
4. Some *S* is not *P* converts to Some not-*P* is *S*

Even where the resulting proposition is known to be true, the conversion is not allowed. If one does know this, he knows it from some other information, and it is this information which he should codify, so to speak, into his propositions. Otherwise what he says, though true, leads to invalid argument.

It can now be seen how some kind of implicit false conversion lies behind many instances of invalid syllogisms. In a school-boy example of the undistributed middle (see #40) and many similar cases, this is very conspicuous: "All asses have ears. You have ears. Therefore, you are an ass." One would not propose this minor premise to a (humorless) superbrain, for the only plausibility comes from the fact that a false conversion of the major premise is assumed: "Only asses have ears" or "All those with ears are asses" (instead of "Some of those with ears are asses"). And in the instance of the Communists belonging to the A.S.C., the speaker leaves it to his audience to make the false conversion and thus justify the inference.

EXAMPLE. A religious pamphlet claims "As all religious men rely on a power beyond human understanding, so no one who relies on such a power can be wholly devoid of religious feeling."

COMMENT. As in most occurrences of logical fallacies, this example disguises itself by a shift in expression. If the writer had said, ". . . so no man who relies on such a power can be a non-religious man," he would have provided a case of false conversion of a universal affirmative proposition, though still not a simple case of it. "No *P* is not-*S*" is a consequence of "All *P* is *S*," right

enough, but not of "All *S* is *P*" ("All religious men rely . . ."). The
actual false conversion is thus a step left out. Persons who indulge
in compulsive superstitious practices are probably not "religious
men" in the sense intended, though they surely can be said to rely
on a power beyond, well beyond, human understanding!

EXAMPLE. Employee Peter exclaims, "Some bosses just can't
take advice. I tried to tell Mr. Henry that the new man isn't worth
beans, and now the fellow's lost three old customers in a week. I
guess most men who are humble enough to listen to advice just
don't become bosses."

COMMENT. Assuming that "are humble enough to listen to
advice," means "can take advice," then Peter has falsely converted,
unless the last sentence is offered independently of the first. This
is quite possible in querulous material, which is notoriously innocent of relevance and coherency.

43 · *Non Sequitur*

False conversion is one kind of *non sequitur*. Any sentence offered
as a consequence of any other is a *non sequitur* unless it *is* a consequence. All invalid arguments, therefore, involve a *non sequitur*
since they at least implicitly assert that the conclusion follows
when in fact it does not. As false conversion, the undistributed
middle, and the like, can be readily explained on their own grounds,
the term *"non sequitur"* is usually reserved for the widely irrelevant
rather than the ordinary invalid conclusions.

In the course of an extended discussion, conclusions are often
immediately put to use as premises for further developments.
Sometimes these premises are converted, reformulated, corrected,
extended. Often it is difficult to judge whether a given sentence
is intended as a valid reworking of one of these temporary conclusions or as a new premise which the speaker introduces in the
hope that it will be unexceptionable. The ambiguity of usage for
such connectives as "so," "therefore," "thus," "hence," contributes
to the difficulty, since these terms, taken literally, promise that the
sentence to follow will be strictly entailed. But in practice they
often serve as mere rhetorical flourishes, smoothing the way and
expressing a feeling that what comes after is somehow relevant

even if the speaker would not wish to maintain that it is a valid consequence of what has preceded.

It is a hair-splitting pedantry to accuse a speaker of *non sequitur* when a reasonable recasting of the forms of his language would more clearly express his probable intention and show his argument to be valid. Just as there is no point in supplying for every suppressed premise in an enthymeme some far-fetched proposition that will make the argument invalid, so there is no need to take every "therefore" as a warrant that the sentence which follows in time will also follow in logic. It may express a closely related fact known to be true on other grounds and suitable to serve as a new premise. There are enough veritable non sequiturs in ordinary disputation, exhibiting a real confusion, on which to exercise ingenuity.

EXAMPLE. A lecturer in modern history: "All the skill and discipline of Hitler's mechanized forces went down before the forces of communism and democracy which *Der Führer* had disparaged and despised. 'Degenerate' democracy grasped control of sea and air; 'inefficient' communism inspired its soldiers with the stubborn resolve that fought on to victory in the rubble of Stalingrad. Thus it was fascism that proved inferior."

COMMENT. The lecturer makes the sort of *non sequitur* which is most commonly encountered, that is, a conclusion not patently preposterous and yet far from supported by the premises. The tremendous efforts through which the British Empire, USA, USSR and their allies achieved victory in World War II do seem to show that both democracy and communism are capable of producing substantial military results. To say that the inferiority of fascism was thereby demonstrated is to assert a *non sequitur*, since the factors of relative resources, manpower and space preclude this as the necessary conclusion drawn from the fact of defeat.

EXAMPLE. A country boy, tiring of small-town life, argues that there is something "courageous and beautiful" about living an "irregular" life in "bohemian" surroundings. "All men who live thus," he exclaims, "have a touch of poetry in their souls. They are not to be judged and censored by ordinary morality." When pressed for his reasons, he says, "Why, many artists live scandalous lives, and we are the richer for it!"

COMMENT. Many is not all. Even if it were, the "all men"

sentence would not follow. There are other non sequiturs in this little effusion.

EXAMPLE. From a scrap-book: "Every reasonable man will want to regulate his life according to moral principles. Yet we all are tempted to make exceptions in our own cases. Therefore, we ought to make allowances for the lapses of others."

COMMENT. A marginal case. The three propositions probably are true in a fairly evident sense, and they are closely related to the same subject. The "therefore" makes them sound like a syllogism instead of a complex observation on life. But what follows "therefore" is no consequence in logic of what precedes. At the very least this is bad writing.

EXAMPLE. "I know what you are thinking about," said Tweedledum; "but it isn't so, nohow."

"Contrariwise," continued Tweedledee, "If it was so, it might be; and if it were so, it would be; but as it isn't, it ain't. That's logic."

COMMENT. Tweedledee's comment is perfectly true—it is indeed logic—but like many other things said to Alice in Looking-glass Land, though miraculously cogent, it is totally irrelevant.

44 · *Trouble with Conditionals and Alternatives*

Sometimes one of the premises is expressed in the form of a conditional—"If the parties agree in principle, a compromise is always possible," "If I arrive before the instructor, I am not really late." Conditionals have the form "If *a* (antecedent), then *b* (consequent)." Now if, in the second premise, one affirms the antecedent, he may affirm the consequent as a conclusion. This form of argument, called the *"modus ponens"* in logic, is a perfectly valid and useful kind of inference—"The parties in this case do agree in principle, so a compromise is now possible." "But I see that the instructor is not here yet, so I am not really late, after all."

A second form of valid inference from conditionals results from denying the consequent and then denying the antecedent as a conclusion—"If it has been raining, the streets will be wet. But the streets are not wet. Therefore, it has not been raining."

If the conditional is true in general, that is, if the antecedent gives a sufficient condition for the consequent, then when the antecedent is true in this particular case, the consequent must be true also. And when the consequent is not in this particular case true, then the antecedent could not be true. *If* it is true that every time it rains the streets are wet, then if it rains now, the streets must be in fact wet. And if it is false that the streets are now in fact wet, then it can not have been raining.

There are two common mistakes in using this form of argument, corresponding to the two valid forms. The valid forms can be summarized as affirming the antecedent, or denying the consequent. The invalid forms are called traditionally "denying the antecedent" and "affirming the consequent." The mistake seems to consist of treating the conditionals as expressing, not only sufficient, but also necessary conditions. Suppose I can affirm that *if and only if* it rains the streets are wet. I can now affirm, when it has not been raining, that the streets will not be wet. Or, in the case when the streets are wet, I can affirm that it has been raining. But the conditional in the if-and-only-if interpretation is false: as a general principle, rain is not a necessary condition for the wetting of streets—the water-wagon may have washed them down. Clearly, in view of this possibility, from the mere fact that the streets are wet, I cannot affirm that it has been raining. Rain is a sufficient condition for wet streets, but not a necessary condition. This being the case, nothing follows from "denying the antecedent" or "affirming the consequent."

Alternatives also frequently serve as premises in argument. The speaker affirms that *a* or *b*; then he affirms that not-*a*, and in a conclusion that, therefore, *b*. When any sentence is substituted for the letters, if the alternative is true, then by denying one of the sentences, the speaker obtains a valid inference to the other. "The chairman is sick, or he would surely be here. But he is not here, so he must be sick." Or, with the same alternative, "I know he is not sick, so he must be around here somewhere."

The improper use of the alternative corresponds to that of the conditional. The speaker supposes that the alternative divides the universe of discourse so that nothing is left over: *a* or *b* is equivalent to *a* or not-*a*. This kind of total division which leaves nothing over is called a "disjunction." Sometimes it is possible to substitute sentences for the letters so that a disjunction results: "It is either raining or it is not raining." "Isn't a student either present or absent?" Unless the alternative is a proper disjunction, it is a fallacy to suppose that the affirmation of one sentence entails the denial of the other. "He is sick, or he will come. But he will come; therefore, he is not sick." He may, of course, come even if he is sick.

Like the other logical fallacies, arguments based on affirming the consequent or denying the antecedent, or on affirming one of the two sentences in an alternative, are often disguised by a shift of expression. Moreover, in common speech there is the ambiguity of "if," which may mean simply "if" or may mean "if and only if." Likewise, "or" may mean "either one or the other but not both," or it may mean "possibly both, but certainly one or the other." In the course of a long argument, speakers often busy themselves producing lengthy evidence that one of the sentences in an alternative is true on the assumption that this disproves the other, or alleging evidence against the antecedent of a conditional, as if this disproves the consequent.

EXAMPLE. A political commentator writes, "If the farmers will organize, they have a good chance of keeping the price supports. But who ever heard of farmers really getting together on anything? They are by occupation and conviction individualists to the core."

COMMENT. This is an enthymeme, and the readers are invited to supply the missing proposition, in this case the conclusion: "Therefore, the farmers do not have a good chance of keeping price supports," an invalid inference. The Administration may hope to retain the farm vote by keeping the supports, even if the farmers do not organize to fight their political battles. This is an instance of the fallacy of denying the antecedent.

EXAMPLE. Peter argues with the reader, "If I don't get B in this course, there is no justice in this world." Later on, surprised at getting a B, he reminds the reader of what he had said and exclaims, "So there is justice in this world, after all!"

COMMENT. It probably was not a logic course. This is another instance of denying the antecedent. Since the antecedent is negative, the denial of it consists in negating a negative: "I did not not-get-B in the course," or, cancelling, "I got B in the course." The denial of the negative consequent operates similarly. But the denial of the consequent does not follow. Translating into an alternative, we have, "I get B in the course, or there is no justice. But I get B." Therefore? These alternatives are not proper disjunctives; one might, for instance, get his B because of favoritism, a form of injustice in the world.

EXAMPLE. Heard on a broadcast sermon: "If a man is self-seeking in all the important crises of life, his life as a whole will become a permanent crisis of lonesomeness, bitterness and futility. No true saint is ever lonesome, even in the desert. Nor is he bitter in disappointment. He may be despised and even persecuted and all his works destroyed, but no one could call such a life a life of futility. The saint, if only by his shining example, is the most dedicated to the service of his fellow man of all the noble classes of human beings. Thus the saint can never be self-seeking, even if he retires from the world to devote himself exclusively to seeking himself, in the sense of seeking his personal salvation."

COMMENT. Here is a typically complicated argument, exploiting all sorts of ambiguities and rhetorical flourishes, operating on complex and vaguely delimited categories (self-seeking, futility), which allow for paradoxical contrasts (not self-seeking though seeking only himself), and a multiplicity of terms, all lumped together. Yet the skeleton of the argument remains clearer than is often the case in practice. "If *a*, then *b*; but not-*b*, thus not-*a*"—a valid inference.

EXAMPLE. Mrs. Peter complains to her neighbor, "When it rains, it pours. This must be my rainy season, as everything is happening to me at once. Just let me tell you . . ."

COMMENT. *When* has the force of *if*. The conclusion is given vaguely, "This must be my rainy season," but it still does not follow from affirming the consequent. Other things might cause "it" to "pour" besides the metaphorical rain.

EXAMPLE. A newspaper editorializes: "The candidate is a fool or a knave. We know that he is not very bright. He played footsie with left-wing groups one day only to turn around the next and make anti-communist speeches. I guess we exonerate him from knavery—while noting that a well-intended dupe often does more damage than a dyed-in-the-wool villain."

COMMENT. Again much freedom with language, yet, again, the form of the argument is clearer than is usual in such writing: "*a* or *b*; but *a*, therefore *not-b*." Invalid. It seems highly likely that many communists, if that is what is meant, are both fools and knaves. Perhaps all of them are, in some sense of these vague terms.

Logicians customarily treat fallacies that take advantage of the imprecisions of language as part of formal fallacies. Ambiguities, doubleness in syntax, and the like, can technically be regarded as instances of what used to be called "the four terms." This is a reference to the rule (#40, p. 145) that syllogisms cannot be validly constructed with more than three terms. Clearly, where a word is used in two several senses, there only *appear* to be three terms, and fallacy results just as surely as if a separate term had been frankly introduced. The following fallacies we treat rather loosely as a group of technical vices or devices that exploit the vagueness of ordinary language.

In the ordinary language a relatively small number of structures must cover a multiplicity of functions. Webster's *Collegiate* says that the preposition *in* is used to show the relationship of containment ("Peter is in the breakfast room."), of part to a whole ("Peter is the dullest boy in his class."), of condition or circumstance ("Peter is in business." "His house is in escrow—it is also in ruins!"), of certain limitations ("Peter argues only in anger—or in circles."), as well as relationships of many other sorts. It is also used in idioms: "in as much as," "in fact," "in particular." Can any two persons be certain that they understand the following sentences in the same sense as to the force of the prepositions (to say nothing of the vagueness of the other terms)?

> In the architectural structure, man's pride, man's triumph over gravitation, man's will to power, assume a visible form. Architecture is a sort of oratory of power by means of forms.
>
> Nietzsche

The process by which language handles different material contexts with the same linguistic forms is called "equalization." Forms logically distinct are equalized. The most notorious fallacies resulting from equalization are the fallacy of ambiguous terms and that of amphibole. Other fallacies that involve a play on vagueness or general ambiguity are those of accent, punctuation, and the like.

45 · *Ambiguous Terms*

As a result of historical development, many words have a large range of meanings. This renders them ambiguous and leads to confusion in argument when such words occur as terms. To show the bare forms of proof and thus escape the ambiguity of language, modern logic dispenses in large part with ordinary vocabularies and reveals the structure of the various relationships in propositions by means of a notation of arbitrary symbols ($a \ v \ \lor \ a$; $a \cdot b \supset b \cdot a$). Most discussion cannot afford to be so abstract as this and must deal with political or social or every-day situations and so employs the rich and ambiguous vocabularies of the natural languages.

What helps control the ambiguity of language? The context will often determine with fair precision in which of its equivocal senses a word is being employed. Puns and homonyms ("raze" and "raise") are not apt to confuse an argument since the very extent of difference in their meanings ordinarily prevents one use from being mistaken for another. The shift in meaning of a single word around a common core is a more usual source of misunderstanding. Here, too, an explicit context is generally successful in defining by use, as it were, the sense intended. To take an instance, the word "speech" is no more ambiguous than many, yet it applies to several situations: "The Provençal speech [dialect, tongue] became a highly developed literary language." "Cicero's First Catiline is a model political speech [oration]." "The actor Garrick learned the brilliant new twenty-line speech [a part of the spoken role] in five minutes between acts." In the contexts the various senses of "speech" become perfectly distinct and give rise to no confusion. A second method of controlling the range is actual definition: "In this treatise we shall use 'speech' to stand for any sounds produced by the human larynx for the purpose of communication." All the kinds of ambiguity important to distinguish for argumentation occur where neither the context nor definition confines the area of meaning to one particular sense of a word.

In the first kind the actual object intended is left unspecified. This sort of ambiguity is trivial, since cross examination could always determine which object the speaker referred to. If in court a witness speaks ambiguously of "the evening I saw Jones," he is frequently required to specify his reference more accurately, "Do you mean the First of April?" Oracles are celebrated instances of this sort of ambiguity, though it is not easy to see how anyone could have been deceived by them.

160   LOGICAL FALLACIES

EXAMPLE. Croesus, King of Lydia, planned to attack Persia. A prudent man, he first enquired of the Delphic Oracle whether Fortune would favor his enterprise. The Oracle declared, "Croesus, having crossed the river Halys, will destroy a great kingdom." Heartened by this, Croesus crossed the Halys, which separated his kingdom from Persia, and was utterly routed by Cyrus. Croesus, bereft of his kingdom, dispatched a messenger to the Oracle to complain of deceit. The Oracle characteristically retorted that the prophecy was correct, for a great kingdom had indeed been destroyed—the kingdom of Croesus.

The second kind of ambiguity is also essentially trivial. It takes advantage of equivocal senses of a word or phrase to make a play on them. In the following example a play is made on the two distinct senses for the phrase "lose no time": "waste no time," "not delay." Thus this is really a pun.

EXAMPLE. Reader Peter is talking to a freshman who comes to his office. "When you turn in your term paper, I shall lose no time in reading it."
COMMENT. The student might well reply, "Then I shall lose no time in writing it."

The third variety has it in common with the second that it hovers between two distinct senses of a word, but the intention may not be a play on them. Sometimes this is by no means funny, as when it is the device of the loop-hole: the language of diplomacy and political concealment. A relatively innocent case is Calvin Coolidge's laconic announcement after two terms in office, "I do not choose to run." Neither newspapermen at the time nor historians since have succeeded in deciphering it. What did the President mean?
"I do not choose (intend) to run."—and I shall do as I intend.
"I do not choose (desire) to run."—though duty may require it.

The final variety we shall distinguish has the traditional name "ambiguous terms." The argument shifts from one sense to another of a term, and what is shown earlier to apply to one sense is later on, often unconsciously, applied to another, simply because the same word commonly covers both. It is this variety that gives rise in argument to the demand "define your terms."

EXAMPLE. Peter remarks to a friend, "It doesn't make any difference whether you win or lose a war. War, as I look at it, is a game which everyone loses."

COMMENT. In this abbreviated example, the shift occurs in two sentences. The words "win" and "lose" in the first sentence seem to refer to military victory and defeat, in the second sentence to the broad advantages of peace over war. It is probably true that nations engaged in modern war must *lose* in the sense of suffering human and material *loss* exceeding any advantages secured. But wars are indeed still "won" or "lost" in the sense of the victor forcing his will upon the defeated. There is a world of difference between winning and losing a war in this latter sense. Peter, it seems, is understandably disappointed with war as a human institution, and his strong feelings account for his being beguiled by this ambiguity.

EXAMPLE. A wife in recriminations against her spouse begins by accusing him of "neglecting" chores: taking out the rubbish, tending the yard, walking the dog. After a few minutes she says fiercely, "You neglect everything. You neglect me shamefully. You neglect your own children."

COMMENT. The first charge uses the term "neglect" in the sense of negligence in taking care of concrete duties. It will be seen that as the woman's feeling begins to mount, she shifts to a more general sense of "neglect." The berated husband is now in a bad way. Whatever he might have to confess concerning the rubbish and dog-walking, what can he say to the terrible accusation of "neglecting" wife and children? If the discussion had been kept orderly, there is at least a chance that the good wife would have seen where she was going in time to keep her sense of proportion. Whether or not she convinced her husband that he was a scoundrel, it seems likely that before she fell silent she convinced herself. And the children, too, if they overheard.

EXAMPLE. A famous philosopher argues that since the meaning of "Peter" is the identical man we knew before, see now, and will recognize tomorrow, the meaning of anything at all is its identity. Moreover, since the meaning of anything to an organism is precisely the value that that something has for the organism, this identical recurrence means the *value* the something has. Thus all value depends on identity. For this reason, pluralistic accounts of the world, as they stress discreteness and change instead of the unity, the identity, of experience, destroy value and are meaningless.

COMMENT. If you do not understand this bit of philosophizing, do not worry: it is unintelligible. It is put in here to illustrate how in actual argument the shift between ambiguous senses of a term often is by insensible degrees, so that it is very hard at times to see that what had been demonstrated by means of the use of one sense is now being applied to something quite different. Characteristically, this philosophical argument originally appeared in an elaborate context, full of illustration, allusion, incidental demonstration. This sort of spell weaving takes time; for that reason no brief examples can seem as plausible as the device often is in fact. Truncated, the shift is too obvious to succeed. .

C. K. Ogden and I. A. Richards, from whom the example is borrowed, wrote a famous book, *The Meaning of Meaning*, to·show that such shiftings about among the accommodating uses of "meaning," even in philosophy, where one would expect some care, vitiate many a discussion. Incidentally, Ogden and Richards complete the argument above in an amusing way. If the identical recurrence of anything is the meaning of it, and if the meaning of anything is its value, the sentence above, "identical occurrence means the value," by cancelling gives "Meaning means meaning." The authors suggest that this sentence loses in force what it gains in clarity. For another philosophical example exploiting the ambiguity of *meaning* and the rhetorical force of *mean*, see #50.

46 · *Amphibole:* "double talk"

This also is a pet device of oracles. Amphibole takes the advantage of the equalization of syntax, that is, of logical ambiguity in sentence structure. In Latin there is often doubt as to which of two accusatives is the subject and which the object of an infinitive. This gave a head start to the oracles. "Aio te, Aecida, Romanos vincere posse," means that you can conquer the Romans— or vice versa. In Shakespeare (2 Henry VI, I, i, 33-34) there is a famous instance:

> The Duke yet lives that Henry shall depose
> But him outlive and die a violent death.

No telling whether this means that the Duke is still alive whom Henry shall depose, or who shall depose Henry. The first line turns on the ambiguity of "that," which can stand indifferently for "who" or "whom," and there is a faulty pronoun reference in the second line, "him." This oracle could be regarded as an instance of verbal ambiguity rather than amphibole, which is ambiguity of syntax—of course pronouns are structure-words, and very different from sense-words, such as nouns and adjectives.

47 · *Ambiguous Accent*

The example in #45 about Reader John would be less ambiguous —and more offensive—if Reader John had accented I: "I shall lose no time in reading your paper!" In a way this would imply that, whoever may lose time, I shall not. Accent, capable of selecting the intended sense amongst various possibilities, is also available for distorting another's intended sense. A malicious person finds endless opportunities for giving false impressions, while staying within the literal truth, by subtle shifts of accent in reporting the words of others. If Mary says, "I didn't *think* to invite him," this becomes, "Mary said—her very words—'I didn't think to invite *him!*'" with scornful inflection on the last word, or, perhaps it becomes, "She said, '*I* didn't think to invite him,'" with the suggestion that the invitation was the fault of another. Even the most obvious and innocent generalizations can become invidious when the speaker cleverly stresses them in a special way. A famous philosopher, who liked to pose as a misogynist, once began an address to a woman's club: "*Man* is a rational animal."

EXAMPLE. Consider how an actor, reading Mark Antony's funeral oration, can vary his inflection to change "But Brutus is an honorable man" from apparent sincerity to open sarcasm.

EXAMPLE. Take some simple sentence such as, "He will come" and accent each word in turn. Note the different contexts implied by each accent.

48 · *Ambiguous Punctuation and Word Order*

The order of modifiers and the placing of punctuation marks can considerably affect the sense of what is said. Everyone is familiar with boners of this sort: "Lost, a fountain-pen by a student half-full of ink," "For sale, Chow dog, eats anything, very fond of children," "See revival of Fred Astaire in *Top Hat* and selected shorts!" These childish jokes illustrate the need for proper disposition of modifying elements in a sentence. They do not prepare for subtle uses of the possibilities of ambiguous punctuation and word order.

Many poets characteristically exploit these possibilities. If, for example, a phrase stands ambiguously between two components, this is a fair sign that the poet intends it to go with both, not to alternate between one or the other, and from this two-way reading expects to get an economy and enrichment. The critic-poet William Empson adduces many examples. In the *Seven Types of Ambiguity* he shows that a part of the effectiveness of poetry depends on this. One instance must suffice. Quoting *Macbeth:*

> If it were done, when 'tis done, then 'twere well
> It were done quickly;

Empson points out that this is "double syntax" since the line end imposes its stop and yet what follows completes the sentence. It is certainly better to do murder quickly, and it is certainly true that no deed of Macbeth's sort is really over with ("done") when it is committed ("done"). Informed readers want the interpretation to *include* both thoughts.

We are not always reading poetry. In argument, we shall want as little of this sort of doubleness as of any other. The importance of watching these elements of punctuation and order is very apparent to legal writers, where care with "and/or" constructions, commas, and all the punctilious details of composition is often carried to what may seem to the layman absurd lengths. Yet cases have turned on carelessness with a single comma in contracts or wills. And issues have often been confused, outside the courtroom, because of divergent interpretations permitted by misplaced modifiers or haphazard punctuation.

EXAMPLE. Peter's will provides, "My son Peter, Jr. shall receive $5,000 per year until he has completed his military service, when he shall receive $10,000 per year and the use of my estate Blackacre, if he is married." Peter, Jr., still a bachelor, completes his military service.

COMMENT. Peter, Jr. will do well to see his lawyer. Does the restrictive clause "if he is married" refer only to the immediate antecedent, Blackacre, or does it refer both to Blackacre and to the receipt of the $10,000 per year? Since the restrictive clause is set off by a comma, a grammarian would apply it to both Blackacre and the $10,000 per year. Courts will not press rules of punctuation to defeat the intent of the parties where the intent is apparent. But what did the deceased Peter intend? Maybe it will take a lawsuit to determine.

49 · *Circular Definitions and Question Begging*

One way to eliminate vagueness and to make sure that abstractions adequately represent constructions is to define the terms carefully. Clear definitions may not solve all difficulties (see pp. 65 f.). Be this as it may, bad definitions multiply them. The most notorious fault with definition is circularity, although formal definitions are circular in the sense that the defining term and the term to be defined are interchangeable. By "circular definition" is meant a definition which attempts to resolve a point at issue by defining a term so as to preëmpt the point. Such a definition "begs the question." Suppose someone is arguing that responsibility cannot be expected of children. His opponent argues, " 'Responsibility' means the ability to distinguish between right and wrong." Then he adds, "Children of six can distinguish between what's right and what's wrong. They are therefore responsible." The answer is correct. "Responsibility" can be defined in this way, and small children can tell you what is right and wrong. The conclusion follows. Far from winning the argument, however, the statement merely leaves the disputants in need of a word to cover what was originally intended by "responsibility."

EXAMPLE. A defense attorney addresses the jury: "These fraudulent charges, long since proved false and unfounded . . ." The judge interrupts to instruct him that whether or not the charges are false and fraudulent is just what the jury is impaneled to determine. Counsel retorts, " 'False' means 'without basis in fact' and 'fraudulent' means 'deceitful.' That is what our side is contending. All I am doing is stating our contention. Are we not to be allowed to answer the charge?"

COMMENT. The attorney's speech begs the question before the court, and his circular definition begs the question as to whether he is to be allowed to beg the question.

EXAMPLE. Sextus Empiricus has an argument for the existence of the gods. He points out that "you do not serve the centaurs, because the centaurs are non-existent." But you do serve the gods. So the gods certainly exist, or else "you could not serve them."

COMMENT. This argument is an enthymeme, but the suppressed elements are suggested by the remark about the centaurs. Let us spell out the whole thing. "If something is non-existent, you cannot serve it. The centaurs are non-existent. Therefore, you cannot serve them. If you can serve something, that something must exist. But you can and do serve the gods. Therefore, the gods exist." Now it is true that there are no centaurs around to be served; moreover, people do not in fact serve them. But how about the first premise "If something is non-existent, you cannot serve it"? From this it follows that "If you can serve something, that something must exist," but this is precisely what Sextus Empiricus ought to be proving. Thus, when we supply for him the premise that will make his argument valid and plausible, we assume the very thing that he wants to prove. The argument is circular. Moreover, as the case of the worship of pagan gods shows, the suppressed premise on which it rests is false. If I should start a new worship tomorrow and establish a ritual to serve Glug-Glug, would this cause Glug-Glug to exist?

Circular definitions are a rather obvious instance of question begging. In its full-blown maturity question begging can go on for volumes, even through whole systems of thought. As can be guessed, the mature fallacy is not easy to handle. There it is, big as the universe (in Hegel, for example), but just how it operates is hard to show in a simple instance. There are some formulas that rouse suspicion in the experienced, such as "It is obvious," "No one can deny" (see #21), and a whiff of vagueness is sufficient to put an old hunter on the scent (see #10). Yet the beast is often elusive: if trapped by an exception, he can be rescued by a distinction.

EXAMPLE. Everything in the world is known through experience. An inexperienced fact is inconceivable. There is, then, a constant equation between fact and experience. Philosophical idealism declares that the world is caused by experience. What evidence is there for anything else? Does not evidence itself involve experience? Now experience obviously requires an experiencing intelligence. Idealism draws the evident conclusion: the universe is mental. Without mind there is nothing.

COMMENT. Notice the vagueness of "fact," "experience," "mental." In this (very truncated) statement of the idealist position, it seems unlikely that by "mental," for instance, can be meant what is commonly meant by that term. And notice "evident" and "obviously." That the universe is mental is a far from evident conclusion, and it is far from obvious that without mind there is nothing, since this is what the argument is designed to prove. Ralph Barton Perry showed that this argument for Idealism rests on the truth that whatever is likely to be meant by "experience," it will attend all knowledge. Perry argued that this kind of constant attendance does not prove a causal relation. Everything that happens in the world is attended by configurations of the stars and planets, what astrologers call the "chart." And this chart is constantly changing. But it certainly does not follow that these changes in the sky cause events they attend in the lives of men. To suppose so is superstition: astrology.

It might be added that the term "experience" is so inclusive that it incorporates "knowledge" and even "fact." When such terms occur in argument, there is open invitation to circularity. The circularity here is *something* like the following: Experience attends everything, and it is mental; the universe is everything; so experience causes the universe; therefore, the universe is mental. Needless to say, idealists would reject such a crude statement of their position. This is what makes exposure of question-begging so difficult.

EXAMPLE. In a picture by the famous French comedian Sacha Guitry some thieves are arguing over division of seven pearls worth a king's ransom. One of them hands two to the man on his right, then two to the man on his left. "I," he says, "will keep three." The man on his right says, "How come you keep three?" "Because I am the leader." "Oh. But how come you are the leader?" "Because I have more pearls."

COMMENT. This apparently satisfies the two thieves. Even this simple-minded example takes several lines to explain, and it is apparent that instances of question begging designed for more than amusement consume time and space. This is especially so, since they almost never occur in pure isolation, but come interlaced with the pearls of shimmering vagueness linked together with false generalizations and the golden chains of Word Magic (see #12).

50 · *Misuse of Etymology*

If context and definition are desirable ways to control the range of senses of ambiguous words (see #45), it does not follow that all ways which attempt to control the range lead to happy results. Some, indeed, lead to further confusion. Speakers have been known to insist on insisting that "education" comes from *"educere,"* a Latin word meaning to draw out. From this etymology they argue that education should be a matter of drawing out the student in the sense of coaxing rather than compelling. Maybe it should, but aside from the fact that the word comes from *"educare"* meaning "to educate," the derivation remains irrelevant to the argument. This fallacy is a form of circularity (see #49), since the audience is asked to subscribe to the conclusion because of the very *meaning* of some terms used in the premises. But simple circularity is hardly apt to deceive, whereas the assumption that words should stick close to etymological sense is a limit on the conventional meaning of words and an unwarranted restriction on the growth of language.

EXAMPLE. Richard Whately cites the argument that since "Representative" means one elected to represent a constituency, why then, the elected Representative should seek the advice of his electors and vote the way they tell him. This argument, Whately rightly points out, is contrary to custom, constitutional practice, and good sense. A representative is responsible to his electors, who may throw him out of office if he fails to represent their ultimate interest, but he is expected in the meanwhile to make a professional study of issues that arise in the legislature and to vote on them according to his conscience.

EXAMPLE. Mystic Peter writes in *The Obscurantists' Quarterly:* "The great physicists, like Newton and Einstein, reduce the vast concepts of Force and Energy to mathematical symbols, but we must never forget that these same words stand for the eternal Power of Life and Spirit that we may use and control in our own thinking."

COMMENT. A little more control in Mystic Peter's thinking and there would be no need for comment here. The words "force" and "energy" occur in physics, but there they are given precise meanings which forever separate them from the vague anthropomorphic associations which Peter is attempting to play on. The sentence is false. Whatever Peter is likely to mean by "the eternal power of life and spirit," etc., the words as used by the physicists do not mean that.

EXAMPLE. Josef Pieper, a contemporary metaphysical philosopher, attempts to show that, not only is leisure of present importance to the spiritual development of Western culture, but that even in the earliest period it was the foundation of it. "That much, at least," he says, "can be learnt from the first chapter of Aristotle's *Metaphysics*." He goes on, "And even the history of the word attests the fact: for leisure in Greek is *skole*, and in Latin *scola*, the English 'school.' The word used to designate the place where we educate and teach is derived from the word which means 'leisure.' 'School' does not, properly speaking, mean school, but leisure."

(Josef Pieper, *Leisure, the Basis of Culture*, trans. Alexander Dru, with an introduction by T. S. Eliot, Pantheon Books Inc., New York, pp. 25-26).

COMMENT. One learns something from the first chapter of Aristotle's *Metaphysics* or any other place in any other book of argument, only if the author's arguments are valid and his premises true. Otherwise, see #15. If Mr. Pieper had been content, in his use of etymology, to limit himself to his statement that the "history of the word attests the fact," *leisure* in its relation to schooling would have constituted supporting evidence of a sort. But he was not content with this. The last sentence is something of a wonder. If "school" does not mean school, how can "leisure" mean leisure or "Pieper" mean Pieper or any word mean anything? "Properly speaking," indeed, clearly does not mean properly speaking. A translation: The English word for school derives from a Latin word for leisure. But this has already been said. Presumably Mr. Pieper is not advising his readers to begin using the word "school" to stand for leisure, but wishes them to remember that the etymology of "school" shows an early understanding of the connection between leisure and education. Thus the use of "mean" in the last sentence is rhetorical, a matter of emphasis, but is concealed in the notorious ambiguity of that term. It is true that Pieper does not use the term in giving the etymologies. If he had written, " 'Skole' meant leisure in Greek," etc., the shift would be very evident. For another example relying on the ambiguity of "mean" see #45.

51 · *Idiosyncratic Language*

There is another common practice which is almost directly opposed to the false kind of control of meaning represented by the fallacy of etymology. This is the sort of paradoxical talk that attempts to sound profound: "The seeming real is the only illusion." It consists in a sort of personal or private charging of words with meanings different from, and sometimes opposite to, the usual range of the words in their conventional contexts. The present time seems peculiarly susceptible to this sort of perversion of the language. Orwell brilliantly characterized the phenomenon in his *1984* ("War is Peace").

It seems particularly hard to describe just what takes place in the cases we have collected. New ideologies—religious, political, philosophical—arise today in a ferment. It is not surprising that language evolved for the needs of past generations is inadequate to express all the new concepts that people wish to talk about. They must stretch old words to radically new meanings or invent barbarous neologisms. They do both, of course, and sometimes with unhappy results. The situation favors some persons and groups who deliberately exploit linguistic confusion. Errors in judgment are described as "treason," conservative statesmen called "fascists," capitalists called "bourgeois imperialistic beasts." Such perversion of language also goes hand in hand with a cynical employment of the emotive power of words (see #13).

EXAMPLES. The "National Museum"—a private enterprise on the site of the Battle of Bull Run.

The "National Socialist rule of law"—a denial of an independent judiciary, equality before the law, certainty of law, *habeas corpus* and other procedural safeguards: in short, a rejection of everything traditionally associated with the term "rule of law."

A "People's Democracy"—a monolithic totalitarian system suppressing free expression of the popular will in control of government.

CONCLUSION

For a conclusion there is one last fallacy—oversimplification. In #3 the example contained the statement, "Increased armaments appear as one of the major causes of European wars." Robert Thouless calls this sort of thesis "tabloid thinking," and analyses it as reducing a complex situation to a simple statement which is inaccurate. False generalizations are often a result of crudely simplifying concepts, but oversimplification is a fault of the explanation. The situation reveals a beautiful complexity, but for purposes of explanation to the uninformed—a fifteen minute radio talk on quantum physics for the layman—it has to be caught up into a vague phrase or two and often tied in with something utterly different or analogous only in a crude way. "Freud teaches that everything is sex." "The atom is a little solar system." "Virgil's *Aeneid* is just a long patriotic hymn to Augustan Rome."

The error is difficult to avoid. In the first place, time generally makes it impractical to elaborate all qualifications. Moreover, in many discussions full exposition of detail would obscure the subject rather than clarify it. For example, textbook writers habitually wrestle with the dilemma of whether to make statements which are, though not wholly accurate, yet clear and serviceable enough for students, or whether to incorporate all the qualifications necessary for accuracy—and drown the student in details. The problem here is to achieve simplification without oversimplification.

In the second place, when the speaker does not possess a detailed knowledge, the very lack of familiarity with the complexity of the subject is apt to increase his confidence in what are his mere "tabloid" thoughts about it. A superficial knowledge may make a complicated situation appear quite simple, like a wide patch of brambles seen from the air. And everybody has to be content with a superficial acquaintance with most subjects. Finally, even where we are well aware of the existence of complexities, we may be tempted, in "the human quest for certainty," as John Dewey argues, to try to cut through them and to set up an oversimplified system with everything tidy and neat.

So, we see, oversimplification produces a sort of false clarity which misrepresents the real nature of the problem. As authors of this book, we hope that our descriptions of common fallacies have not often fallen short of a proper balance between directness and accuracy in explanation. And we are sorry for any statements which make the error of oversimplification.

This book began by quoting a cynical sentence or two from Schopenhauer. The authors should like to end it by quoting a sentiment which seems to come from another world, the world of John Henry Cardinal Newman. On defining a gentleman, Newman says, "He is never mean or little in his disputes, never takes unfair advantage, never mistakes personalities or sharp sayings for arguments, or insinuates evil which he dare not say out." This noble disputant, Newman continues, acts towards an enemy as if he were one day to be a friend.

> He has too much good sense to be affronted at insults, he is too well employed to remember injuries, and too indolent to bear malice. . . . If he engages in controversy of any kind, his disciplined intellect preserves him from the blundering discourtesy of better, perhaps, but less educated minds; who, like blunt weapons, tear and hack instead of cutting clean, who mistake the point in argument, waste their strength on trifles, misconceive their adversary, and leave the question more involved than they find it.   Cardinal Newman

It is the "blundering discourtesy" of minds that leads to *oversimplification*. And Newman is right; it is a paradox of bluntness and dullness that they leave the question more involved than it was to start with. Only the clear-thinking and well-informed mind can cut through complexity and achieve something of the true simplicity that mathematicians call elegance.

Exercises

Introduction (pages 1-9)

A. True or false?

1. The factual sentences of scientific observation are the premises of arguments in science.

2. All scientific laws are mutually consistent.

3. Scientific laws lead to predictions.

4. When the predictions come true, they "confirm" the scientific laws.

5. To "confirm" the laws means to modify them.

6. Einstein confirmed the laws of physics.

7. If only one predicted observation confirms the laws, they become then discarded hypotheses.

8. The laws are never fully proved: they remain hypotheses.

9. The facts never contradict the hypothesis.

10. There is no logical contradiction in denying the laws.

11. It leads to logical contradiction to say that the sun rises in the west.

12. It leads to logical contradiction to say that $2 + 2$ is not equal to $3 + 1$.

13. The laws can be regarded as generalization without known exceptions.

14. Compared to scientific laws, our ordinary common sense seems hopelessly inaccurate.

15. The problem of the every-day situation, in which there are so few reliable generalizations, is how to act sensibly.

B. The following words are important in understanding this section. Use each in a correct sentence, looking them up in a good dictionary if necessary:

1. rhetorical	2. misfunction	3. observation
4. prediction	5. (logical) contra- diction	6. complex

7. generalization	8. lattice	9. induce
10. verify	11. fictions	12. tenets
13. confirm	14. hypothesis	15. abstractions

1 · *Faulty Generalization* (pages 10-17)

A. Illustrate the following:

1. a statistical generalization
2. a generalization in a matter not yielding to statistical treatment
3. the limited ways in which generalizations are expressed.

B. Each of the following statements indicates some evidence for a generalization. What, if any, further evidence would you like to have before accepting or rejecting the generalization? Where you find a need for further evidence, state whether you are trying to avoid making a hasty or an unrepresentative generalization.

1. The type of service one can expect doctors to give under socialized medicine is shown by the English physician who boasted of examining eighty patients in three hours. Yes, this was after England adopted a socialized medicine plan.

2. A mixture of equal parts of sulphur and saltpeter will explode if placed upon a cement floor and struck with a hammer. I know this because I tried it once.

3. I didn't realize what the most popular soft drinks in this locality were until my son began collecting bottle tops in the park last Sunday. He got a good supply from the refreshment stand, and he arranged them in rows on the rug when we got home. The rows turned out this way:

Fizzo	58
Pinkpop	40
Steinola	16
miscellaneous	5 or fewer for each

So now I know which companies are doing the best business in soft drinks around here.

4. We made a poll on the main street in town on the question of a five-percent tax raise to improve the school system. The replies of the first hundred people we asked are pretty conclusive: yes—56, no—14, don't know—30. It is obvious that of the interested citizens a vast majority want better schools and are willing to pay for them.

5. Now that over a generation has passed since the last grizzly bear was shot in California, it seems safe to assume that the grizzly is extinct in that state.

6. I have been riding up and down in that elevator every day for the past ten years. Now they come around to inspect it! Hasn't it proved safe already?

7. As a Congressman, I feel obliged to vote according to the clear will of my constituency. My mail in the past weeks has proved to me that my duty is to vote against the budget proposed by the Administration in its present form. My constituents are two-to-one against the foreign aid sections.

8. In shopping on the Via Veneto in Rome I never encountered a clerk who did not speak very good English. It is not necessary to speak Italian to shop in Italy.

9. Spaghetti with green sauce is made with anchovy and parsley. We never eat it. My wife got sick on it last summer in Naples. It's wise to leave fish alone in hot climates, even canned anchovy.

10. Crime never pays. It is true that a certain percentage of criminals escape detection and punishment, but the case of Jasper Holmes, who made public restitution for robbing the poor box, shows that even the man who "gets away with it" will be hounded by his conscience.

11. Since Jones manipulated the receipts of the charity fund to his own advantage, we can never trust him again with financial responsibility.

12. Cats are man's best friend. I know two separate cases where they saved the lives of people by jumping onto the bed and waking them when the house was on fire.

2 · *Faulty Causal Generalization*   (pages 17-21)

A. Economic conditions are a fertile field for all sorts of faulty causal generalization. Assume that you have encountered the following statements during a bull session. For each assertion, frame a question which will indicate that the cause may be more complex than suggested.

1. The constant demands of labor for higher wages are the cause of inflation.

2. Heavy installment buying is to blame for the inflation.

3. Inflation is the result of our tremendous national debt.

4. We're importing too many goods—that's why we have an inflation. There's too much stuff to buy.

5. The cause of the rising prices is that commodities are relatively in more demand than the money required to buy them.

6. The big businesses are pushing prices up. They don't really compete, you know.

7. The cause of inflation is the abundance, that is, the cheapness of money relative to demand for commodities.

B. The following examples are all derived from general science or common knowledge. In which of them does "the cause" require a broad interpretation, such as, "a prominent cause," or "the determining condition, everything else being equal." Give your reasons.

Model: "According to the germ theory, germs or viruses are the cause of disease." In order for this statement of the germ theory to be literally correct, the presence of germs or viruses would have to be both necessary and sufficient condition for illness: if and only if germs or viruses, then disease. But we know that some persons can carry disease organisms while remaining immune to the disease. We also know that some diseases, such as vitamin deficiency, are not caused by organisms. "The cause" in this statement requires a broad interpretation as "the usual cause," "the cause to look for," or something of the kind. It is, of course, possible to use "disease" in a special sense: "that illness which is always caused by germ or virus."

1. The cause of forgetting a person's name, according to Freud, is the unconscious desire to be rid of the person or to repress some circumstance in connection with him, such as the memory of an embarrassing encounter.

2. Glacial action is the cause of moraines, that is, certain large scale accumulations of earth and rock.

3. Television is the cause of the decreasing attendance at spectacle sports.

4. Proper cutting is the cause of brilliance in gems.

5. The real cause of juvenile delinquency is the disintegration of moral or social standards throughout the land.

6. Uncertainty about defense spending is the cause of the recurrent fluctuation in the stock market.

7. The strain and tension of business competition is the cause of the rise in the rate of stomach ulcers.

8. *The* cause of cancer is undetermined.

3 · *Assuming the Cause: "post hoc* reasoning" (pages 21-22)

A. Is the assumption of causal relationship justified in the following cases? Give reasons for your answers.

1. Soon after the black cat ran in front of me, my tooth started to ache. Don't tell me that there's nothing in the saying about black cats bringing bad luck!

2. When President Peterson came to our state university twenty years ago, there were only 2500 students and an outmoded plant. Today we have over 8000 students and new buildings stand all about us! There could be no more impressive evidence of the administrative genius of our President.

3. All I did was to put *Easyway Weed Killer* on my lawn. All the dandelions and witch grass died right away—just as the label predicted. It certainly made all the difference this year. I'm recommending it to my friends.

4. My cold began to get better the day after I took *Sniffleless*. So there is one medicine that I can recommend with confidence.

5. Anybody ought to know how to vote in this election. Only the present administration could have brought peace and general prosperity. These achievements can't be gainsaid.

B. In medical research it is customary to show that a certain result follows after a certain treatment *and* that a different result occurs where the treatment is not given. Why is this procedure employed?

4 · *Faulty Analogy*   (pages 22-27)

A. 1. What is an analogy? Define and give an example.

2. When will an argument by analogy be good reasoning?

3. When will an argument by analogy be faulty reasoning?

B. True or false?

1. Any analogy may break down.

2. If an analogy is made between members of a narrow class, there is a high probability that the analogy will hold within the area of the similarities which determined the class.

3. A class with many members cannot offer strong analogies between the members.

4. Things which are analogous in some respects may differ widely in other respects.

5. A figurative analogy may be useful for illustration.

C. Point out the similarities and differences which should be considered in evaluating each of the following analogies. Then evaluate the strength of each.

1. The play *Trees Are Green* is a lively farce which has won a good reception in Boston. Producer and cast alike are confident of a long run when they hit Broadway next month. And with reason, too.

2. Professor Peter gave an excellent course in English literature of the twentieth century. I'll bet his course on the nineteenth century would be a good one, too.

3. A dangerous criminal, like a wild beast, threatens the security of the people. Society is the gainer when dangerous beasts are destroyed, and so it must gain when criminals are extirpated.

4. Sound financial policies for a nation are comparable to the prudent management of a household. If, year after year, the householder goes into debt he must eventually face bankruptcy. So, too, the state that neglects to balance its budget is pursuing a course that can end only in bankruptcy.

5. Paul, age twelve, is being taken to an evening movie while his brother Peter, age eight, is being left at home. "If Paul goes, I should get to go, too," wails Peter.

6. The State of Washington distributes liquor through state operated stores. Public bars are prohibited; only a private club may supply

drinks to its members at a bar. In my opinion, the state monopoly of liquor dispensing has worked well in Washington and the problems in liquor control there are the same problems we face in California. Therefore, I favor California adopting a liquor control law similar to the Washington statute, except that the clause permitting clubs to maintain bars should be changed since it has led to abuses. California liquor control would then be as good as liquor control is in Washington and, so far as the phony "club" situation is concerned, it might be better.

7. In number 6, substitute "Pakistan" for "California." Evaluate the strength of this new analogy.

D. A series of cases known to lawyers as the "turntable cases" has established that a railroad will be liable for damages where a child is injured when playing with a turntable which has been left unlocked or otherwise unguarded. A "No Trespassing" or other warning sign is not sufficient to avoid liability. The theory is that a turntable is an "attractive nuisance" which tempts trespassing children to turn it in play and, thereby, run a risk of injury.

A child entered the property of a Chemical Company and discovered a large abandoned quarry filled with apparently clear water. The quarry was distinctly posted "No Swimming." The child went swimming and was injured by chemical wastes which had been disposed of in the quarry.

Should the theory of the "turntable cases" be applied to hold the Chemical Company liable for damages? Argue the case on both sides. Use analogy to the "turntable cases" when arguing for liability. Distinguish the "turntable cases" when arguing against liability.

E. 1. Cartoons often depict analogies. Bring in three cartoons of this sort and evaluate the analogy in each. Possibly you will regard some cartoons as effective even though the analogies they depict are not valid arguments. If so, state why the cartoon appeals to you as somehow cogent.

2. Fables and parables also are often couched in analogy. Cite one instance of each and evaluate the analogy proposed. What is the purpose of the analogy used in the fable that you cite? In the parable?

5 · *Composition and Division*   (pages 27-30)

A. Define "composition" in a single short sentence. Do the same for "division." It is easy to confuse the terms, so be sure you have the definitions clearly in mind.

B. Explain why arguments based on composition or division are fallacious even though a whole and its parts often do share the same characteristics.

C. Point out for each of the following:

   a. Whether the situation is one of composition or division,

b. What sort of evidence is needed to establish the point which is being falsely assumed.

1. The people of Sweden are law-abiding, so Gustav Anderson (a Swede) couldn't have broken the law.

2. Eastern University is the nation's most outstanding school, and that means that the paleontology department there will have an outstanding faculty and facilities.

3. Oh, if only we could have an all-star cast, the play would be a matchless performance.

4. A grocery chain offered $80,000 for the block of land on Kelley Avenue. Sam owns a quarter of that block, you know. Well, one old lady wouldn't sell her lot, so the whole deal fell through. But at least Sam found out what his parcel is worth, a cool $20,000!

5. If every railway operates its line efficiently, it stands to reason that the country will enjoy an efficient railway system.

6. Saving is a virtue. It contributes to individual prosperity. So if every individual saved up his money then everybody would prosper.

7. Since payrolls are the backbone of consumer demand, the monetary interest of the individual businessman actually is to pay his own labor force well.

6 · *The All-or-Nothing Mistake*   (pages 30-32)

A. 1. Advocates of every hue—lawyers, salesmen, legislators, debaters—are apt to indulge in all-or-nothing arguments. Why so?

2. A thoughtful member of an audience generally will place little confidence in any speech that treats a public issue as a matter of unqualified praise or blame. Why so?

3. The adage "There are two sides to every question," taken literally, is false. Cite an example to expose its falsity.

B. Underscore all phrases in the following passages which indicate an all-or-nothing approach to the problem. In each case decide whether the problem fundamentally has only two sides or whether it has more than two sides. Do not assume that an all-or-nothing assertion is necessarily wrong.

1. "The West must make up its mind about Nasser.

"Shall we write him off, let the Reds have him, seek other friends in the Middle East? Or shall we support him in his plans for Egypt, come to some kind of terms with his new nationalism?

"On the answer may depend whether the Middle East will be on the side of freedom—or go the way of Red China."

Edwin Muller, "Egypt's Nasser: Hope or Menace,"
Reader's Digest, August 1956, p. 98.

2. "The reason they [i.e. price and wage controls] do not work is that they are bad in principle; they treat symptoms instead of treating

the disease. In wartime, with a patriotic motive to aid them, they work well briefly but the erosion of their effectiveness cannot be delayed long. In time of peace in this country they would not work at all; they were not working at the close of World War II."

Editorial, *Los Angeles Times,* September 4, 1957.

3. "Poverty never begets extravagance, and frugality is never the offspring of wealth. Poverty is productive of every human exertion, while wealth is the parent of every form of corruption. The richer a nation is in time of peace, the poorer it is in time of war."

Homer Lea, *The Valor of Ignorance.* N.Y.:
Harper & Bros, 1909. p. 65.

7 · *The False Dilemma*   (pages 32-36)

A. Distinguish a false dilemma from a true dilemma.

B. State two ways in which a false dilemma may be refuted.

C. Identify the following as true or false dilemmas, and show how each false dilemma might be refuted.

1. If the children are provided with a TV set they will become spectators at the expense of healthful play out-of-doors, and if they do not have a set they will miss part of the culture of contemporary times.

2. Those who are famous suffer the personal disaster of lack of privacy, while those who are not must ever feel the ignominy of being damned to oblivion.

3. To go to the geology lecture is a waste of time, but not to go might mean that I'd flunk another quiz.

4. Either a nation must support its allies without reservation or its friendship will be regarded as worthless. So the public will have to reconcile itself to all the unhappy actions which grow out of this painful truth.

5. I don't approve of the policies of one of the major parties and I don't care for the candidate put up by the other. The minor parties don't express my views either, and not to vote at all is to leave the decision to others. So I'm in a fix. I guess it's the usual predicament of the voter.

Trouble with Constructions   (pages 33-36)

A. Reread this section carefully. Define the following terms in the sense in which they are used in the text:

   1. situation
   2. construction
   3. name

B. Why do people make up new classifications?
C. Answer briefly:
   1. In the bag of marbles what is the "situation"?
   2. What are the marble-constructions of the little girl?
   3. Describe the situation in a game with which you are familiar and explain the constructions as if to someone who had never heard of them before.
   4. In your game described in 3 are all the essential elements separated by the constructions? Do these elements have distinct names or descriptions?
   5. Look at the same situation, that is, the game you have described in your answer to 3, and see if you can divide it up in an entirely different way, describing and naming new constructions to fit the new classification.

8 · *Faulty Classification*   (pages 36-39)

A. Test the following classifications according to Rules 1 and 2, that is, try to decide whether or not all important elements are covered under the headings and are clearly separated.

1. Games are either competitive or not. In competitive games one player pits his skill against others (chess, golf) or one team opposes another (football, bridge). In non-competitive games the player always tests his skill against chance or luck (pinball, old maid).

2. The tasks of gardening are twofold: first, there is the care required to keep the garden in good condition; second, there are the jobs you do today looking forward to a future result. The day-to-day care includes watering, weeding, pruning, etc. The long-range jobs are illustrated by making cuttings, planting bulbs and seeds, and the like.

3. Popular magazines are either slick or pulp. Slick magazines are middle-class and rely on advertising. Pulp magazines rely on wide circulation.

4. There are two kinds of games, games of skill and games of chance. If chance enters into a game of skill, it is only incidentally and will even out over a period of time. In games such as bridge and chess a skillful player will always win out over the tyro in the long run. This is also true of many sports such as football and golf. In games of chance, if there is present an element of skill, it is less important by far than luck and cannot be relied on, as many gamblers have learned at their cost.

5. The tasks of gardening are twofold, planting things to grow and digging things up. You prune undesired growths or trim off dying blossoms—to say nothing of killing weeds—quite as much as you help things to grow. Gardening is as much a process of destroying growth as encouraging it.

6. Popular magazines are all either uplifting or merely entertaining. The stories and articles are often simply intended to amuse—western, adventure, science-fiction magazines seldom point a moral beyond the obvious one that good guys are good and bad guys are bad. But there is a growing trend even in the fiction of certain popular magazines to tell the readers something, to inculcate an attitude towards a complicated moral situation, or, more rarely, even to instruct the reader on conditions, such as health problems, which the editors feel the reader ought to know about.

B. Classify TV programs according to some simple method of division. Prepare to defend yourself in the classroom against the charges that there is no place in your classification as stated for an important kind of program or that a certain kind of program seems to fall indifferently under two heads.

8 · *Faulty Classification* (continued)   (pages 36-39)

A. General principles of classification (pp. 33-36). Classify the following situations in two ways. State clearly the purpose behind each classification.

Model: kinds of good students.

1. Good students are either naturally bright students who are conscientious about doing their assignments or dull students who work very hard, even harder than necessary. The purpose of this classification is to characterize good students according to the relation between their native ability and their study habits.

2. Some students are good because they find a challenge in a subject or technique (Greek, violin playing) and become more than temporarily interested in it. Others become good students because they have a powerful incentive *not* related to their interest in the subject. This incentive may be praise, prizes, scholarships, subsidy, future job placement, or a desire to show well in competition—or merely self respect. The purpose of this way of dividing up good students is to lay stress on the importance of motivation.

1. successful marriages
2. juvenile crimes
3. types of storms
4. causes of failure in life
5. reasons to travel

B. General principles of classification (continued) (pp. 33-36). By way of review, consider your classifications in answer to "A" above and ask yourself:

1. Are all important elements of the situation taken care of?
2. Do the divisions clearly separate all important elements so that none occurs under two coordinate headings?

9 · *Misconceptions about Classification* (pages 40-53)

A. If you have ever observed an infant beginning to talk, describe the way he learned the correct use of general terms or abstractions (such as, "baby," "red").

B. Suggest in broad outline the *reduction* of the underlined terms in the following sentences:

1. Is this your *book?*
2. I am her *brother*.
3. The knife is *sharp*.
4. The Governor is very *ambitious*.

C. Reread the examples in the text. Cite an instance of reification from your own experience and explain which of the examples it most resembles.

D. Consider the following personifications. Suggest a use of each that takes it as more than an imaginative symbol, that is, that mistakes it for an entity in the world.

Model: Santa Claus is the spirit of Yuletide.

Small children of course would not understand this sentence beyond the reference to Santa Claus, whom they regard as a real person rewarding good children with presents at Christmas. (See exercises to #29 *personification.*)

1. The Rain God is angry. (See p. 115.)
2. There walked the goddess of inexorable revenge. (See pp. 198 ff.)
3. The Earth is a nourishing mother to her children.
4. Automation is an electronic monster, subjugating our industry to a veritable robot tyranny.

E. Reread the example of King James and the comment (under *Faulty Analogy*, pp. 25-26). Compare this with 3 and 4 in "D" above. A personification can be used to introduce a figurative analogy. If this is done, what are the limits to the conclusions that can be based on such personification?

9 · *Misconceptions about Classification* (continued) (pages 40-53)

A. What does it mean to say:

1. that the purpose *determines* the classification?
2. that the situation *limits* the classification?

B. Reread the section about the marbles (pp. 35-36).

1. Show how the purposes of the boy and his sister determine their differing classifications of the marbles.
2. Show how the situation limits the classification.

C. Consider again the model for "A" in the exercise on the general principles of classification (p. 182). How does the situation limit the two classifications of good students? State the limiting action of the situation to the classifications you made according to the instructions of that exercise.

D. In the comment to the example on p. 53 an analogy is suggested between the "verdict" of history and the verdict of a jury. Is this analogy justified? Explain. At what point would you expect this analogy to break down?

E. In your own words, explain the broad philosophical basis upon which each of the following rests.

1. To the relativist, no moral code has universal application to all human beings.

2. To the Platonist, morals are an ideal code which immutably binds all human beings, regardless of time or place.

10 · *Unnecessary Vagueness*   (pages 53-64)

A. General:

1. What is the "general direction of use"? Give examples of your own.
2. Explain and illustrate "unmistakable examples."
3. What is a construction-for-convenience?
4. How is there a danger of reification in the use of vague constructions such as *chivalry?*
5. Vague usages are permitted in argument with two qualifications. Which are they? Explain with examples of your own.

B. "Without such vagueness modern advertising would be impossible; it's of the essence."

1. Find two examples.
2. Prove that these usages (your examples) are too vague for "responsible discussion."
3. If the terms were carefully defined, would the claims still be justified by the product? If not, why not?

C. Study carefully the sociological example on p. 63. The comment says that the speaker may be trying to say something interesting. See if you can find a way to clarify his constructions and define or exemplify his terms so as to avoid unnecessary vagueness. Be prepared to discuss this in class. (Note: the first thing to do is to look for unmistakable examples.)

11 · *Over-Precision*   (pages 64-68)

A. True or false?

1. The use of a term is justified only if all cases are clear.
2. The use of a term is justified if it is clear within the context where

it is used and the classification is as well constructed as feasible.

3. Vagueness is, in degree, unavoidable.

4. It never is over-precision to demand a more precise definitior where the meaning of a term in the context in which it is used is not clear

5. All uses of a term should reduce easily.

6. If some uses of a term do not reduce easily, then the term is un necessarily vague.

7. There can be no meaningful discussion of a subject so long as vaguo terms are used.

8. Precise terms are not always essential to a meaningful discussion.

9. Over-precision involves a rejection of serviceable uses of a term on the ground that the term is vague in other contexts.

B. Engage a friend or classmate in a discussion about a current social problem. As the argument warms up, attempt to make your opponent sharpen his constructions, even beyond the point of reasonable precision. When he begins to complain of your hair-splitting tactics, confess to him what you have been doing. Together review the course of the argument and find, if you can, the place at which the constructions were serviceably clear and after which your demand for further definitions and distinctions was obstructionist.

12 · *Word Magic*   (pages 68-75)

A. Give a brief answer to each of the following:

1. Why is a belief in unicorns not necessarily Word Magic?

2. Why is a Platonic reification not necessarily Word Magic?

3. Why is a belief today in the "ether," in "phlogiston," etc., not excusable as a case of mere ignorance, that is, why is it likely to involve Word Magic?

4. Why does a belief in destiny automatically involve Word Magic?

5. What is hypostatization? (Consult a good dictionary.)

B. What distinguishes Word Magic from other forms of reification? Explain with examples of your own.

C. Find or invent several sentences involving Word Magic—that is, serious uses of "destiny," "luck," "inevitable," "bound to," or the like. Try to translate these sentences into sentences containing no names of reifications or constructions not reducible in principle. Are the sentences equivalent to their translations?

PART II. PSYCHOLOGICAL FALLACIES

13 · *Emotive Language*   (pages 77-82)

A. For each sentence given below, note all terms with pronounced connotations, whether favorable or unfavorable, and substitute neutral words for these terms.

Model one:

"Johnson admitted that it was two in the morning" becomes "Johnson stated that it was two in the morning."

(The word "admitted" has an unfavorable connotation that implies some special damaging significance is attached to the assertion that it was two in the morning. The word "stated" is without any prejudicial emotive overtones.)

Model two:

a. "He firmly opposed the tax assessment" or
b. "He made a fuss over the tax assessment" becomes
c. "He objected to the tax assessment."

(The terms in this example have connotations which are (a) favorable, (b) unfavorable, and (c) neutral. Notice other possibilities such as, "He challenged the tax assessment," "He assailed," etc., "He denounced," etc. Some of these expressions have slightly different denotations, but the difference in connotation ranges from strong approval on the part of the speaker to blame or ridicule.)

1. The suspect squandered the funds in Reno.

2. After his long fast, Ghandi was downright skinny.

3. The Secretary of the Treasury is a miser with the people's money.

4. You have no right to drag up scandal from the candidate's remote past.

5. The union is struggling to achieve a pension plan.

6. The suspect invested other people's money at the gaming tables and race tracks.

7. After his long fast, Ghandi was gaunt.

8. The Administration is doing its best to repair the damage done by the last Congress.

9. The Commonwealth will never yield to the demands of blackmailers.

10. The union is trying to force through a pension plan.

11. The Japanese slaughtered the green recruits that the Chinese threw into battle outside Fouchow.

12. There has been considerable uninformed prattle about overloading the ship.

13. Whether or not the accident was his fault, it's dead certain that he was driving a rattletrap.

14. One faction in the management wants to hike up the prices.

15. The candidate's supporters are out garnering in the all-important signatures.

16. The foreman made the men slave overtime.

17. It was a brilliant *coup* of diplomacy.

18. The foreman managed to get the men overtime pay.

19. Before the hearings, the press secretary was effectively gagged.

20. A responsible group of the management concede the possibility of lower profits.

21. The envoy delivered a curt note, flatly rejecting the demands.

22. There is considerable crowing at Jonesberry College over a marginal victory.

23. The noted architect complained that the campus is a hodgepodge of styles.

24. It took courage to stand up to them.

25. Wherever a problem has a solution some man of vision will at last see it.

B. Advertisements often rely on extravagantly emotive language to create a demand for products. Find at least five examples in current newspapers or magazines. Here are a few specimens: "Friendly Handshake Tiregrip," "Smartly Different Luggage," "Zephyr Creme Rose Soap," "Angel Baby Tydies, the best in children's underwear."

C. Underline the words or phrases in the following quotations which carry strongly emotive meanings. Explain the emotive effect of each term and of the quotation as a whole.

1. "For the benefit of those representatives who have not been here before this year, it may be useful to explain that the item before the General Assembly is that hardy perennial called the 'Soviet Item.' It is purely a propaganda proposition, not introduced with a serious purpose of serious action, but solely as a peg on which to hang a number of speeches with view to getting them into the press of the world. This is considered by some to be very clever politics. Others, among whom the present speaker wishes to be included, consider it an inadequate response to the challenge of the hour."

Speech by Mr. Lodge (USA) to the U. N. General Assembly, 461st Plenary Meeting, 30 November 1953.

2. "The war-mongering character of all this flood of propaganda in the United States is admitted even by the American Press. Such provocative and slanderous aims clearly inspired today's speech by the United States representative, consisting only of impudent slander against the Soviet Union, to answer which would be beneath our dignity. The heroic epic of Stalingrad is impervious to libel. The Soviet people in the battles at Stalingrad saved the world from the fascist plague and that great victory which decided the fate of the world is remembered with recognition and gratitude by all humanity. Only men dead to all shame could try to cast aspersions on the shining memory of the heroes of that battle."

Speech by Mr. Baranovsky (Ukrainian SSR) to the U. N. General Assembly, 461st Plenary Meeting, 30 November 1953.

D. In the following passage, the first paragraph of Melville's *Moby Dick*, note the use of words and phrases to express attitudes. Artistry in the control of connotation in language is indispensable to literature, and no one can, without long practice, expect to master literary effects in his own style. But one can make a beginning by observing such touches as, "and see the watery part of the world" (for "see the oceans"), and "whenever it is a damp, drizzly November in my soul" (for "whenever I am ʹlepressed").

> *Directions.* a. Pick out several literary usages in the following passage and describe their function.
>
> b. Find *two* prose passages of literary merit and report briefly on the emotive language employed in them.

Call me Ishmael. Some years ago—never mind how long precisely —having little or no money in my purse, and nothing particular to interest me on shore, I thought I would sail about a little and see the watery parts of the world. It is a way I have of driving off the spleen and regulating the circulation. Whenever I find myself growing grim about the mouth; whenever it is a damp drizzly November in my soul; whenever I find myself involuntarily pausing before coffin warehouses, and bringing up the rear of every funeral I meet; and especially whenever my hypos get such an upper hand of me, that it requires a strong moral principle to prevent me from deliberately stepping into the street, and methodically knocking people's hats off—then, I account it high time to get to sea as soon as I can. This is my substitute for pistol and ball. With a philosophical flourish Cato throws himself upon his sword; I quietly take to the ship. There is nothing surprising in this. If they but knew it, almost all men in their degree, some time or other, cherish very nearly the same feelings towards the ocean with me.

Melville, *Moby Dick*

14 · *Ceremony or Setting*   (pages 82-83)

A. Though setting is always irrelevant to argument, its practical contributions to persuasion account for its general use. Note the effects sought through setting in each of the situations described below:

1. A young man seeking a job as a bookkeeper holds an interview with a prospective employer. Before appearing for the interview, he is careful to put on a suit with a press and to have his hair cut.

2. A British judge wears a wig and a black gown. A bailiff announces his arrival, and all must stand when he enters or leaves the courtroom.

3. A political candidate is asked to speak at a clambake. Although it does not happen to be convenient for him to do so, he goes to some

trouble to appear in a sweater and other outdoor clothing similar to that
worn by the group.

Cite from your own experience or reading three or four examples
similar to those given above.

B. Cite one or more instances from your own experience where you
observed an inappropriate setting which was a practical hindrance to
effective argument.

15 · *Appeal to Authority*   (pages 84-89)

A. True or false?

1. A source of information is personally reliable if it will render an
honest judgment, unswayed by bias, and based upon conscientious investigation.

2. It is proper for a speaker in argument to offer as an authority any
source which he knows to be technically qualified even though not
personally reliable.

3. An authority is personally reliable in the same way that anybody
else is.

4. The best indication that an authority is technically qualified as an
expert is the wide use of that source by laymen.

5. No person can be an authority in more than one field.

6. A conflict between authorities usually indicates that human understanding of the matter in question has not reached a high level of
certainty.

7. A layman should accept as provisionally true whatever is asserted
by a competent authority speaking within his special field.

8. Expert opinion is most satisfactory when applied to technical
questions which can be reduced to accurate evaluation by human beings.

9. Where a question cannot be reduced to accurate evaluation, it is
not useful to consider so-called authorities in the field.

10. All authority becomes obsolete after a few years.

11. Things which have been asserted by the really great men of
history should be accepted as the opinion of authority.

12. An authority is identified if his name is known.

B. Cite an authority who satisfies all five conditions required before a
source should be accepted as technically qualified.

C. Is it always feasible to establish whether or not a source satisfies all
the five conditions? Illustrate your answer with an example.

D. Can you add to the kinds of practical difficulties mentioned in the
text which are often encountered when trying to determine whether or
not a source is technically qualified?

16 · *Appeal to Tradition or Faith*   (pages 89-92)

A. Some of the following appeals are justifiable reference to tradition, others confusions of the issue. In each case, argue whether the appeal is justified or not.

1. It is proposed to tear down Sheridan Hall, a college building erected immediately after the Civil War. A memorandum is read to the Board of Governors at a meeting called to consider the problem:

"We, the undersigned, favor the retention of Sheridan Hall as a monument deserving a rightful place in the history of American architecture and in the traditions of the college. We consider that its importance in these respects overbalances any inconveniences which the Hall may possess when compared to the facilities of a new building."

(*Hint:* It is proper to point out the value of maintaining a tradition where the action involved would destroy this value. Of course, those supporting the tradition must show that it has a value, and argue that this value exceeds any disadvantages incurred in preserving it.)

2. A proposal is made to transfer jurisdiction over matters of marriage and divorce from the states to the federal government. Mr. Fairwell addresses a meeting, saying:

"This field has been governed by state laws since the founding of our country; the constitution assures us that the regulation of these matters close to the lives of us all shall be reserved to the states and to the people. Therefore, we should resist this encroachment of the federal authority."

(*Hint:* The question at issue is, should the tradition be changed? This question is not answered by a mere repeating of the tradition without showing that it has value.)

3. "Son, you ought to attend Yellowstone College. I went there and so did your grandfather. It's a family tradition."

4. The annual meeting of stockholders of a large corporation is held at Walden, N. Y. A stockholder attends the annual meeting. He points out that the main office of the company is located in New York City, that the company does a nation-wide business, and that the practice of holding meetings in Walden is inconvenient for the great majority of the stockholders now interested in the company. He concludes his speech by making a motion to designate New York City as the location for future stockholders' meetings. In opposition to the motion, the Chairman of the Board of Directors points out, "As I am sure everyone here knows, this company was founded in Walden as a local business, and stockholders' meetings have been held here throughout all the sixty-three years that the company has operated. I am opposed to changing such a long established practice. Call it sentiment if you will."

5. A proposal calls for reducing the numbers of jurors from twelve to seven for cases of misdemeanors carrying sentences of not over one year. A famous judge writes in opposition to the proposal, "Freedom for the individual is a sacred tradition of our scheme of government. Liberty is of priceless value. We must resist each little chip that cuts it away."

6. A company personnel board is discussing the age limit to be specified for applicants for a certain job. One member of the board argues, "This company has always followed the policy of taking only young men into its labor force. So the younger we set the age limit, the better."

B. Let the student cite (a) a valid appeal to tradition, and (b) an invalid appeal. In each case the student must defend his classification.

17 · *Impressing by Large Numbers*   (pages 92-94)

A. Each of the following contains an attempt to impress by numbers. In some cases the reference to numbers contributes to the argument; in others it has little or no merit. State your reaction to the reference to numbers in each problem. Give your reasons.

1. Advertisement: "Carlson's Weatherstripping outsells all its competitors."

2. Neighbor to a new arrival in town: "I go to Dr. Tweedle, the most popular dentist here. And popularity is a good recommendation."

3. Hardware clerk to a customer: "If you want to paint a wooden boat, I recommend *Newseal No. 1*. It is widely used by yachtsmen in this area."

4. Architect says to a friend: "Everybody's buying stocks now. If you've got any money to invest, you ought to buy some too."

5. Housewife says to neighbor: "I don't know much about the case, but I am impressed by the strong feeling of the public. The governor, the president of the state university, and other leaders have all expressed the opinion that guilt is plain. So I suppose he is guilty."

6. Machinist to his wife: "The lawyers in town have voted 314 to 62 against reelecting old Judge Smith. The vote was taken at a Bar Association meeting. It is a non-partisan election, and both candidates happen to be Republicans. I'll go along on the theory that the members of the bar know who would make the best judge."

7. Overheard on a bus:
"Everybody says it's a good show, so we decided to go tonight."
"Who do you mean by 'everybody'?"
"Why, everybody I've talked to. I haven't heard so many favorable comments about a show for years."

8. Businessman to a rancher: "Phillips got elected county sheriff by the biggest majority in sixty years. I think that's a good sign. The county ought to have some good work out of the sheriff's office for a change."

B. Find two advertisements that owe their appeal to impressing by large numbers.

18 · *Popular Passions*   (pages 94-96)

A. Identify the "popular passion" to which each of the following appeals is addressed.

Model: A speaker addresses his audience, "We favor extending social security. Isn't that the American thing to do? And we are trying to reduce racial discrimination. Isn't that the American thing to do?" etc.

By claiming that various policies represent the "American" way, the speaker seeks to emphasize their desirability. The speech is obviously *ad populum* to some American audience; it would be inconceivable to any other audience.

1. "Let us leave the rarified atmosphere of social planning to those who like to talk about situations being 'normalized,' or submitted to 'indigenous' control. All the situation boils down to is . . ."

2. "The man of common sense is not going to fall for the weird forms which are conjured up and dignified as 'modern sculpture' in these fast moving times. Forms that can't be recognized, torsos with holes in them, vacuous distortions carefully placed on expensive pedestals: the public has the good sense to ignore all the neurotic host of objects that too commonly get admitted to the galleries."

3. "A good job means a union job with fair wages paid, fair standards followed, and fair profits earned. One can be proud to deal with an outfit that cuts no corners."

4. "I'm not a man who had all the advantages, who was sent to prep schools and then to an Ivy League college. I worked my way through college, I did any job and I took every job that I could get. I went to the school of hard knocks, but it paid. So when I say that we ought not to coddle labor as we do these days, then. . . ."

5. "Teachers are people who never got out of school. They don't have to worry about competition, prices, payrolls, strikes, government red tape, and so on. It's a good life in the ivory tower. Schools have their place. But when it's a question of deciding the practical problems of a city planning commission, then we need a man with business experience. You are businessmen and you know what experience is."

B. Find (or construct) and answer arguments based on each of the following popular prejudices.

1. For the self-made man
2. For the little businessman
3. Against monopoly
4. a. For experts
   b. Against "egg heads"

19 · *Damning the Origin*   (pages 97-99)

A. Pointing out the origin of an idea has both its legitimate and its illegitimate uses. Justify this statement.

B. Analyze the following references to origin and point out any ways in which they seem to you justifiable and any ways in which they do not.

1. A state legislator remarks to his secretary: "This bill prescribes the succession of property in the event of a 'common disaster,' that is, in cases where two people—say husband and wife—die at the same time. An insurance company lawyer drafted the bill and the insurance companies seem to want it passed. Well, I am going to find out what their interest is before I vote on it."

2. A businessman says to a friend: "I won't pay any attention to what Jones says about the strike. He's a labor leader, so he couldn't be impartial even if he wanted to."

3. A taxpayer remarks to a friend: "The Socialist Labor Party wants to raise the tax rate. I'm pretty hard to convince when it comes to raising taxes, and when *that* party suggests the raise, then I'm stubborn as a mule."

4. Young man to his wife: "My father was against Proposition 'A' as soon as he heard that the unions were for it, and your dad says that he's for labor and the things that labor wants. So I guess we'll have to read the Proposition and decide for ourselves."

20 · *Personal Attacks*   (pages 99-101)

A. Point out for each of the following personal attacks:
   a. What the basis of the attack is,
   b. How you would answer the attack.

Model: A newspaper has made itself the advocate of a certain slum clearance project. An editorial declares:

> "The man who opposes this slum clearance project is the very arch conservative who has opposed every forward step in this town, particularly every step that might cost the taxpayers money. Today he is financing opposition to this civic improvement."

a. The basis for this personal attack is the supposed popular hostility (see #18) to a demon individual labeled "arch conservative." If one accepts the allegation that this individual represents only the view of saving money for taxpayers and that he is financing opposition to the project, then one will look at the arguments that he advances with the extra care needed in evaluating a biased or unreliable source. Imputing bad motives may arouse suspicion, but motives do not invalidate a position.

b. An answer to the attack would be to point out its nature as vague personal abuse, and to direct attention to the evidence showing the costs and expected benefits of the slum clearance project.

1. A company officer is talking to a colleague: "Archibald Henry DePaugh, playboy of the Board of Directors, who devotes Monday, Wednesday and Friday to fast cars and women—and who thinks he can run his granddaddy's business on Tuesdays and Thursdays! So now we've got to talk him out of opening a branch in Canada."

2. A dismissed teacher charges that the teaching load in the Pleasant-ville School District is actually heavier than reported. At a teachers meeting, the Superintendent of Schools remarks: "Every school district has to expect incidents like this from teachers who have proved them-selves misfits, and who are dissatisfied and uncooperative."

3. A newspaper editorial argues: "The gas bill met with a deserved veto. It was a justifiable rebuke for the arrogance of the Oil Lobby Senator and the high pressure methods which were used to secure its passage. Though no one succeeded in proving corruption, the veto comes as a welcome discouragement to dirty politics, whatever the merits of the bill."

4. A railroad executive comments on a plan for eliminating the need to change trains in Chicago: "Mr. Clearway has got a nice idea about ending the shuttle system for passenger service going through Chicago. It would be a change, that's for sure! Well, I happen to know this fellow Clearway; he's a thwarted subordinate who never got where he wanted to in the engineering world."

5. A teacher addresses a women's club: "Every time there's an international crisis of one sort or another, the hue and cry goes up to do some tinkering with our immigration quotas and admit flocks of refugees. The man who is behind the present maneuver is just the fellow who will be championing the next 'liberal' issue, whatever it may happen to be."

B. A personal attack usually is combined with the fallacies of popular passions (see #18) or of origin (see #19). Show how an argument often mingles a personal attack with one or both of these fallacies.

18, 19, 20 · *Popular Passion, Damning the Origin, and Personal Attacks* (pages 94-101)

A. In your own words distinguish a personal attack from an instance of damning the origin. Make your distinction clear by finding or inventing concrete examples of each.

B. Identify the fallacy or fallacies involved in each of the following:

1. I suppose Mrs. Stevens is all right—if you can stand that type.
2. I heard him. He gave a pompous, over-confident speech. What would you expect from an ex-sergeant in a position of power?
3. He is a "whisky-drinking, poker-playing, evil, old man."

4. I'll not take advice from a city know-it-all.

5. At the very kick-off of this campaign, let me say that if anyone is arrogant enough to use smear tactics against our President, I will meet these tactics with merciless exposure.

6. He hopes to become the head of our local unit on the basis of arduously having sat out the war in Washington, I suppose.

7. Well, so far as *they* are concerned, I say to let the men of Main Street revel in their Babbitry.

8. Opposing military training on this campus is the unenviable privilege of a few misfits and pacifists.

9. The aluminum trust is behind the bill, and that means there's some scheme afoot to subvert the public interest.

10. It's a fine thing for Smith to propose a bypass around this town. He ought to attend to his flower business and let others wrestle with the traffic problem.

11. Yes, yes, we all know Boston is the seat of Culture, leader of Learning, home of Puritanism and moss-back Conservatism.

12. As for Johnson, he has as fine a record of missing the point as any man I know.

21 · *Forestalling Disagreement* (pages 101-102)

A. Arrange the following sentences in order so that the italicized phrases range from mild to strong attempts to forestall disagreement.

1. *No one would seriously doubt that* the next war will end civilization.

2. *Everybody agrees that* the next war will end civilization.

3. *Of course* the next war will end civilization.

4. *Everyone in his right mind knows that* the next war will end civilization.

B. You are undecided whether or not the next war will end civilization. Devise a tactful sentence which would open the problem to discussion after each of the above attempts to preclude disagreement.

C. Underline all terms in the following passage which are used to forestall disagreement. Explain how they are used.

"Surely this group is too experienced to award the *Grand Prix* to an artist who exhibited his first paintings only a year ago. Any well-informed person knows that artistic works are not produced by novices and, obviously, this man is a novice. I think that this painting should receive some award appropriate for the work of a promising beginner, but anyone who has at heart the interest of encouraging the arts will deplore awarding the *Grand Prix* to such an amateur."

D. Make up a tactful answer to the above argument which exposes its nature to third parties in the audience.

22 · *Creating Misgivings*   (pages 102-104)

A. Analyze and answer each of the following attempts to create misgivings:

1. So McCall wants to put through the new tunnel to drain the silver mines around Leadville. Well, I wonder what's in it for him.

2. Yes, I know the court acquitted John of the embezzlement charge. Courts acquit lots of people, you know, but you can bet the J. K. Smith Co. won't be hiring him if I have anything to say about it.

3. The British have come up with a new plan for policing the area jointly with the USA. It's just a maneuver to get us involved in their colonialism. As ever, perfidious Albion.

4. I don't know what the affair that George got into was all about. At any rate, "Where there's smoke there's fire," and I'll not have my daughter going out with him.

5. They say Karl used to go with a pretty radical set when he lived in Los Angeles. I wonder if he didn't pick up some pinko ideas.

B. How can one try to insulate oneself from misgivings spread about by malicious or ignorant persons? Why is it hard to be wholly successful in disregarding unsupported gossip?

23, 24, 25, 26 · *Self-righteousness, Finding the "Good" Reason, Wishful Thinking, Special Pleading*   (pages 104-109)

A. True or false?

1. Good motives are the best guarantee of truth.

2. "Finding the 'good' reason" commonly employs faulty premises to reach the desired result.

3. An argument will be special pleading if it serves the interests of the party advancing it.

4. Standing for one proposal and against another, when both are governed by the same principles, is a mark of special pleading.

5. In wishful thinking there is a failure to look at the evidence fairly.

6. The avoidance of rationalization is mainly a psychological matter.

7. Where one suspects special pleading, the only safe thing to do is to disregard the argument.

8. The fact that most human conduct springs from complex motives makes it easy to offer "good" reasons for one's actions.

B. You suspect rationalization in the situation given below. For each "example," provide a "comment" describing and naming the rationalization stratagem involved.

1. "John won't fail. After giving so much time and effort to the association, I'm sure he deserves a better reward than that."

2. Peter has often expressed belief in the following ideas: (a) Prisons should rehabilitate their inmates so far as possible. (b) Prisoners should perform useful work in order to reduce the cost of prisons to taxpayers. (c) Assigning useful occupations to prisoners contributes to their rehabilitation. (d) Enforced idleness is demoralizing. Faced with a proposal to have the local prison supply furniture to all state institutions, Peter writes his state senator: "As one of your constituents who has been a supplier of furniture to several institutions, I wish to express my opposition to Senate Bill 321, which provides for making furniture with prison labor. This is unfair competition."

3. "The United States and Russia are going to get along together because for them to disagree would open the way for World War III." (This one was asserted by millions during and for some time after World War II.)

4. Harry to a friend: "I got fired by that outfit. Instead of doing any work down there, all they do is play office politics."

5. "The reason the management must reject any increase in wages at this time is nothing less than a genuine concern for the well-being of the whole country. Any increase would have to be passed on to the consumer in the form of higher prices. This in turn would increase inflationary pressures, and the whole nation would suffer, including labor."

6. A union negotiator: "The company has had the two most prosperous years in its history. This should make the management willingly grant the wage increase requested. It is only fair to share the general prosperity with the labor which has made those profits possible." On another occasion, the negotiator is dealing with a company which has not been making money. "The wage increase proposed is slight and is in line with the pay scales in effect elsewhere in the industry. I realize that the corporation barely broke even last year. Wages are not profits; they are the laborer's reward for working and they determine his standard of living— how he and his family will eat. Declining profits are not a reason for refusing a wage demand."

C. Cite an instance of rationalization from your own personal experience. Name the kind involved and show how it fits into this class.

27 · *Lip Service*   (pages 109-111)

A. 1. Everybody on occasion preaches what he does not practice. Explain why this is so in terms of the relation of the individual to his culture.

2. If actions speak louder than words, why does lip service so often go undetected?

B. A politician has just given a speech advocating the following:
   a. a balanced budget
   b. better schools

c. racial equality

d. lower taxes.

You are impressed, but you do not want to be a victim of lip service. How would you endeavor to check?

C. Lip service generally arises because the individual's personal conviction or self-interest is opposed to some cultural norm. Point out one instance of lip service arising from each of these sources.

28 · *Apriorism*   (pages 111-115)

A. Write a "comment" to each of the following "examples," showing the operation of apriorism in them.

1. A small child refuses to hang his stocking at Christmas time, as he has just found out there is no Santa Claus.

2. A wife tells her husband to wear his raincoat to work as the papers predict rain. The man leaves his coat behind, arguing that the rainy season isn't due for two months.

3. A man refuses to read a new book on the grounds that it is a novel. He disapproves, he says, of novels because they are fiction and prefers to read history and biography. "Life is stranger than fiction, so I don't care how good the book is."

4. An elderly woman refuses the advice of her attorney to invest the $10,000 she has stored in a safety deposit box. The attorney argues that because of the inflation idle money actually decreases and melts away: that is, it loses some of its purchasing power. The woman replies, "A penny saved is a penny earned. I am going to save that money."

5. A club votes against engaging a noted physicist to address them. The vote is taken after an argument offered by the chairman to the effect that all the interesting developments of contemporary physics are classified for security reasons. "All we could expect from this speaker is broad generalizations about new discoveries, enough to whet our curiosity without satisfying it."

B. Reread #15, 16. Show by examples how some appeals to authority or dogma are apriorist in their cast of mind.

29 · *Personification*   (pages 115-117)

A. Do you yourself have, or do you know someone else who has, a favorite personification? Explain. Could this personification conceivably lead to a false belief and thus, perhaps, affect an argument?

Model: Though Peter has not, of course, believed in Santa Claus since he was a small child, he likes to think of Santa Claus as a symbol of the Christmas spirit, the embodiment of generosity and good feeling. He taught his own children never to pass a street-corner Santa without tossing money into the pot.

The man in a fake white beard and red costume, ringing a bell on the street corner is *not* the Santa Claus who, in Peter's fancy, is the symbol of the Christmas Spirit. Peter would have done better to teach his children to investigate appeals to charity. They should "throw their money into the pot" of worthy causes only, without regard to Christmas trappings.

B. Reread "reification" (pp. 41-49). Explain how reification is related to personification.

30 · *Cultural Bias*   (pages 117-119)

A. If you have ever traveled to a distant region or foreign country, recount the social customs that struck you as strange. Do these different customs seem to you more "sensible" or less so than the ones you were used to? Why?

B. What has the cultural bias got to do with argument? How does it lead to fallacy? (Remember that fallacy occurs *in argument*.)

31 · *The Gambler's Mistake*   (pages 119-120)

A. The examples in the text are not cast precisely into the form of argument. Rewrite them into argumentative situations, making such changes as you choose.

B. The text says that the failure to realize how a slight possibility of something happening is still a possibility is a sort of "failure of the imagination." The example given concerns military planning. Can you think of an instance from ordinary life where judgment refused to take account of the unexpected? For instance, urged to draw up his will, Peter replies, "Oh please. Tomorrow will be time enough for that!"

32 · *Humor and Ridicule*   (pages 122-124)

A. From your own experience, describe an instance where this fallacy was used in a discussion.

1. Do you consider that the use of the fallacy was effective in putting over the contention of the party employing it? Why?

2. State how the fallacy could have been countered by the party against whom it was employed.

B. Do you think that ridicule or humor is ever justified in argument? If you do, specify the kind of case you have in mind. If you do not, give your reasons.

33 · *Demand for Special Consideration* (page 124)

A. Write your own comments for the two examples in the text, bringing out in detail the fact that these appeals to pathetic circumstances are irrelevant to the arguments.

B. Cite one such appeal from your own experience.

34 · *Clamorous Insistence on Irrelevancies* (pages 124-125)

A. The text characterized this fallacy as "the patron saint of those being overwhelmed in argument." Why so?

B. How many red herrings do you find in Hitler's Düsseldorf speech? (See pages 121-122.)

C. In the broadest sense, all fallacies are also irrelevancies: one cannot imagine a relevant fallacy. Those fallacies classed under the heading *Diversions* often are clear-cut instances of obfuscating argument by introducing irrelevant material. Glance through the examples given for the three diversions discussed so far and point out those which are also clear instances of irrelevancy. (See pages 121-125.)

35 · *Pointing to Another Wrong* (pages 126-128)

A. "Two wrongs don't make a right," affirms the popular adage. Cite an instance where you have encountered this adage, or, if you cannot recall such a case, make one up where you would use the adage to counter an argument.

B. Despite the idea that one wrong does not justify another, there are situations where a feeling of "it's the rule of the game" or "everybody is doing it" does seem to mitigate action which one should otherwise denounce. For instance, where there is a large-scale black market, those who try conscientiously to limit their purchases of the necessities of life to rationed goods, whose supply has been syphoned off by the black market, may subject themselves and their families to intolerable privation. In such cases, does pointing to widespread practice justify the wrong? In your answer, consider carefully the meanings you give to "situation," "right," and "wrong."

C. Answer the arguments advanced below:

1. Your son brings home a piece of wood from a house under construction. You order him to take it back. "I don't see why I have to. Everybody helps himself," protests your son.

2. You suggest to a friend that the violence of crime comics is a factor conducive to juvenile delinquency. "Well," remarks the friend, "many fairy tales abound in violence and lurid scenes of horror. So if you're going to condemn crime comics, you'll have to take a stand against fairy tales, too."

3. You are a company official discussing pay increases for some of the employees. You oppose giving a raise to a certain salesman on the ground that he is not a hard worker. Irritated, one of your colleagues chides you, "Look who's talking! If you think that you rate as one of the hard workers of this office, then you're the only one with *that* delusion. I wouldn't have the nerve to argue against this little pay raise, if I were you."

36 · *The Wicked Alternative* (pages 128-129)

A. Find two positions, A and B, so related that an attack on A constitutes legitimate support for B. (*Hint:* the two positions will have to be true opposites, for example, political indifference *vs.* active participation in civic affairs.)

B. Construct an answer to this argument: "Memorized material is soon forgotten. The ineffectiveness of compelling students to remember quantities of particular events, rules, or formulas shows that progressive education is the method which schools should adopt."

C. Attacking a straw man can be effective with an unobservant audience. Explain how this device works, and state how you would rebut it.

37 · *Nothing but Objections* (pages 129-131)

A. Raising objections to a proposal can hardly be called a fallacy. What, then, is the fallacy of *Nothing But Objections?*

B. What makes a "decision by default" a special case of this fallacy?

C. When the Constitution of the United States was submitted to the states for ratification, so many objections were urged against it that several states ratified by the slimmest of majorities and two states rejected the plan, entering the Union only after Washington's inauguration. If you had favored the plan, how would you have argued to prevent the proposal from being smothered by objections?

D. The Treaty of Versailles, including the League of Nations Covenant, was not ratified by the United States Senate. There were many objections, particularly that membership in the League would involve the United States in foreign entanglements. Give an answer designed to prevent objections from being over emphasized. You may have the benefit of hindsight.

38 · *Impossible Conditions*   (pages 131-132)

A. It is one thing to point out ideals toward which men should strive
and quite another to argue that action should wait upon the development of more perfect men. Does this mean that ideals should not be
discussed when deciding upon a practical course of action? Defend
your answer.

B. The conclusion that the solution of a problem lies in reform of the
human heart is probably the most pessimistic of all possible conclusions.
Why so?

C. Answer this call to perfection: Disarmament pacts, arbitration treaties,
world organizations of various sorts are well intended illusions . . .
"Since war begins in the minds of men, it is in the minds of men that
the defenses of peace must be constructed." So says the UNESCO constitution itself. We must go to the heart of the problem; we must educate man in ways of peace.

39 · *Abandonment of Discussion*   (pages 132-133)

A. Why is abandonment of discussion not always obvious?

B. Lawyers and newspaper reporters often become adept at identifying
and turning back attempts to choke off or abandon discussion. Can you
cite an instance? How was the discussion put back on the track?

C. Imagine that you were engaged in the following dialogue:

Yourself: Civil service examinations should be given without allowing preferences to veterans or any other group. Giving special advantages to some people can only result in a less competent public service,
both by qualifying individuals who otherwise would not qualify and
by deterring others from applying for jobs where they must compete
against those receiving artificial preferences.

Peter: I'd be ashamed to make the proposal that you are making.
Why, many a veteran has served his country in ways that money
couldn't pay for—and *you* don't want to concede a thing for all that!
It's the most ungenerous suggestion I've heard for a long time.

Unwisely, perhaps, you do not want to have discussion choked off
on these terms. How do you answer Peter?

PART III. LOGICAL FALLACIES

Introduction (pages 134-142)

A. Which of the following sentences are *logically* true?

  1. Food nourishes.

  2. Tomatoes are a food.

  3. Tomatoes contain vitamin C.

  4. If mangoes are a food, then they are edible.

  5. One man's food is another man's poison.

  6. Your brother or sister is your sibling.

  7. Your brother is your male sibling.

  8. Not all people have siblings.

  9. You either have siblings or are an only child.

  10. Every mortician (if you look closely) will turn out to be an undertaker.

  11. If a man is called a "mortician," he is an undertaker; Peter is called a "mortician," so Peter is an undertaker.

  12. By "mortician," we simply mean "undertaker."

  13. Either he is on time, or he's late.

  14. Either he is punctual or he is not.

  15. "To be punctual" means in English "to be on time."

  16. "Punctual" means "on time"; my friend is never on time, so therefore, by definition, he is never punctual.

  17. Mathematical proofs are arguments without disagreement.

  18. In ordinary usage "argument" suggests disagreement.

  19. Premises are either true or not.

  20. If an argument is valid, then by definition of "valid" the conclusion follows from the premises.

B. Which of the following arguments are valid?

  1. If you wish hard enough, you always get your wish. You did not get your wish; so you did not wish hard enough.

  2. If I wish hard enough, I will get my wish. But I am not wishing hard enough; so I won't get my wish.

  3. All tulips grow from bulbs
    All begonias grow from bulbs
    So all begonias are tulips.

  4. All grass plants are seed plants
    All seed plants are weeds
    So all grass plants are weeds.

40 · *The Undistributed Middle Term*   (pages 142-147)

A. Some of the following syllogisms are not valid. Which are they? (List by number.)

1. All men are capable of charity
   All dictators are men
   So all dictators are capable of charity.

2. No psychotics are rational
   All dictators are psychotic
   So no dictators are rational.

3. All undertakers are solemn
   Some cheerful persons are undertakers
   So some cheerful persons are solemn.

4. No men are infallible
   Some communists are men
   So some communists are not infallible.

5. Foresight always begins right in the home
   True charity is a matter of foresight
   So true charity begins at home.

6. No jealous man is a trusting individual
   Some trusting people get a rude surprise
   So some jealous men avoid (do not get) a rude surprise.

7. A well-trained child is self-sufficient
   Some well-trained children are not happy
   So some happy children are not self-sufficient.

8. No alcoholic is reliable
   Some completely honest men are alcoholics
   So some completely honest men are not reliable.

9. All Protestants believe in interpreting the Bible themselves
   Some Anglicans do not believe this
   So some Anglicans are not Protestants.

10. All important cities today are vulnerable to air attack
    The cities of Western Europe are especially vulnerable
    So the cities of Western Europe are especially important.

11. Jason is not an important city
    Even Jason is not safe
    So no city is really safe.

12. All American cities are entirely safe from air attack
    West Berlin is an American city
    So West Berlin is safe from air attack.

13. No American city is safe
    Paris, anyhow, is not an American city
    So Paris is safe.

14. All of us ought to live where we are safe
    There is no place that is really safe
    So there is no place where we *ought* to live.

B. Specify the rules violated by the invalid syllogisms above.

C. Regard the premises in the above syllogisms as instructions and show the relations among the classes by drawing circles.

41 · *Suppressed Quantification*   (pages 147-148)

A. Supply the quantifying word ("all," "no," "some," etc.) needed to make sound arguments of the following:

1. If it's true, as you say, that GI's don't like their officers, then they don't like discipline, because that's what officers represent—discipline.

(Try "some GI's." Is it necessary in making a syllogism of this argument to state "All officers represent discipline"? Does it follow that some GI's don't cotton to all—or only some—representatives of discipline?)

2. American men often go overboard on their hobbies. American men spend too much money on what they go overboard on. So it's not surprising that they spend up to half their income (*i.e.* too much money) on their hobbies.

(The first sentence *is* quantified. For practical purposes here "some" can substitute for "often.")

3. Logical exercises are for the birds, and what's for the birds is not for yours truly. These exercises are not for me.

B. Construct three sound arguments using "some" in one of the premises.

42 · *False Conversion of Propositions*   (pages 149-152)

A. Convert correctly the following propositions.

Note: For purposes of conversion treat "most," "many," etc. as "some," and translate propositions with "always," "often," etc., as if quantified in the traditional way. Thus, "The good always die young" becomes "All the good die young." "The good often die happy" becomes "Some of the good die happy." "Everybody in the theater was laughing" becomes "All people in the theater were laughing."

1. All bakeries use preservatives.
2. No cigarette filters cut out the dangerous tars.
3. Some fungus is edible.
4. Some fungus is not edible.
5. Fungus is sometimes not unappetizing.
6. Preservatives usually contain dangerous chemicals.

7. Many laws regulate traffic.
8. Highway engineering regulates some traffic.
9. Penalties are imposed by most traffic laws.
10. Everybody is an exception.
11. Americans occasionally make enthusiastic travelers.
12. The globe-trotters of the last century were usually British.
13. Not all Americans can afford to fly.
14. Nobody likes to stay home.
15. Few are free to travel.
16. Only considerate travelers are ambassadors of good will.
17. Everybody wants better schools.
18. Not everybody is willing to pay the higher tax rates.
19. There are those who actually like commercials.
20. Everybody cannot always have everything the way he wants it.

B. Choose five of your conversions of the above propositions and, using each as a *premise*, construct a valid syllogism.

C. Proceed as above and use each sentence as the *conclusion* of a valid syllogism.

43 · *Non Sequitur*   (pages 152-154)

A. An enthymeme is an argument with a step left out, which may be premise or conclusion (see page 3). The difference between an enthymeme and a *non sequitur* is one of degree. If many steps are omitted or if it is difficult to see just what bridge could be built reasonably between the grounds and the consequence, then the argument may be fairly judged a *non sequitur*. In the following truncated arguments the missing propositions are fairly obvious. Supply the missing premises in each of the following enthymemes:

1. He is a fool, so he will soon be parted from his money.
2. Fools and their money are soon parted. He will be soon parted from his.
3. They did not learn from their mothers, so they don't know their prayers.
4. The project will be wasteful since it is conceived in haste.
5. Why does he love company? Because he's miserable, that's why.
6. As it is a hot day, it is a day for watering the fuchsias.
7. The "price" of money is its relative purchasing power. Its price determines the cost of living.
8. Teachers are always on fixed salary. So they are among the first victims of inflation.
9. This is a real inflation, so nobody prospers.
10. All those who prefer quick profits are short sighted. Some business men do not prefer quick profits.

B. Supply the parts needed to complete the following arguments:

1. All those who prefer quick profits are short sighted. But some business men are not short sighted.

2. TV is a popular art, so it is commercialized.

3. All highbrows resent reasonable advertising. No TV fan resents it.

4. Only those who buy any old thing like insistent advertising. Few TV fans buy any old thing.

5. All Martian traders speak Pidgeon Phnu, which is a dialect of Saturnian.

6. All musicians get seasick. People who get seasick always lack a sense of humor.

7. Only people with a sense of humor are musicians. Few drummers have a sense of humor.

8. None of the children can tell the difference. Those who read terror comics can always tell the difference.

9. Magic spells are seldom effective in Wales. All heartfelt yearnings are effective in Wales.

10. No blood from a turnip!

C. Which of the following are *non sequiturs?* Which enthymemes?

1. A proper suit bid shows at least thirteen points. So I had confidence in my partner.

2. He always comes on time. He must have had an accident.

3. The Knights Templar fought the Saracens. They found this profitable. Therefore, their motives were not religious, but economic.

4. I am a turnip, so you can't get blood from me.

5. Wise shoppers buy name brands. They like to know what they are buying. So they like the purple and orange stripes of Zebra Cream Soap.

6. Student themes sometimes jump to conclusions without preparation either in logic or in fact. This is a consequence of being scatterbrained.

7. I am a man like any other. I, too, shall some day die.

8. The Supreme Court is trying to upset the balance of government functions because it doesn't care whether or not Congress approves of its decisions.

9. There are eighteen different pretenders to the vacant thrones of Europe. Which goes to show that unemployment is here to stay.

10. Brand names guarantee quality. So Zebra Cream Soap is amongst the products of a guaranteed quality.

44 · *Trouble with Conditionals and Alternatives*
(pages 154-158)

A. Determine which of the following arguments or enthymemes are valid.

1. If I write tomorrow, I ought to get an answer by the first. But I can't write for a couple of days. So I won't get an answer by the first.

2. Nobody knows the trouble I'm in, or they'd take it easy—which they don't. So nobody, I say, knows the trouble I'm in.

3. Peter: Either I have a head for logic, or this test is a threat.

Instructor: But the test is no threat to you.

Peter: I see. I have a head for logic.

4. If you don't have a head for logic, the test is a threat. The test isn't a threat to anybody here.

5. If you are unwilling to establish credit, you will never get a good credit rating. And you seem unwilling to establish credit.

6. Paul: Either establish your credit or don't expect a good credit rating.

Peter: Well, I don't expect a good credit rating.

7. If there is air on Mars, there can be vegetation. There is vegetation on Mars. There must be air.

8. If there is vegetation on Mars, there must be an atmosphere. There is vegetation, so there is an atmosphere.

9. You can either read or listen to music. Oh, I see you are reading, so you won't be listening to music.

10. At this time I always either read or listen to music. I am not listening to music, so I will be reading.

B. In two steps draw a valid inference from each of the following propositions.

1. If you expect help, you have to pay for it.

2. If you aren't ready, I won't wait.

3. If we don't take the pills, we may get malaria.

4. If we don't pay the bribe, they won't help us.

5. If one brings water to 100° C. at sea-level pressure, the water will boil.

6. Either expect no help, or be ready to pay for it.

7. You be ready, or you'll find I won't wait.

8. Don't bring water to 100° C. at sea-level pressure, or don't be surprised when it boils.

9. Take the pills, or you may get malaria.

10. Pay the bribe, or they won't help us.

45 · *Ambiguous Terms*   (pages 158-162)

A. Find or invent an example of each of the four kinds of ambiguous terms discussed in the text. Show in each case how to eliminate the ambiguity. Note how what may before have seemed interesting or plausible now becomes flat or trivial.

Model: Peter is trying to persuade Paul to address the Dahlia Growers Association of Pebbleville. "What do you mean you can't make a speech? You have a lot to communicate about the growing of dahlias, from the 12-foot tree variety to the Unwin dwarfs. Anybody who has something to communicate can tell his friends about it. Anybody can make a speech, Peter!"

This is an ambiguity of the fourth variety, exploiting a shift in meaning between "speech" in two of the senses of that word mentioned on p. 160. Paul is not denying that he can "tell" about the growing of dahlias to his friends; he apparently is simply saying that he cannot "make a speech."

B. Show by an example how a syllogism containing a shift between the ambiguous senses of a word is an instance of violation of the rule against four terms. (See p. 145.)

46, 47, 48 · *Amphibole, Ambiguous Accent, Ambiguous Punctuation and Word Order* (pages 162-165)

A. Look up "oracles" in a book of reference and find example of amphibole (#46). While you are at it, also find examples of the first type of ambiguous terms (#45, see pp. 159-160).

B. Find or make up a short eulogy. Show how changes of inflection could turn the passage into sarcasm. Indicate the changes by underscoring or by notes in the margin.

C. Look through a recent piece of your own writing (letter, theme, etc.) and see if a more careful ordering of some elements would not make for greater clarity. Would more explicit punctuation help?

Model: "The opposition don't appreciate the difficulties of government. How could they? They are very many, I think, some of them are made by the opposition."

Does the second "they" refer to the opposition or to the difficulties? Does "I think" go with "They are very many"? Probably not. Rewritten this all becomes, "The opposition don't appreciate the difficulties of the government. These difficulties are very many. I think some of them are made by the opposition."

49, 50, 51 · *Circular Definitions and Question Begging, Misuse of Etymology, Idiosyncratic Language* (pages 165-170)

A. Consult books of reference or logic books and look up circular definitions and question begging. Try to recast the examples you find in a way to eliminate circularity. Does the fault seem a matter of carelessness or is it essential to whatever effectiveness the arguments might seem to have for the unwary?

B. In the same way look up the fallacy of etymology. Do the examples need the etymologies for plausibility?

C. Find instances of the fallacy of idiosyncratic language in George Orwell's *1984*. What seems to you to be the motive behind the appropriation of words such as "peace," "democracy" by movements which do not pursue these goals in practice?

Review Exercises for Part III   (pages 134-172)

A. Construct valid arguments to prove the following conclusions. You may use either the syllogism or the other forms of valid arguments given in the text.

> *Model:* Conclusion: So some courageous men are subject to panic.
>
> Argument: All men who lack discipline are subject to panic. Some courageous men lack discipline.
>
> Or: Either all courageous men are unflinching or some courageous men are subject to panic. But not all courageous men are unflinching.

1. All wrong doing is involuntary. (Or: No wrong doing is voluntary.)
2. Certain people better watch out.
3. All haste makes waste.
4. All Frenchmen are Protestants.
5. No baboons are marshmallows.
6. Some zeugmas are lampoons.
7. Some lampoons are not zeugmas.
8. Cousins are natural enemies.
9. No raw fish is edible.
10. Some raw fish is edible.

B. Employ the following sentences in valid arguments, either as premises or conclusions.

1. All pennies saved are pennies earned.
2. No friend is like an old friend.
3. Some haste makes waste.
4. Some savage beasts are not unaffected by music.
5. All roads lead to Rome.
6. Many mansions are in my Father's house.
7. Strathors are seldom star-happy.
8. Few eggs are ovoid.
9. Only savages understand nature.
10. Reprieves never arrive on time.

C. Translate the following alternatives into conditionals and derive valid conclusions from them.

1. Either you are able to do these exercises, or you are not well prepared.

2. Either you are not able to do some of these exercises or you are really able to do them all.

3. Either today is not Tuesday, or it is the third day of the week.
4. They are either friendly or on to us.
5. Men must work or their women must weep.

C. Translate the following conditionals into alternatives and derive valid conclusions from them.

1. If he went to sleep on Tuesday and slept twenty-four hours, then he woke up on Wednesday.
2. If any man gets tired enough, he can sleep the clock around.
3. If the expression "1400 hours" means "2 P.M.," then "0200 hours" must mean "2 A.M."
4. When I am sick, I sleep all the time.
5. If you are able to do some of these exercises, you are really able to do them all.

Appendix

SOME LOGICAL PARADOXES

This discussion is appended for those who might have an interest in modern logic. It is not generally known that some of the apparent paradoxes of material implication also occur in the ordinary language, where they are used for special effects.

The logical relations between sentences hold even when the sentences are relevant to one another only in the largest sense, their truth values. Thus the usual interpretations in logic of the terms "or," "if," and the like, has no regard for the content of the sentences related by them, but considers only whether or not the sentences are true. Persons untrained in logic find some of the examples used by logicians very paradoxical: "Today is Tuesday, or Truman is President. But Truman is not President, so today is Tuesday." This is a perfectly valid inference, and every Tuesday since the inauguration of Eisenhower, it has yielded a true conclusion. The mutual irrelevancy of the two sentences leads to a feeling that it is not very good reasoning to decide the day of the week on the grounds that somebody is not President.

The logician is not interested in the grounds of belief in so far as they involve content other than truth value. His grounds for affirming or denying a conclusion are the relations obtaining among true or false sentences when they are combined according to exactly determined operations. An even more striking instance of this attitude results from what is called "material implication." This is a rule of interpretation which takes every complex sentence of the form "if a, then b" to be syntactically equivalent to any compound sentence of the form "not-a, or b." It is evident that in all cases in common speech, in fact in all cases whatever, where the conditional is true, the corresponding alternative is also true. "If it rains, the streets are wet" has the same truth value as "It does not rain, or the streets are wet."

Rule: If a, then b is equivalent to Not a, or b.

Yet one feels that a compound sentence expresses a weaker relationship than a complex sentence. In this case they have the same truth values, of course, but in an accidental sort of way. The conditional seems to *show* a relationship, to *express* a tighter, more essential connection between the two facts. And when one considers some of the consequences of the equivalence that Bertrand Russell and other logicians

212

have explored, one finds them shocking to common sense. A few examples will illustrate this feeling of paradox.

An equivalence, of course, works both ways. Not *a*, or *b* is equivalent to If *a*, then *b*: "Red is not a primary color, or the earth revolves around the sun." The first sentence is false, the second true, and thus the compound sentence, as a whole, is true. This is already bad enough, though we are familiar with this use of "or," to show that one side or the other must be true. But when we translate into the conditional, according to the rule, we get "If red is a primary color, then the earth revolves around the sun." This seems to suggest that a truth about colors is grounds for the astronomical truth. But the point here is that *any* true sentence can be the consequence of *any* other true sentence, in this interpretation.

Suppose we put a true sentence on each side of the alternative. "Arsenic disagrees with me, or the moon is a heavenly body." We are also familiar with the use of "or" which allows both sides to be true: "I'll phone or drop in to see you" remains true if I do both, though, of course, I must do one or the other. Now the arsenic-and-moon example translates to "If arsenic agrees with me, then the moon is a heavenly body." (Note: "not disagrees" equals "agrees.") As this case is entirely representative, we can say that *any* false sentence implies *any* true sentence. Yet a known false sentence is strange grounds for believing a true sentence, even one surely known to be true.

So far we have seen that any sentence, true cr false, is "grounds" for affirming any true sentence. What of false sentences? We already know that any false sentence implies any true sentence. It now develops that any false sentence also implies any other false sentence. To take an example, "If Carroll is a figment of the Red King's dream, then Brooklyn is the capital of Ethiopia." This is equivalent by the rule to "Carroll is not a figment of the Red King's dream, or Brooklyn is the capital of Ethiopia," perfectly true, since the first member is true.

These paradoxical results of the material interpretation of If *a*, then *b* as Not *a*, or *b* are often summarized as follows: a true sentence is implied by any sentence, true or false; a false sentence implies any sentence, true or false.

The feeling of "paradox" arises from two facts of common usage. The first has already been mentioned, that language characteristically employs conditionals to express general principles. This is to say that the conditionals are themselves general principles or are particular applications of them. Take the case "If $7 = 3 + 2$, then $7 = 2 + 3$." Not bad; though the hypothesis is false, the conditional does express a general principle about the meaning of "=" and "+". Apparently we don't mind reasoning on false hypotheses when a condition of relevance is preserved, that the conditional express a general principle: "If Hoover is the uncle of Washington, then Hoover is a man" is a fanciful but clear illustration of the general principle "If x is the uncle of y, then x is a man." Now if one should say, "If $7 = 3 + 2$, then daffodils bloom in the fall," this condition of relevance is lacking. There is no general principle expressed here; that is, the sentence is itself no general principle about the meaning of relations like "=", nor is it a special application, like the uncle sentence, of some principle, say, about the meaning of "7" or "daffodils," or the like. The conditional is true but vacuous. Our feeling is as if, turning from the street, we opened the front door of a house and stepped through into a vacant lot. We've "entered," all right, but we have got nowhere—like a Hollywood set.

The second fact of usage is that ordinarily we don't start with sentences already ear-marked "true" or "false." When we use conditionals, we are trying to give our grounds for affirming that some proposition is true or false. Yet there are occasions when ordinary people speak rather like logicians. These are the cases when people want to demonstrate their conviction of the certain truth of a proposition. This works very well for alternatives: "Today is Tuesday, by heaven, or my name is mud!" "I paid you back that five dollars, or I'll eat my hat." Something similar also occurs in conditionals—we have seen how alternatives can always be translated into conditionals. "If today is not Tuesday, my name is mud!" Falstaff is very fond of this form of asseveration. "If manhood, good manhood, be not forgot upon the face of the earth, then am I a shotten herring." "An [if] I have not forgotten what the inside of a church is made of, I am a pepper-corn." "If I be not ashamed of my soldiers, I am a soused gurnet."

Falstaff's semi-oaths are a reminder that these paradoxical uses are perfectly valid. When the conditionals are true, a true conclusion can be derived from them. Since arguments based on the material interpretation are valid, it is a fallacy to reject these arguments as invalid, no matter what feeling of paradox they arouse. The exploration of the forms of valid inference based on the nature of logical operations is a proper study of logic. We must conclude our discussion with a few examples of misunderstandings of the nature of the logical enterprise.

EXAMPLE. Paul, who knows some logic, argues with Peter. "Either you should take a logic course, or if you should take a logic course, then you should not take a logic course." Peter exclaims, "And talk like Gertrude Stein! If I ever in my life heard an invalid argument, that is one."

COMMENT. This certainly sounds like nonsense. Presumably Paul would explain that all complex sentences in the form of "*a*; or if *a*, then *b*" are necessarily true. Examination shows that, as one side or the other of this alternative must be true, therefore, the alternative is true. If we suppose *a* to be true, there is not a problem: one side *is* true. The whole conditional on the right side will be false, in Paul's argument, as it says that a true sentence *a* implies its contradictory. Now if we suppose *a* to be false, then the right side is true, for the conditional will simply state that a false sentence implies some other sentence, in the example its contradictory, a true sentence. But every conditional whose antecedent is a false sentence is, as we have seen, necessarily true. If Paul had said, "You should study logic, or at least if you should study logic anything is possible," the nature of the argument might have been clearer to his friend.

EXAMPLE. Paul tries again, "You should study logic or if you should study logic, then you are able to profit by it." Peter throws up his hands and turns on the radio very loud.

COMMENT. The same tautology—a vacuously true sentence, but nevertheless, true. If it is true that Peter should study logic, then what follows the "or" can be false. If it is false that Peter should study logic, then either he should study it or . . . , and for the dots we must supply a true sentence. As we just saw, on the hypothesis that "a" is false, "if a, then b" is necessarily true, as any false sentence implies any other sentence, true or false. True then: "If you should study logic (but you shouldn't), then you are able to profit by it" even though you wouldn't learn a thing.

Again, suppose Paul had said, "You should study logic, or by heaven, if that's false, then anything else goes in this idiotic world—such as that *you* could learn something from it." In this form, for some mysterious psychological reason, the argument seems convincing.

Index

abstractions, 16, 43, 45, 68
ad hominem, 94, 99-101, 127
ad personam, 96
ad populum, 94-96
affirmative propositions, 143, 149-152
affirming the alternative, 156
affirming the consequent, 155-157
all, 11-14, 28, 34, 143, 148-151
alternatives, 154-158, 212-215
ambiguity, 137, 146-147, 152, 156, 157, 158-165
ambiguity of "all," 28
analogy, 22-27, 122
analogy, figurative, 25
animism, 115, 117
antecedent, 154-157
a posteriori, 113
apriorism, 111
argument, model, 5-6
Aristotle, 2, 3, 60, 169
authority, 84-88, 99

Bacon, Francis, 95, 127-128
"bad man" argument, 101
band wagon, 92, 94
Beard, Charles, 50
Benedict, Ruth, 117
Berkeley, Bishop, 133
bias, 111-121
big-lie technique, 103

Caesar, 107
cause and effect, 17-22
ceremony, 82
characteristics, 34, 41, 49, 51, 60
circularity, 165
classes, 23, 34, 68, 141-152
classification, 34-52, 60
classification, non-exclusive, 36, 38, 39

classification, non-exhaustive, 36, 37, 38
classification, rules of, 36
Clemenceau, 123
Cocteau, Jean, 48
conclusions (of syllogism), 2, 3, 5, 9, 139-147
conditionals, 154-158, 212-215
connotation, 78
consequent, 154-158
constructions, 33-35, 40-53, 56, 57, 61, 65, 68, 69
contradiction, 136, 139
conversion of propositions, 147-152
counter instance, 13, 14, 15
cultural bias, 117

Darwin, 85, 123
decision by default, 130
definition, 65, 88, 136-137, 159, 160, 165-168
denotation, 78
denying the antecedent, 155-158
Dewey, John, 60, 171
dilemma, 32-36
disjunction, 155
Disraeli, 123
distribution of terms, 143-147
diversions, 121-133

Einstein, 6, 86
either-or, 30
Eliot, T. S., 49
emotive language, 77-82
empirical truth, 135
Empson, William, 164
enthymeme, 3, 146, 147, 152, 156, 166
equalization, 158, 162
evidence, 9

expert, 84-89
extension of argument, 26
extreme-case criterion, 57-64, 65, 66

fallacy, defined, 3
Falstaff, 214
forestalling disagreement, 101
four terms, 158
Frankfurter, Justice, 30
Freud, Sigmund, 65
fundamentum divisionis, 36, 39

Galileo, 112, 113
Gallup poll, 14
generalizations, 10-22, 69, 112
generalizing, 148
general terms, 40, 43
Gibbon, 51
glittering generality, 81
guilt by association, 147

half-truth, 100
Hannibal, 51
Hegel, Hegelian, 48, 75, 160
Hitler, 15, 16, 30, 31, 73-74, 83, 97, 103, 104, 121, 127, 153
Hobbes, 80, 93
Hume, David, 6, 136
Huxley, Thomas, 123
hypocrisy, 110
hypostatizing, 43, 68, 69

idea, 41
idols of market place, 95
if-then, 135, 154-157
induction, 8

Jackson, President, 52, 53
James, William, 12
Johnson, Dr. Samuel, 133

Kent, Jack, 47
King Aroo, 47, 48
Koestler, Arthur, 127

Laplace, 138
lip service, 104, 109-110, 126
logical truth, 134-137
loop-hole, 160

Madariaga, Salvador de, 48
Mark Antony oration, 95, 96, 163
Marx, Marxist, 29, 47, 75, 109

material implication, 212
Mead, Margaret, 65
middle terms, 142-147
Mill, J. S., 7, 110
modus ponens, 154

name calling, 81, 95, 96
"necessary connection", 6
negative, 143-145
Newman, John Henry Cardinal, 172
Nietzsche, 158
nominalist, 49
non sequitur, 152-154
not, 135, 149-152, 213

observations, scientific, 5, 6
Ogden, C. K., 79, 162
only, 147-149
or, 155-158
origin, 97-99, 132
Orwell, George, 80, 170
over-precision, 65-68
oversimplification, 171

particulars, 41, 42, 43, 50, 144
Pascal, 120
pathetic fallacy, 115, 116
Perry, Ralph Barton, 167
personification, 48, 115-117
persuasion, 1
Phaedrus, 41
Pieper, Josef, 169
Plato, 41, 44, 59, 68, 76, 79, 97
Platonism, Platonic, 40, 41, 42, 46, 49, 64, 68, 72
post hoc, 21
prejudice, 94-104
premises, 2, 3, 4, 5, 9, 10, 135, 138-147, 154
propaganda, 30, 31
propositions, 10-33
proverbs, 14

quantification, 147-148
question begging, 80, 101, 165-168
quoting out of context, 88

rationalization, 16, 104-111, 112
red herring, 124, 132
reduction, 43, 44, 58, 64, 65, 68
Reichenbach, Hans, 79
reification, reify, 40-49, 58, 64, 65, 68, 69, 72

relativism, relativist, 40, 41, 49-53, 64
Richards, I. A., 8, 11, 54, 56, 79, 162
ridicule, 132
rumor-mongering, 104
Russell, Bertrand, 79, 117, 212
Ryle, Gilbert, 48

sampling, 12, 14-15
Schopenhauer, 1, 2, 76, 172
semantics, 9, 136
setting, 82
Shakespeare, 162-163
Sieyès, Abbé, 33
situation, 34, 40, 41, 49, 50, 51, 68, 69
smear, 100
Smith, Adam, 28
Socrates, 97
some, 34, 148-152
"soul searching" fallacy, 127
Spengler, 75
stereotyping, 26, 27

syllogism, 2, 106, 139, 141-147

tabloid thinking, 171
Talleyrand, 104
tar with same brush, 100
tautology, 137
Teggert, F. J., 50
therefore, 152-154
Thouless, Robert, 171
Toynbee, Arnold, 51, 75
tradition, 89
tu quoque, 98

universals, 40, 143, 149-151

vagueness, 53-64, 65, 158, 166-167
validity, 134, 138-142

Whately, Richard, 130, 168
Wilberforce, Bishop, 123
William of Occam, 47
Word Magic, 63, 64, 68-75